Saving Higher Education in the Age of Money

Saving Higher Education

IN THE

Age of Money

JAMES ENGELL and
ANTHONY DANGERFIELD

University of Virginia Press   Charlottesville and London

University of Virginia Press

© 2005 by the Rector and Visitors of the University of Virginia

All rights reserved

Printed in the United States of America on acid-free paper

First published 2005

9 8 7 6 5 4 3 2 1

Library of Congress Cataloging-in-Publication Data

Engell, James, 1951–

  Saving higher education in the age of money / James Engell and Anthony Dangerfield.

     p.   cm.

  Includes bibliographical references and index.

  ISBN 0-8139-2331-X (cloth : alk. paper)

  1. Education, Higher—Economic aspects—United States.   2. Commercialism in schools—United States.   3. Universities and colleges—United States—Sociological aspects.   4. Education, Higher—Aims and objectives—United States.   I. Dangerfield, Anthony, 1956–   II. Title.

LC67.62E44 2005

338.4'3378—dc22

                                     200402133

For Ainslie

For Anne and to the memory of Mary Jo Lewis

The ancient kings regarded education as the first important factor . . . in a country. That is the meaning of the passage in the Advice to Fu Yue *(by King Gaozong of the Xia Dynasty) which says, "Forever occupy your thoughts with education."*

—CONFUCIUS, *BOOK OF RITES,* FIFTH CENTURY B.C.E.,
TRANSLATED BY LIN YÜTANG

CONTENTS

ACKNOWLEDGMENTS

This book would not have been possible without the assistance and wise council of many individuals and institutions. Colleagues, students, friends, and critics read drafts of chapters, commented on them, offered correctives, and gave sound advice. They took the time to talk and correspond with us at length regarding their own ideas of higher education and, in many cases, their very extensive experience in it. Their intelligent conversation, letters, and e-mail messages taught us much. We cannot list all our debts—they are too numerous—and apologize in advance for oversights. The annotated bibliography at the end of the volume stands as a supplement to the acknowledgments expressed here.

We thank particularly Daniel Aaron, Carolyn and Kenneth Andrews, James Basker, Derek Bok, David Breneman, Peter Cohen, Jill Ker Conway, Andrew Delbanco, John and Judith Dowling, John Engell, Karen English, Daniel Goroff, Dudley and Georgene Herschbach, David L. Kirp, Erika Kiss, James T. Laney, Gregory Maertz, John L. Mahoney, Michael S. McPherson, Jack Miles, David Perkins, Ruben Quintero, Henry Rosovsky, Marc Shell, Michael Shinagel, Gary Setnik, Roger Shattuck, Judith Shklar, Donald Summers, Giorgio Tagliacozzo, Janice and Patrick Thaddeus, Sanford G. Thatcher, Kevin Van Anglen, Donald Phillip Verene, Michaele Whelan, and Thomas Winship.

We extend gratitude to several corporate bodies, first to members of the Cambridge Scientific Club and the Saturday Club for their astute and delightful conversation touching on this subject over the course of more than a decade. Our work would have been blind without the Harvard University Libraries, their superb librarians, and staff. We thank especially Nancy Cline and Sidney Verba, as well as the research and reference librarians at the Harry Elkins Widener Memorial Library of the Faculty of Arts and Sciences and the Monroe C. Gutman Library of the Graduate School of Education.

An earlier version of chapter 4 appeared in the May–June 1998 issue of *Harvard Magazine;* we are indebted for the encouragement and editorial improvements provided there by John Rosenberg and Jean Martin.

We thank Joel Meyerson and Maureen Devlin at the Forum for the Future of Higher Education. They prompted what has in the present volume become the second chapter, a shorter version of which appeared in *Forum Futures 2001*. Members of the Forum at its 1999 meeting provided suggestions and guidance. An earlier version of chapter 3 appeared in *Loyola Magazine.*

At the University of Virginia Press we have been blessed with Cathie Brettschneider as acquiring editor. Her high enthusiasm is matched by her professionalism, a rare combination. Ellen Satrom and Ruth Melville have provided clear production assistance and sound editorial direction. We thank David Breneman and the anonymous reader for the press; the diligence, care, and acute corrections given by those two readers characterize the kind of helpful, expert reports that all authors seek but not all receive.

Publication of this book is supported in part by a grant from the Hyder E. Rollins Fund of the Department of English and American Literature and Language at Harvard University. Rollins published many works still regarded as standard five decades after their first appearance. He used to say, "There is no such thing as a perfect book." The criticism, help, and information we have received from so many individuals and institutions have been generous and unstinting, but errors no doubt remain and for those we alone are responsible.

We thank our families for the support, understanding, and love that place all intellectual work in perspective. They also contributed immeasurably to the substance of this volume. Our greatest debt is acknowledged in the dedication.

1

THE NEW STATUS OF MONEY

The true life of a university depends finally not so much on the abundance of its means, as on the character of those that use them.

CHARLES ELIOT NORTON, 1890

This book examines how a new and growing culture of money both shapes and distorts higher education. In the past forty years, that culture has altered almost every aspect of colleges and universities in a manner unprecedented in the history of those institutions. This book does not advocate a return to some era when money exerted little or no force in higher education. There was no such era. Wealth has always played a major, though a different, role from the one it does today. Historically, colleges were the province and privilege of the well-to-do. Now, however, college is a necessary passport into the middle class. Often, and in a new manner, the influence of money has spread and deepened. In many ways this has been admirably meritocratic, yet in other ways money is becoming the end rather than a means for the whole enterprise. A new, more complex money ethic pervades the external, macro level: it largely directs how higher education and society interact, how colleges and universities serve, increasingly, an economic ethos. The recent money ethic, to an overpowering degree, also dictates the internal, micro level of educational institutions: it now determines which fields and pursuits within the academy expand and flourish, and which ones retract and shrink.

The newly ascendant and expanding force in American higher education is not love of learning, nor a desire to teach, study, or conduct research. It is no longer the hope of imparting ethical and cultural values, nor the critical turn of mind that questions or modifies those values. It is not the democratic intention to educate citizens who are asked, as soon as they reach college age, to make complex decisions at the ballot box. Nor, despite the vital importance of higher education to a greatly expanded number of citizens, is the strongest force of higher education dedicated to providing equal opportunity without regard to socioeconomic circumstances and background. America pursued that ideal as long ago as the creation of public institutions under the Morrill Act of 1862, and reaffirmed it in the mid-twentieth century with the GI bill and increased scholarship aid to many needy students. But continued dedication to that ideal is far from guaranteed.

The fastest-expanding and often strongest motivation in American higher education is now money. While other aims and functions certainly persist, they are increasingly eclipsed by the ultimate goal of wealth accumulation. There are many names for this, revenue streams or revenue enhancement, lifelong earning power, social utility, product testing, pre-professionalism—they are all tied to money. Money, rather than a means, is becoming the chief end of higher education. The rationale to pursue and to practice higher education is now routinely predicated not on learning but on money. With growing frequency, the ends are not cultural values or critical thinking, ethical convictions or intellectual skills. When these goals are pursued, it is often not because they offer multiple uses and relevance but because they might be converted into cash.

This book therefore also treats the inversion of means and ends in higher education. It examines how ends are diminished or forgotten, and then how easily means are elevated above, mistaken for, and then finally substituted for the ends they should properly serve. Goals that are tangible and quantifiable enjoy a huge competitive advantage over goals that are ideal, broad, and, at their most ambitious, never fully attainable. The former speak for themselves, the latter need advocates to plead their case. Fortunately, their case is a good one, for high and ideal goals are not merely among the most honorable ends that higher education can seek. They are the only ones that, being pursued, will guarantee its continued vitality and strength.

Schools, academic counselors, insurance companies, financial advisers, and economists, many themselves employed in higher education, bombard parents and students with the message that a college education boosts lifetime income by an average of more than a million dollars, and that the more selective the college attended, the higher the ensuing income. In the last three decades, this advantage has not remained steady. It has grown dramatically. Marvin Kosters estimates that the "earning advantage for those who attend college . . . has doubled to about 60 percent from 30 percent in the early 1970's" (Stille 2001). College is now regarded as a monetary investment to be repaid, with considerable interest, over a lifetime. After the purchase of a home, and barring catastrophic medical bills, higher education is the largest expense most families incur. In less than twenty years, between 1985 and 2003, the real cost of attending a four-year college, adjusted for inflation, has more than doubled (Elfin, 9). Some students amass debt so large that it becomes the deciding factor in choosing a career. For a family with several children attending private—or even public—colleges or graduate schools, the combined tab will likely exceed the cost of the family home.

What the state of Massachusetts did for 2003–4 mirrors a trend across the country. It increased public university tuition and fees 28 percent while lowering available scholarship aid by a sadly coincidental 28 percent. In that academic year, many other public universities significantly increased tuition for in-state undergraduates: the University of Virginia added 20 percent to the cost, the University of California climbed 27 percent, and Arizona State University soared 40 percent, all in one year, not "the first time state universities have jacked up costs during a soft economy—just when many families already are having a tougher time affording college" (Chaker).

Some businesses, when not treating campuses as targets for advertising, see college education as the way to supply an "educated" workforce, that is, educated in skills businesses want. Other skills may seem superfluous. The university often conceives of itself not only metaphorically but also literally as a business. Stanford advertises itself as a "start up since 1091." It is easy to infer, and perhaps it is implied, that the whole enterprise and its leaders are entrepreneurial in a fashion that puts economic gain in primary place.

So many decisions are keyed to, measured, strongly influenced, or even determined outright by the measure of money: where to apply to college; who gets accepted (students from well-to-do families are generally favored, not just because of the educational advantages their money has already procured, but because they can more easily pay the tuition); how much aid is offered (rarely based on financial need alone, because fewer than 1 percent of colleges both practice need-blind admissions and provide sufficient financial aid—"full-need aid"—to all those admitted to enable them to attend without incurring huge debt); what majors are chosen and what possible majors are rejected; what "star" professors are well known; who are selected as trustees; how the job of president or provost is defined (as fund raising); how endowments are built; who can be hired as low-end, low-paid teaching drones (despite holding the highest of academic degrees); how university presses are expected to pay their own way, even make money; how big-time college sports operate; how distance learning is configured—the list is long. While, ironically, "star" faculty often do not teach much and in some cases do not teach at all, crude enrollment figures for courses can determine other faculty salaries.

It has become common practice in the last decade to declare that students paying tuition are consumers or customers, not students. The common denominator of these phenomena is an overwhelming concern, even an obsession, with money. One-third of all active college and university presidents sit on the board of at least one for-profit corporation. Writing in 2003, Tamar Lewin reports, "At all the highest-paying universities, presidential compensation has increased at least twice as much as faculty pay over the last five years." Yet, aside from seeking more money for their institutions and, in some cases, for themselves, leaders and administrators in higher education have been hesitant to indicate to their own institutions, let alone to the public, that money has become the main concern.

Higher education in America, being a segment of American culture, both exhibits and contributes to the character of that culture. It has its own distinctive features, but higher education displays and sometimes magnifies the peculiarities of its milieu. Popular culture is entranced with means: not the product, but how the product will be marketed; not the quality of information, but the speed of its transmission and manipulation; not achievement, but the reputation of achievement; not the uses of wealth, but wealth in and of itself. In short, means are mistaken for ends. As a human foible, this is nothing new, but recent history has given it new force because society is now so adept at creating, improving, and refining means. Not long ago, heavy loads went by ox cart, food sat unrefrigerated, dentistry was extraction, plumbing was outdoors. Means that improve at all are a relative novelty; no wonder it is bedazzling when a year or two is sufficient to improve them beyond recognition. The trend in higher education is to take means—one of whose synonyms is "money"—for ends in themselves.

For higher education to share in this phenomenon is not surprising. Since 1940, academia has been called an "ivory tower," a term coined by Charles-Augustin Sainte-Beuve in the nineteenth century. But it is not and should not be. Its campuses are in the world and the world is in them. Yet, should the academy become just another container for ambient cultural practices? Should its innate strengths—the disinterested pursuit of knowledge and the resolve to impart learning and cultivate critical judgment—be contravened? As Norman Birnbaum stated in 1973, just at the time the new culture of money was taking hold on higher education, "The university can never be wholly adapted to society . . . [because] the ideas and values it cultivates must transcend and collide with the present organization of power and the average conception of the way life should be led." He noted that the university can cultivate such values "only at risk to itself—the risk of incurring the wrath of those whom it will offend by challenging (if only implicitly) their sloth, culpability, or greed. A university unable to make the challenge, however, is a university unworthy of its traditions" (1973a, 29; 1973b, 479).

In the last four decades, higher education has gone a long way toward accepting and declaring as exclusive and all-important one of its several missions, a mission first proclaimed in the late nineteenth century, universally recognized by 1970, but dominant, even supreme, by the start of the twenty-first: to foster economic growth in the nation, to assist the citizenry in securing lucrative employment, and to serve practical purposes. To borrow Richard Hofstadter's categories, this means elevating intelligence over intellect: "Intellect . . . is the critical, creative, and contemplative side of the mind. Whereas intelligence seeks to grasp, manipulate, re-order, adjust, intellect examines, ponders, wonders, theorizes, criticizes, imagines. Intelligence will seize the immediate meaning in a situation and evaluate it. Intellect evaluates evaluations, and looks for the meaning in a situation as a whole" (25).

Money and economic contributions have always been and should always be part of higher education. Yet, for hundreds of years, in Europe, in the North American colonies, and then in the new republic, money and economic gain did not form the basic premises of higher education. Then, beginning in the late nineteenth century, the idea of economic advantage established itself in colleges and universities. After the Great Depression and World War II, the trend grew. That trend, confirmed as one key and advantageous feature of higher education, accelerated from the mid-1960s to the present to become its chief and defining characteristic (Eulau and Quinley 1970). Without a clear demarcation between economic and educational interests, the two have been merging. But can they serve each other best if they become identical?

The internal effect on higher education of making money an end rather than a means works this way. Faculty salaries, number of new positions created, number of degrees given, relative growth in enrollments, standardized test scores, alumni donations, departmental budgets, elimination of departments: taking *any* of these measures it is clear that any field now ranking higher than the mean of all fields fits one or more of three criteria:

(1) the field promises more money in lifetime earnings to its graduates, though the promise may be illusory;
(2) the field studies money; or
(3) it receives significant money from federal grants or private funding.

Within higher education, any and all fields promising money, studying money, or receiving money are now thriving. Any field not doing at least one of those three has been slipping for decades. If differences between the money fields and the others formed a constant, steady state, one might not bat an eye. But what has happened is more dramatic and telling. Between the fields that promise money, study money, or get money and those fields that meet none of those criteria in any obvious way, the differences are growing, often at an *increasing* rate. (For elaboration, see chap. 4.) This is a new phenomenon, one unknown until about 1965.

Gaps in salaries, in degrees awarded, in new positions created, in buildings built and programs established, in alumni interest, and in support from politicians and business leaders have become striking, so much so that the liberal arts and sciences now represent not only a minority of college education but a very small minority. Fewer than 10 percent of colleges and universities in this country now offer degrees primarily in the liberal arts and sciences. Since the mid-1970s, the percentage of liberal education degrees conferred has slipped significantly, and some liberal arts and sciences schools, even elite ones, are discovering how hard it is to keep their identity (McPherson and Schapiro, 47).

Yet, ironically, social scientists and economists rightly identify those liberal arts and sciences schools as the first home in higher education for many students who later achieve leadership, intellectual and public prominence, and strong lifetime incomes. To explain why this is so—when those institutions do not stress, and many do not offer, professional or occupational courses let alone majors—is a telling absence in many reports. This type of institution, the college of liberal arts and sciences, has traditionally set apart American higher education from its counterparts around the globe. If higher education in this country is unique and recognized as a world leader, then this eminence is due in large measure, along with specialized graduate and professional programs, to the existence of these schools for whom money remains a means to education, not the end of it.

Scope of the Argument

It is impossible for most statements to apply equally to all institutions. A reader might rightly remark that a particular condition "is not true at my school." There is not one system of American higher education. In 1973 Kenneth Minogue noted, "What saves the university from the more extreme consequences of error is its sheer plurality. The universities do not, in most respects, constitute a single system" (61). As

Michael Davis observes, "The land-grant universities have never maintained the distance from the world's work that Princeton or the University of Chicago have" (79). In 2003 more than half of all college students were not the traditional college age of eighteen to twenty-two; women outnumbered men six to five. Community colleges are a crucial part of the mix. Differences within the system can contribute to the overall strength of American higher education. While universities have been segmenting and diversifying in some respects, mostly to serve the needs of a larger, more diversified group of students, they have also, as a group, grown more bureaucratic, managerial, and corporate.

The focus in this book is on liberal arts and sciences colleges, private research universities, and flagship public institutions. Those private and public universities usually contain within their precincts a college of liberal arts and sciences, and frequently other kinds of colleges as well. The intention is to discuss features and problems significant enough to attain national scope. Concentrating on institutions that might be identified as select serves several purposes. They are not necessarily held up as models. However, they clearly set a tone and exert an almost disproportionate influence. "Simply put, the executive leaders of these institutions exert a tremendous amount of political, economic, and social power and truly play an instrumental role in molding and shaping the politics of higher education" (Losco and Fife, 56). Time and again, other institutions emulate what they perceive to be their success and prestige. Further, one might expect that the more elite and well-funded institutions would be in a better position to resist certain economic forces and pressures. These institutions and many of their students enjoy the option to consider freely the whole range of motives for educational and institutional decisions. This freedom should not be curtailed or constricted; ideally, it should spread to more institutions and more students.

• • •

In the United States the land-grant universities—named for the method of funding in the Morrill Act of 1862 (though several institutions predate that legislation)—and in Great Britain the nearly contemporaneous civic universities, such as Owens (later Manchester), London, Liverpool, and Bristol, brought practical intelligence directly to bear. Farming interests, primarily, in the United States and industrial interests, primarily, in Britain demanded answers to agricultural and industrial issues and also required the training of new generations capable of implementing chemical and mechanical engineering. The older universities soon modernized their curricula, especially in the physical sciences. The idealism of those pioneers of modern higher education (literally so in the American

West), their civic pride and concern for local interests, their dream of democratizing education at all levels, their struggle to make science where they found pseudoscience or none at all, their continued respect for liberal education and their desire to spread it beyond the moneyed elite, their huge share in creating national secondary education—all these changed higher learning. As new and present needs challenged the halls of established disciplines, professional scholarship often rebuffed the incursions of blinkered "common sense." This dynamic interplay of competing demands has contributed much to create the best of modern culture.

The idea that colleges and universities should be engaged with society and, as one development publication from the Ivy League now puts it, "solve society's problems," that they should not exist in and for themselves, is not uniquely American. However, the combined influence of American ideals, geography, and form of government gave a distinctive and successful shape to this engagement. Soon, American universities were producing prototypes of applied knowledge. They thus became, especially when compared with universities in other countries, very successful "endogenous" institutions, and continue to be so (Rosenberg, 36–57). They produce economically useful knowledge. In addition, the belief that humble origins should not impede talent remains part of the national ethos. It made sense to Americans that not just government but education should be "of the people," just as it made sense for political and geographic reasons that, every state having its own government, every state should establish its own university. Wisconsin, UC Davis, Michigan, and Texas, to name a few, now rank among the most distinguished institutions of higher learning anywhere. Yet, success in academia is, ultimately, academic success. In many states, the rising eminence of the flagship public university, with more of its funding often now from private rather than public sources, has shifted the burden of democratizing education to less well funded state campuses and to even less well funded community colleges. It remains vitally important work, and the challenges faced by public institutions are as daunting as those faced by the early land-grant universities.

One uncomfortable new dilemma is that while the dignity of education as learning rather than as simple usefulness has fallen, its dollar price to the student has gone up. Add to this that "surveys measuring what undergraduates learn—or, more accurately, don't learn—underscore a decline in academic standards" (Elfin, 9). Of course, generations ago standards could be, and often were, depressingly low. The "gentleman's C" meant the work was in reality D or F, yet it passed. It is hard now to imagine the days when mere social rank counted for so much in the admissions process, and when future scholars like Josiah Willard Gibbs and George Lyman Kittredge attended lectures at the most august institutions with other gentlemen who could barely write a sentence. The decline Elfin laments has been occurring over the last thirty years. It has not spared the elite schools, and there, bizarrely, it has taken place against a background of ever more academically demanding admission standards. Nevertheless, with enormous social pressure and perhaps individual desire to get a college degree, students and parents for whom rising tuition means real financial hardship and years of debt are understandably anxious that college education not chalk up, in the long haul, a net financial loss. This legitimate fear is among the pressures that over the last few decades have redefined the usefulness expected of higher education so that a narrowed and narrowing set of needs are now typically regarded as the ones that colleges and universities must chiefly accommodate. Pressure on families has translated into their demand—explicit and tacit—for more institutional focus on a valuable but not intrinsic service provided by higher education: a path cutter through the wild and ever-shifting landscape of the contemporary job market.

A nominal apprenticeship at the college level demonstrates interest in the work, and it supplies a rationale for a job application to both applicant and prospective employer in a world where stable occupations are a dwindling minority. In this way, a need that colleges and universities can help to address is more and more perceived as the single one they are designed to address—and if this is the case, they are very wastefully designed. Meanwhile, the equally genuine needs that colleges and universities are the appropriate and not just the adventitious means of answering can be slighted or forgotten for lack of advocacy: the need to provide people from all walks of life the chance to rise to an educational level suitable to their abilities and interests, the need for an educated electorate and educated leadership, the need to provide knowledge that can be activated by later applications, the need for information and advice crucial to local occupations, the need to preserve and bring alive local as well as national and international history and issues, and with these needs the larger need to build a sense of both local community and national society.

The cost of education is an alarming issue, especially for less-affluent families and institutions. Remedies for it are hard to devise and to implement, and the situation should concern every citizen, just as the rising cost of health care does. However, where the economic pressures on institutions and faculty, students, and families are less onerous and emergent, where fewer choices are forced and where there are more of them, there is something insidious in the vague concept of vocational usefulness used as a trump card. The gratuitous contraction and reduction of the needs that the select liberal arts and sciences colleges and major research universities can or should serve is a disturbing phenomenon. It reveals acceptance of an attitude that disparages one of the finest things higher education was designed to foster and perpetuate, the multifarious accomplishments of the human intellect in all the sciences and arts, no matter where they may lead.

Thus, to repeat, this book concentrates on an upper echelon of institutions, public and private. For better or worse, the most renowned and wealthiest colleges and universities set the standard in American higher education. Acute budgetary necessity does not exert the same degree of leverage on decision making at these institutions that it does at most community colleges, second-tier state campuses, and regional private institutions. Where there is more freedom of choice, reductive notions of utility are less plausibly construed as iron necessities and appear as what they actually are, elective attitudes to what education can and should do.

• • •

It may seem a paradox for this book to argue at the same time that higher education does and should have economic benefits: personal, institutional, corporate, and national. Yet, those benefits have proved greater when relatively unforeseen. Their final utility has broadest impact when not narrowed at the start. The central problem is not the link between higher education and money. That's natural, legitimate, and inevitable. The endogenous, economically useful nature of American universities is indeed *one* of their strengths. The negative effects accumulate when the connection between education and money is linked to two other attitudes: first, when it attaches to the idea of Olympic-style competition, as if measuring complex institutions, students, faculties, teaching, research, and different institutional histories and objectives could be done in the manner of the finishing order of a swimming race or the 1500-meter run. Measuring people and institutions suggests something more like judging figure skating, diving, or style points in ski jumping; in fact, it is more like combining *many* such complex judgments and measures, each one inherently subjective, though all based on actual performances. But in a society where competition habitually produces "standings" (pennant races, the Fortune 500, the Forbes 400, the major market indices), and where standing is determined by wins and losses or by a dollar amount, money seen competitively crowds out less-tangible values. Thus, the second way in which money becomes dangerously predominant is when the several other purposes and goods associated with education (see chap. 2) are diminished or forgotten, when money, as the winner, takes all. Just as winning a bronze medal is reported as a "failure," not maximizing money at every stage can be seen as a sin. When money becomes the chief or only goal, when other purposes and goods, such as discussing values, promoting social justice, enhancing aesthetic appreciation, grasping historical causes, and simply learning more, or educating citizens to make intelligent choices in their self-government, forming personal judgment, and—most intangible, but still fundamental—becoming a better person, when these are squeezed or squeezed out because attention to them hampers the accumulation of money, then money has triumphed as the single end.

Every constituency of higher education now proclaims and reinforces the new status of money. A vast majority of students regard economic and utilitarian ends as exclusively personal, a fact validated by every poll and questionnaire published in this area. The idea of competition for gain has changed the rationale for learning; it has altered the perceived raison d'être of colleges and universities. Moreover, when leaders in higher education identify the ends of their stewardship, they often reveal signs of drift and confusion. Alvin Kernan, a scholar who held key administrative posts at Yale and Princeton, notes these pronounced larger changes and speaks of the "old dreams of absolute truth and great learning," how these "failed," and how the universities, now governed by "relativism and politicization . . . are fragmented, nervous, uncertain, demoralized" (1999, 272). However, leadership and scholarship do not and, in fact, never did depend on some shibboleth of "absolute truth." They require rather judgment and courage, a desire to attain a more ample truth, a truth clearer than that previously known.

The open advocates of the new status quo would not have undue influence were it not for the acquiescence of those who are unsettled in thought, but passive in action, about trends now becoming entrenched. A large number of thoughtful, well-informed observers of the reconfiguration of American higher education have reviewed the situation and elected to call it healthy. Part of the caution, mild optimism, and lack of alarm emanating from high-ranking university officials results, paradoxically, from a growing admission of impotence to effect real change. They often feel "like Gulliver at the hands of the Lilliputians" (Kerr and Gade, 30–31), tied down by myriad tiny threads, but nevertheless hopeful that the general drift of things cannot be all that bad.

But what chiefly keeps this group of eminent minds in a state of passivity is, on the one hand, a vested interest in defending a system they lead, one through whose administrative ranks they have risen diligently, usually for decades. Fewer and fewer university administrators are long-time teachers or researchers. This opportunity for advancement gives the optimists reason to continue cheerful. On the other hand, defeatism consoles the well-placed pessimist with the assurance that there's little to be done and that "change" must be managed. The system is too complicated, the flaws too ingrained, for basic reform. Market forces will resolve whatever problems exist. This position negates individual judgment and courage because it posits forces larger than ourselves that will decide the hardest questions. This immobilizes leadership in any meaningful sense. Leadership in higher education today is weak and hesitant.

The sheer pace of change has been adduced as necessitating a thorough housecleaning of institutional and disciplinary structures in the academy. Science and technology now do change more rapidly—and are capable of yet more rapid change—than was imaginable even in the days when astronauts walked on the moon and organ transplants were becoming standard surgical procedures. Though far from solving all the challenges that confront society—global warming, nuclear waste, famine, AIDS, the ozone hole—technological capabilities have expanded with unprecedented rapidity. In order to keep up, everyone must move faster.

Yet, the related and often conjoined imperative to move ahead as fast as possible carries the tacit assumption that it is clear what needs to be done, that some impersonal guidance system like "the market" or "history" will determine what to do, or that it doesn't matter what is done. Adaptability to new circumstances is a necessary attribute of wisdom, since many circumstances change whether people will them to or not. Moreover, consciously creating change rather than succumbing to it has always been the better part of wisdom and foresight. But reactivity—reflexive adaptation to every new thing—is not wisdom but hysteria. It can create a sense that immediate needs are the only ones worthwhile. The physicist and economist of science John Ziman makes an eloquent plea for a circumspect attitude. He notes that "the suggestion that all research will eventually relate to problems arising in the context of application has profound consequences." When this is "combined with the demand for accountability in the formulation of problems, it opens up the whole of academic research to the influence of external interests." Ziman argues that the only way to counter that trend is to return to "the central tradition of academic science." For him, this "was, quite simply, patronage. It was the convention by which society provided resources for the production of knowledge without insisting that they should be accounted for, in prospect or retrospect, in utilitarian terms. This convention may now seem elitist, irresponsible, and inefficient, but it worked remarkably well in its time. We abandon it at our peril" (153).

Current Debate

In the mid- to late 1990s, the increasing influence of money and commercialization on higher education finally began drawing attention proportionate to its importance. Timely now, the issue will only become more urgent. In *Academic Capitalism* (1997), Sheila Slaughter and Larry Leslie present a broad yet detailed treatment of the issue. Their book opened the eyes of many to what had already been going on for more than two decades. In 1996 Bill Readings published *The University in Ruins,* which develops the related observation that, largely under economic pressures and temptations, universities are changing the priority of their primary functions and becoming more like corporations.

Writing from a point of view similar to Readings's, Stanley Aronowitz pursues more-specific arguments in *The Knowledge Factory* (2000). He distinguishes three functions of postsecondary institutions: vocational or professional training, education, and learning. Education, he argues, tends to reinforce and reproduce the norms of a culture, its social organization, and its prevailing political climate. Learning, in contrast, is free inquiry driven by curiosity, and while learning cannot escape the context of its own time completely, it eventuates in a critique that encourages "difference, debate, and even dissent" (35). This consciously echoes a classic work, Thorstein Veblen's *The Higher Learning in America: A Memorandum on the Conduct of Universities by Business Men* (1918). Aronowitz contends that since the 1960s, American universities have increasingly offered training and education but not much in the way of learning. They have acted as partners and servants of corporations, government research interests (often military or defense related), and entrenched financial powers, including a rather broad plutocracy, but a plutocracy nonetheless. Universities do not lean into the wind but, according to Aronowitz, blow with it. Starting with Clark Kerr's "multiversity" of the early 1960s, Aronowitz chronicles a series of developments that lead him to this conclusion: "The notion that the university has a critical as well as a research function has disappeared" from the commitments of university presidents and "leaders" (50). As a result, he calls for "dismantling the corporate university." This may sound polemical and ideological, and there is no doubt that Aronowitz might fairly be called a leftist. He is also learned, his arguments cogent, and his critique worthy of serious engagement rather than airy dismissal.

In 2003 more titles took up economic motives and higher learning. Derek Bok's *Universities in the Marketplace* consists of three extended examples: athletics (with which Bok has extensive personal and administrative experience), distance learning, and university research with commercial potential. Bok's warning that commercialization is encroaching on academic turf—and academic values—is welcome if only because, coming from a former, long-term president of Harvard, his views automatically receive wide attention. He sharpens his warning when he contends that the encroachments are growing, often unchecked, in ways that the governance of most universities seems ill equipped to resist or control.

The Knight Foundation Commission's report on intercollegiate athletics, *A Call to Action: Reconnecting College Sports and Higher Education* (2001), should be read as a supplement to Bok's commentary on that topic. Its condemnations are harsher than Bok's, and it calls for greater direct reform. Distance learning, Bok's second example, has not lived up to projections of its more enthusiastic supporters. While serving certain needs for teaching selected subjects to targeted populations, it is clear that clicks will supplement bricks in only a limited way. In fact, 44 percent of private four-year colleges (and more than 30 percent of all colleges) have no plans to offer courses through distance learning in the near future. Half of all national enrollments in distance learning occur at two-year public institutions (*CHE* Almanac 2003, 14). It is in the call to examine ties between business and research that Bok strikes a major chord. However, even there, he implies that many conflicts and challenges can be handled. The irony is that in the 1980s, when "technology transfer" and patent possibilities were newer forces, Bok was saying much the same thing: these problems can be dealt with. Now, twenty years later, he must admit that the problems have grown in number, scope, size, and that they have stiffened in their resistance to remedial action.

Two prominent national reviews of *Universities in the Marketplace* contend that its arguments fall short. Jonathan Yardley, writing in the *Washington Post,* applauds Bok's "astute and fair-minded" views, "but a pinch of anger is in order as well, and it is a pity that Bok chooses not to toss it into the pot." And however accurate Bok's observations, they are limited to a few specific categories. He misses the enormous power exerted not so much by commercialization in the usual sense but by the overall motive of monetary gain that permeates higher education. As Yardley puts it, "There are other aspects of commercialization that he minimizes or overlooks." He cites as examples administrative bureaucracies and a view of students "as cash cows." These represent not commercialization per se but the primacy of economic over intellectual and educational motives. Bok's assessment reveals the kind of caution and "melancholy" (Bok's own word) that in less morally alert minds might contribute to the very problem he identifies.

Anthony W. Marx, who assumed the presidency of Amherst College shortly after he reviewed Bok's book in the *New York Times,* writes, "Yet as chilling as Mr. Bok's warnings are, they could go even further." Marx's examples include the "competition for admission selectivity and higher rankings" among colleges, and the competition "for star faculty, paying large salaries to attract celebrity professors who demand lighter teaching loads." The title of the review is "Academia for Sale (Standards Included)." To repeat, then, the problem is not the commercialization of higher education alone, it is also the deep penetration at every level, and for every constituency, of the imperative of money and of the competition for prestige that promises money.

Eric Gould's *The University in a Corporate Culture* (2003) presents a case that might be characterized as one of constructive or accommodating defeatism. "Liberal" capitalism is here to stay, he claims (a discovery?), and it has to a large degree been embraced by universities, which are not going to let go of it. Therefore, any sharp critique is, for Gould, "nostalgic" or "utopian." He is ready to push aside many figures in the humanities, such as Matthew Arnold and John Henry Newman, author of the classic *The Idea of a University,* as irrelevant or outdated. Gould's primary contribution is to call for a renewed sense of education to serve democratic processes and governance, a call that should certainly be heeded. However, if his purpose is to effect a "pragmatic" or "modern" compromise with commercial forces threatening what Bok rightly calls academic values, then his compromise sounds more like capitulation. His analysis and his answers to the forces he is analyzing avoid the potential and at times the very real conflicts between academic standards and commercial forces. His argument makes idealism seem obsolete. And it overlooks the fact that democracy regulates capitalism—for good reason. (As Bok notes, Teddy Roosevelt regulated not only monopolies but college sports as well, and was in part responsible for establishing the NCAA, the National Collegiate Athletic Association.) Fred Donnelly, a professor of history at the University of New Brunswick, laments in a review of the book that "Dr. Gould seems to have assumed too much, too easily." His "blind spot is exemplified by . . . giving little coverage to those events we have been so familiar with, where corporate powers have tried to limit academic freedom and disseminate research results to fit their own narrow commercial interests. . . . Without an analysis of such conflicts and points of friction between 'societal' interests and academic interests, Eric Gould's efforts at compromise fall short."

Sheldon Krimsky, in *Science in the Private Interest* (2003), warns that standards of scientific research are under attack and losing ground. In consequence, Krimsky makes no case for the kind of compromise Gould espouses. For him, scientific integrity is at stake. He reminds us that much of the money used to fund research is our money, taxpayers' money, and that conflicts of interest increasingly undercut the quality of scientific research. Aronowitz's final verdict is worth considering: "Without efforts to produce new forms of governance and of learning, the drift toward the corporate university will turn into a tide" (163). Debate and discussion continue and intensify. The problems and behaviors outlined in these books and in the present volume are not going away. They are growing. Their influence and impact are accelerating.

Weakened by Division

Marketers care little whether a student wants anything more from Yale—to pick one of many possible names—than a Yale T-shirt, and some commercial interests see profit as the best inspiration a researcher could ask for. But for veteran educators to forget that the whole enterprise—at every level—is powered by, guided by, and justified by the recognition of one's own ignorance and the passion to know more, *that* is the widening concern of the current state of affairs.

An almost blind reverence has arisen for the "prestige" of institutions, measured in ways that often reflect scant connection with daily teaching and research. Acceptance of the lockstep credentializing function of higher education as a kind of upper-class, white-collar union card makes education seem, first and only, a dollar imperative. This acceptance, once it becomes a conviction, drives out other motives because other motives prove incompatible. The university and college become high-visibility sites for advertising, recruitment, and access to intellectual capital. Everyone admits that conflicts of interest and conflicts of commitment occur, yet every administrator, while confidentially suspecting their existence elsewhere, confidently declares their absence at home.

Dozens of scholars have charted these recent "broad changes in higher education, often focusing on how the center of the academy has shifted from a liberal arts core to an entrepreneurial periphery, describing the increasing 'marketization' of the academy and detailing the rise of research and development . . . with commercial purpose." Faculty involved in this academic capitalism—and they constitute a growing, influential number—"act more like their counterparts in commercial organizations" (Slaughter and Leslie, 208, 222). While certain universities pursue economic activity much more than others, and while some still practice long-standing policies of self-regulation, the point is, such behavior has become a desideratum, an infallible sign of a "successful" university, a "successful" president or dean. Yet, ironically, as such activity in colleges and universities expands, "the apparent conflict grows between their academic responsibilities and their vested financial interests," interests which coalesce "into a service mission that is largely autonomous from the academic goals of universities" (Geiger, 71–72). In the early 1980s, when the trend to academic capitalism intensified, partly as a response to the beating that America seemed to be taking in a new global economy, university presidents such as Donald Kennedy (Stanford), Derek Bok (Harvard), and Steven Muller (Johns Hopkins) welcomed this academic capitalism, not uncritically but definitely. However, Muller's formulation that "independent colleges and universities need the support of private enterprise, and private enterprise needs the independent sector of American higher education" (21) is too neat, too balanced. In reality, private enterprise needs higher education more than higher education needs private enterprise. So it should come as no surprise that private enterprise should try to shape higher education to satisfy its own ends. This shaping influence takes many forms, among them harnessing the research of professors, demanding that students receive certain training advantageous to particular kinds of enterprise, establishing professorial chairs and underwriting research programs, even exploiting students as captive consumers. Some of these links are advantageous to higher education. But when they become pervasive, and when decisions to enter into agreements between educational institutions and entities whose interests are not primarily educational are driven by fiscal concerns rather than educational values, eventually the border between the two kinds of institutions dissolves.

Moreover, the university divides itself into units, schools, programs, and faculties, each on the lookout for new support and revenue. And when the university ceases to act as "a corporate, spiritual, or intellectual whole," then it more easily falls prey to decisions that compromise its integrity while serving instead the demands of government or business (Shils 1997a, 203). To repeat, win-win arrangements exist, but some become win-lose. David L. Kirp, professor at the Goldman School of Public Policy at Berkeley, puts the case succinctly: "What is new and troubling is the power that money directly exerts over every aspect of higher education. There is surely a place for the market in academic life, but the market needs to be kept in its place. The critical question is how to draw, and how to maintain, this line" (2000, 27).

The temptation to let fiscal concerns alone govern education becomes enormous. Higher education is massive in its own economic right. In 1993 the almost four thousand colleges and universities employed 2.6 million people, more than those employed in "the manufacturing of every kind of food product, *combined* with all apparel and textile manufacturing." From 1970 to 1994 higher education revenue rose by a factor of more than eight, tuition income multiplied eleven times, and government spending on education increased almost sevenfold over what it was in 1969–70, all adjusted for inflation, an astonishing increase in twenty-four years (Weingartner, 8–9). From 1994 to 2002 these increases in costs, budgets, and revenues continued to climb, in some institutions at faster rates.

For parents concerned with their children getting into a "good school" and enjoying a better life afterward, it may be helpful to consider first what happens while they are in school, what kind of education they decide to pursue once they have examined several alternatives. They will grow as individuals; they can realize a vision of knowledge and of society drawn from different fields of endeavor. They can become citizen stakeholders in a democracy. These students will emerge in a position to make their own adult choices in a way suited to their expanded interests, cultivated talents, disciplined temperaments, and higher aspirations. College as a credential for this or that job is not a higher education. And it is sobering to realize that when college degrees are common, such a credential no longer guarantees a good job at all. A college experience aimed at one particular career is a limited and limiting one.

Yet, no Invisible Hand will gather together many fragmented "interests" into a grand general good called Learning. A large part of the thesis of this book, outlined directly in chapters 2 through 5, is that higher education has a set of essential purposes, and that a great many of the unwelcome developments in the academy are the progeny of forgetting—or treating with benign neglect—those larger, communal ends. Learning is more than its parts. It is not a "brand" or "branding." It is hard to measure or to rank, yet the work it produces is palpable. It is more than a student's job offer, a professor's career, a departmental budget, or a university's reputation. Learning can flourish and grow without any of these, while once that love of learning is extinguished, none of them is based on anything real. When that belief is lost, the university becomes a jumble of things: a patent office, a job fair, a place to advance one's career to stardom, the R&D arm of corporate society. In 1971, seeing that a new culture of money was beginning to take hold, John Kenneth Galbraith put it this way in a trio of pithy, prophetic sentences: "The industrial system has induced an enormous expansion in education. This can only be welcomed. But unless its tendencies are clearly foreseen and strongly resisted, it will place a preclusive emphasis on education that most serves the needs, but least questions the goals, of that system" (373–74).

"Winning," Vince Lombardi is reported to have said, "isn't everything. It's the only thing." Whether this detestable maxim is applicable to professional athletics or not, it would at one time have been incomprehensible as the motto of a university. But is that still the case? Getting ahead as individuals and as institutions is emerging as the one agreed-upon objective of academic life. Competition among students and among institutions is inevitable and healthy—to a point. It is commonplace and correct to say that competition is good, but it is not an unqualified good. Unbridled competition predicated on personal gain rather than on intellectual achievement, and on prestige and rankings rather than on unique institutional qualities in depth, will administer a systemic poison to higher education.

Why shouldn't the university exist simply as the loose aggregate of its separate parts, providing for each individual the maximum economic benefit possible according to a self seeking course of action? Because it cannot. Capital markets provide for this in society, but it must be understood that the university is not primarily a capital market. It serves other purposes not inimical to the markets—often beneficial to them—but not identical with those markets. It is a cooperative enterprise that produces many different goods, and these goods must be balanced against, and with, one another. One or a limited number of goods cannot be permitted to drive out the rest. The student seeking only an employment boost will be narrowly educated. Such a student will discover that the utility promised by occupational education becomes obsolete, whereas critical thought, skill in communication, and strong powers of analysis never do. If professors spend increasing time on research, consulting, and private business, soon scantily paid adjuncts, part-timers, and graduate students will be the predominant classroom instructors, advisers, and managers of curriculum and requirements. They now teach more than half of all classroom hours nationwide, with full-time tenured and tenure-track faculty teaching well less than half. If the loyalty of a professor is increasingly reserved for his or her field and not given to the institution called home, then the desired goal becomes a wandering celebrity status. If administrators scramble over "star" faculty and engage in bidding wars, it will not produce a tide that lifts all boats. There will just be less money for other purposes. A Hobbesian state of higher education will eventually exhaust its constitutive resources in internecine combat and cut its own throat. A few will be left standing, the "victors," but the battlefield, the campus, will look like defeated Carthage.

A generation ago Wayne Booth, then dean at the University of Chicago, stated, "It is hard to see how the American college can survive as an institution functionally distinct from graduate and professional schools unless in some sense we can agree on a knowledge most worth having" (1967, xi). For Booth, the question was intellectual. At the end of the twentieth century, Paul Neely, publisher of a prominent newspaper and a trustee of Williams College, put the changed situation this way: "If results are increasingly measured in dollars, liberal arts colleges will suffer—unless they are seen even more clearly as the precise antidote to that way of measuring the world" (44).

One type of corruption is direct, ugly, and venal. While higher education has not been exempt from this type (Roche, 150–51, 234–35), almost without exception its professionals abhor unethical enrichment and extravagant living. The interest in this study rests with a second type of corruption, more insidious because it is not direct but insinuating and obscure. In the end, it does more damage. In this form of corruption, the nature of an enterprise becomes perverted or institutionally turned away from its essential goals and independent functions, goals and functions that other institutions either do not pursue or do not pursue nearly so well. Corrupted in this way, higher education begins to serve interests and ends extrinsic to education rather than continuing to pursue its own ideals of learning and the complex, common, yet not always practical goods that such learning makes possible. (A similar, not unrelated argument can be made about political processes and campaigns. While tainted at times by the personal venality and greed of individuals, they are more deeply warped by the pervasive influence of money, the need to raise enormous sums of it, and the access and leverage it procures.) This type of corruption happens by degrees, as it did in some big accounting firms in the 1990s. Various forms of articulate rationalization always defend it. But it is, nevertheless, corruption from within and should be faced honestly. Ethan Bronner, education editor of the *New York Times,* notes that "increasingly, as we seem to be in a 'knowledge-based' economy, people want to come to these places [universities] so they will then be able to go out and make a million bucks. Universities are struggling to ride that wave and, at the same time, to hold it back" ("Future of the Research University," 49). However, no one holds a wave back by riding it. While higher education benefits from ties to corporations, industry, government, and applied technology, it is in danger of losing its own identity if it becomes effectively synonymous with them.

Higher education best predicates its unique institutional existence on a set of coordinated ends and goods. As discussed in the next chapter, these goods and ends together form an entelechy, a term meaning a set of goods or characteristics ordered in relative worth and function, then put into coordinated motion together such that they realize the ideal potential of the whole. Throughout this book we argue that higher education can be saved only if its multiple goals—individual, social, economic, civic, ethical, and intellectual—form a set of mutually reinforcing aims. Placed in a stark winner-take-all competition with the others, any one goal would ultimately gorge itself on the others, ensuring its own eventual demise as well. In the premodern world, the purely contemplative life may have threatened to imprison the academy in cloistered protection, demoting utility and losing itself in jargon, scholasticism, or Alexandrian complexity. Today, the clearer pitfall is the denigration of a free, disinterested discourse of ideas and information in favor of knowledge that can quickly be converted into utility.

Method of a New Dialogue

While at times focusing on how the money ethic has wounded a larger sense of ethics and has helped the humanities wound themselves, the argument is not that the humanities are separate from other fields but that they are inseparable. There is no reason to pit the humanities against the sciences, basic or applied. All these fields are part of something larger. Calling them separate no more makes them so than the statutory border between Iowa and Minnesota makes those states physically distinct. The humanities are inseparable from the natural and social sciences and intrinsic to all considerations of how any knowledge that can affect life and conduct might be applied. We do not claim that the humanities are predominant. The aim here is a more modest one: to prevent the humanities from marginalizing themselves and to integrate them with other disciplines. The history of modern thought, especially over the last century, is characterized not by the radical, increasing separation of disciplines but by their intermingling and overlapping: linguistics and mathematics and philosophy, chemistry and psychology and biology, physics and chemistry and astronomy, economics and history and mathematics, systematics and ontology, anthropology and literary criticism, and on and on.

Denunciations, exposés, political appeals, impassioned defenses of "absolute truths," or attacks calling for their demolition are inadequate to revitalize higher education. That task requires a broad, capacious vision, one that polemics and ideology cannot supply. But in the very fields, the humanities and social sciences, where one might expect common goals and dialogue aimed at mutual understanding, strong forces have split along political or ideological lines to the point of bad habit. A polarized rhetoric degrades intellectual debates and national conversations. There is something more important at stake than adding another voice to the "left" or "right" balance pan measuring out gunpowder in the culture wars. This book takes no deliberate part in fighting the internal battles that have split and demoralized the humanities. Behaviors on both sides of this polarized rhetoric are, to use David Bromwich's phrase, symptoms "of the same disease."

The arguments contained in these chapters do not blame one ideological group; no slogan is a panacea; partisan politics are not the answer. Although concrete suggestions are made for improvements in higher education, no "step" program is offered. The analysis that Cary Nelson and Stephen Watt voice in their lively study entitled *Academic Keywords* is apt: "Higher education is in genuine trouble. There is no conspiracy to uncover, but there are multiple, uncoordinated forces working to alter higher education for the worse, not the better" (xii).

2

PRESTIGE, MONEY, AND THE ENDS
OF HIGHER EDUCATION

*New inventions, fresh discoveries, alterations in the markets of the world
throw accustomed methods and the men who are accustomed to them out
of date and use without pause or pity.*

    —WOODROW WILSON, "WHAT IS A COLLEGE FOR?" 1909

A Model

Various explanatory models have been imposed on higher education
for the purpose of judging what it is doing, what it ought to be doing, and
how it might do what it does better, faster, or more cheaply. The diversity of higher education makes this a hard task. Models can reflect economic, historical, managerial, or philosophical concerns.

The first step in creating an effective model is to ascertain the purposes and functions, the *entelechy,* of higher education generally and of
its component institutions individually. Entelechy, as noted at the end of
the previous chapter, means the striving for perfection in a series of goals
taken together as a whole. The word derives from the Greek *enteles,*
meaning "complete" or "full," which in turn comes from *telos,* "goal" or
"end." It is an extremely important concept. To understand and then to
pursue an entelechy requires envisioning how to fulfill the potential of
the whole by coordinating and giving proper weight to a set of varied
goals and the goods they seek to achieve. After having identified the entelechy or general concept of higher education in its entirety, one must
apply this understanding to individual institutions, each with its own
particular inflection, history, and emphasis. This sense of institutional
direction (or the lack thereof) impinges on every college and university
activity—hiring and promotion, budgets and endowments, admissions,
physical plant, libraries, laboratories—and no sensible administrator attempts to ignore it. "The single most serious problem of our universities
is their failure to adhere steadily to their own purposes," warns Hanna
Gray, former president of the University of Chicago. "No university is

strong," states Bart Giamatti, who led Yale for almost a decade, "if it is unsure of its purpose and nature" (Axtell, 213–14).

• • •

The general entelechy of higher education produces three instrumental functions, one economic, one social, and one civic. These three instrumental goals or goods rest ultimately on two final goals. One final goal concerns the ethical application of knowledge and its relationship to human conduct. The other final goal is intellectual, the fundamental search to discover and to order knowledge and ideas. This intellectual goal or end is the definitive one. It is the final cause of the ethical goal, as well as of the economic, social, and civic functions.

Education acts inevitably as an *instrumental economic good;* it readies individuals to undertake specific tasks, careers, and professions. A sound education serves this function and indeed serves it best collaterally. The instrumental economic function of education should not be problematic, and it would not be so were it not blown up to gargantuan size by a bad combination of overfeeding and early underperforming. If we were sensible enough to get children to a genuine twelfth-grade level of literacy and numeracy (admittedly, a large "if"), this economic instrumental good would be well on its way. Much education as an instrumental good must occur by the time mandatory schooling ceases. In a technological, complex society, higher education and professional schools continue this instrumental function, which, as an economic good, is assumed, supported, and promoted by colleges and universities.

But concentrating everything in education, whether elementary, secondary, or higher, on maximizing its positive effects for specific economic activities does not best strengthen the economy; rather, it denatures and deforms education and robs it of its greatest long-term economic potential. That seems almost too paradoxical to accept, but some ends are best achieved by direct aim while others, even superficially similar ones, are not. A marksman aims a rifle bullet, but any successful pitcher will confirm that it is counterproductive to aim a baseball. Direct aim and open campaign are proven routes to high public office, but scarcely advisable as the shortest ways to a seat on the Supreme Court. The instrumental economic good certainly includes some specific and immediate practical applications of knowledge, but developing these alone reduces the huge potential of economic benefits derived from unforeseen, future applications of new knowledge.

Yet, some private and especially public universities, such as the system in Massachusetts, advertise immediate economic utility not only as their chief but as their *only* asset for applicants to consider. When former governor Tom Ridge of Pennsylvania advertised his state's schools on national TV, he said the schools graduated thousands of students each year in computer science and various engineering fields, "ready for the workforce." That's important and admirable. But no other fields and no other conceivable purposes of higher education, aside from immediate job training, were mentioned. They didn't rate. The word *success*—meaning individual economic success—punctuates college advertisements and redrafted mottoes. Politicians press hard for it. Parents demand it. Insurance companies remind clients of it. Businesses often see it as the raison d'être of education.

Increasingly since the early 1980s, money has come to be seen by many Americans as a good in itself, an end rather than a means, something automatically conferring status, class, power, even *virtue* (Lapham; Taylor, 1–21). Some economists, such as Paul Krugman, worry about the rise of a plutocracy. It is not uncommon to see commentators in publications such as the *New York Times Magazine* proclaim, without irony, "In America . . . money is ubiquitous. But most of all, money is virtuous" (Brooks, 88). Moreover, in terms of economic changes and behaviors, aren't parents and students acting rationally when they seek a prestigious institution (even if it's not a good match), when they accept scholarships based on merit rather than need, bargain for aid, and elect a major for its perceived economic value? Studies reveal that a school's name correlates with later earnings; the college major, other studies suggest, also correlates with earnings after graduation. If "rational" means to act in ways seeming to promise more money, the answer is yes. And in a competitive society this behavior is self-reinforcing. As long as hiring and salary decisions are made categorically, the spiral will tighten and steepen. There are choices here: actively support or passively accept this system as "rational," let it increasingly drive applications, admissions, majors, "intellectual" choices, and institutional competition; or, question this system, create incentives to counter it, even fight it as potentially allowing the economic function to swallow the other functions and make the economic instrumentality of education its sole good.

This "rational" behavior intensifies in part because higher education is neither regulated nor self-regulated heavily. Governments impose certain accounting procedures, but institutions are free to set salaries, build buildings, target applicants, solicit funds, merge, advertise, outsource, compete, offer varied scholarships and loans, establish branches, invest, specialize, diversify, even monopolize. A market of higher education so unregulated and competitive contains a paradox: many institutions are presumed to pursue the same general ends—intellectual, social, civic, economic, and idealistic ends that serve learning and society—but the same institutions compete against each other in doing so. In order to best serve those larger, shared goals, *to what extent* should they compete? Or cooperate?

Bart Giamatti became commissioner of major league baseball for more than love of the game. However different their activities, suggestive similarities exist between professional sports and higher education. Both groups of institutions serve a complex set of national and communal ends—recreative, economic, social, and educational. Both are presumed also to promote larger ideals. It cannot be the object of one team to drive others out of existence. Beat them on the field, but don't bankrupt them. Yet, after the advent of free agency, it became painfully obvious that in those sports less regulated, wealthier teams bought the best players. Those players, often having won a championship, now leave as soon as better offers come along. Frequently, the team that buys them can't afford to keep them. Case in point: the former world champion Florida Marlins. Correlation of team wealth and win-loss records is a scandal in major league baseball. From 1995 through 2001, only 3 out of 189 postseason baseball games were won by teams ranking in the bottom half of total player payroll amounts! To combat these inevitable, increasing imbalances, some leagues regulate themselves contractually through salary or payroll caps, guaranteed minimums, unionization and arbitration, rules for drafting and free agency, mandatory sharing of TV revenues to even out major and minor markets (pro football does this), procedures to add or move teams, and the power of commissioners to act beholden to no one owner or clique. This self-regulation serves the health of the sport and is condoned by law. Nothing like this really exists in higher education. (Professional sports lack tenure, but everyone on the roster must be full-time with all fringe benefits.) If the federal court decision banning schools from sharing financial aid information is any indication—a decision only MIT had the courage to fight—then the courts do not grasp that higher education serves larger, less tangible communal goods as well as individual, tangible interests. Higher education might at least be accorded some options analogous to those open to professional sports, such as antitrust exemption (Collis); and education, a unique form of commerce and trade, might best be treated uniquely.

Higher education acts as an *instrumental social good* when it promotes awareness of, and derives benefit from, the lives of all participants. This is a communal benefit—it builds communities and supports social responsibility. Empathy is a hoped-for result; the broader aim should be critical reflection and reasoned discussion, an ideal identified in Renaissance courts, Enlightenment salons, and American colleges by the same word: *conversation*. Learning, then, creates a social and socializing experience, one intensely intellectual when those jostling together are gifted, reflect different backgrounds, and harbor heterogeneous ideas, values, and interests (Hansmann; Goethals, Winston, and Zimmerman). In its March 1998 report "Reaping the Benefits: Defining the Public and Private Value of Going to College," the Institute for Higher Education Policy concluded on the basis of hard data that higher education enhances certain social and public benefits of education in general. Among these are lower crime rates, increased community service and charitable giving, an appreciation of social diversity, and an improved ability to adapt to and use technology,

Freedom of choice is essential to democracy. An understanding of several fields is key to complex choices of self-government. The issues faced by a citizenry asked to decide them through their representatives require that education also act as an *instrumental good for civic and political reasons* in a way analogous and allied to, but not identical with, its economic instrumentality. Scholarly debate is, or should be, the standard for a democratic society's procedures of verification and dispute over ideas and policy. If all inquiry serves vested interests and is circumscribed in advance, then in time few inquiries (and none of them controversial) will be pursued to their ends. No one fears this outcome more than defenders of a free press. But political wisdom cannot be achieved by pursuing economic competition alone. Leo Marx, a keen exponent of American studies, states, "The utilitarian idea of the multiversity, and the fragmented . . . conception of knowledge which it favors, are at odds with our presumed commitment to democratic . . . values" (12). George Washington realized the democratic value of general education when he urged in his Farewell Address, "Promote, then, as an object of primary importance, institutions for the *general* diffusion of knowledge. In proportion as the structure of a government gives force to public opinion, it is essential that public opinion should be enlightened." Education as exclusively an economic instrumentality characterizes authoritarian and totalitarian regimes, not democracies. It coexists comfortably with control of the media, a caste system of jobs, early specialization, and even censorship.

• • •

Already possessing vast stores of knowledge, society and individuals naturally ask what possible uses that knowledge might or should serve. To question whether potential applications are, on balance, ethical goods— with benefits, evils, trade-offs, and possible consequences all weighed together—engages *the moral or ethical goal* of higher education. This questioning differs from the pursuit of knowledge, though it usually accompanies the application of knowledge to produce economic usefulness or to solve specific problems. Yet, to ask the possible ethical ramifications of knowledge obtained is a venture not limited to specific practical questions. Properly speaking, it is philosophical and humane. It forms the basis for organizations such as the Union of Concerned Scientists and International Physicians for the Prevention of Nuclear War.

The history of unlocking the atom offers a series of cautionary examples. First came theoretical knowledge sought for its own sake. No one in the early days of nuclear physics worked in order to produce weapons of mass destruction or any other "product," not Planck, Schrödinger, Bohr, or Einstein. Only later did the exigencies of circumstance and the sophistication of technologies assembled for one purpose permit practical applications: power source, food preservation, medical advances, extreme destruction. Each use entails various decisions to implement it or not: whether to build nuclear power plants, irradiate food, use radiation therapy, or deploy the weapon—a political, military, and moral judgment based on values established and debated since before the founding of nation states. Some decisions override economic incentives.

Genetics presents a similar case. The monk Gregor Mendel did not envision interferon to treat hepatitis. Rosalind Franklin, James Watson, and Francis Crick did not conjure cloned sheep or trade wars triggered by genetically altered crops. Mendel wanted to interpret the patterns of heredity; from studying generations of smooth and wrinkled peas he formulated general laws. How that knowledge and all it engendered should now be used entails, again, ethical and economic decisions. Though the results of knowledge can be perverted, we cannot prevent abuses before the fact nor predict favorable outcomes. How to use knowledge is rarely a matter of obvious application; it is a long test—essay, not multiple choice—a contest of values, and, at times, a calculated risk. In the humanities, results can be misused, but, more often, the methods and approaches can be trivial, foolish, or twisted by prejudices of all kinds (Bate, 217–18).

Yet, none of this could be considered if those in education did not first give rein to innate curiosity. Needs that are specific will find specific solutions, but general needs are the hardest to supply. The Promethean spark came before Bessemer furnaces or Dr. Frankenstein's creation. An irreducible element in the search for knowledge is the unpredictability of its application. If society ceases to recognize this, it can spend down intellectual capital and fail to replace it. The capacity to wonder, to be curious, will atrophy. The wellspring of advancement remains the open yet baffling quest for new knowledge. This quest is *an end or good desired for itself*. It is the *final cause* of all the other goods in the entelechy (Popper, 5). It does not overshadow the other goods but undergirds and cooperates with them all.

In education—a pale word for the species's innate quest to answer the riddles that surround us as we hurtle on a speck of cosmic dust falling through the most tremendous room—to seek knowledge and ideas and then to debate the ethical application of that knowledge in an intellectually disinterested fashion: these are *goods in and of themselves*. Following from them come the economic, social, and civic instrumentalities of higher education.

The sense of a whole group of goals as the object of higher education is also called a "bundled view of learning." Stanley O. Ikenberry, former president of the University of Illinois and then president of the American Council of Education, remarks that this bundled view "is what we think and speak of as the 'purpose' of a college education." But, he warns, new communications technologies invite—they encourage—unbundling, "partly because of economic incentives and realities. . . . Teaching, or the sharing of knowledge and skills, tends to be unbundled from the creation of knowledge, or research. Likewise, information transmission tends to separate analysis and synthesis" (59). This is intellectually dangerous because it suggests that analysis and synthesis can be done in isolation from each other, something the philosopher W. V. Quine argued is intellectually counterfeit.

F. Scott Fitzgerald says that the ability to keep seemingly contradictory ideas simultaneously in one's mind defines intelligence. The entelechy of higher education means several coordinated ends regarded together as producing different kinds of goods. Thus, it is both possible and necessary for the entelechy to serve all these functions: welcome higher education as an economic instrumentality, hope for it as a social asset, trust in it as a civic or political benefit, insist on it as a good in itself—as a final cause—when it seeks knowledge and ideas, and nurture it as a moral good when it investigates, in a disinterested way, the ethical application or potential of the knowledge and ideas it establishes and transmits.

Economic Pressures

However, education as an instrumental good geared to competitive economic gain, coupled with competition for prestige among educational institutions, can form a juggernaut threatening to annihilate the other goals and, ironically, subvert its own. To aim only for the instrumental while ignoring the general pursuit of knowledge is like expecting a roaring spring stream to power a mill for the entire year without first taking the trouble to dam it into a pond. To see higher education simply as an economic instrumental good—in other words, to derogate the belief that the pursuit of knowledge is self-justifying, to dismiss it as too uninvolved to perform civic good, and to belittle education as a social good in the process—is too easily a consequence of first following short-term economic "incentives."

In a technological, capitalistic society whose aim is to create more wealth and be not merely competitive but first, economic incentives will always be linked to practical problems. But an unregulated, competitive, instrumental economic good seen itself as the final cause will slowly but surely choke the other goods. All this, as Galbraith saw in *The New Industrial State,* "suggests how readily we assume that education and research must be subordinate to the needs of the industrial system," which wants to bypass "the university administration to adapt education to its requirements." Or, if the administration cannot be bypassed, perhaps it can be co-opted. However, Galbraith remarks that education and research "need not be subordinate if it is realized that the educator . . . is the source of the factor of production on which industrial success depends; he must realize this and exert his power, not on behalf of the industrial system but on behalf of the entire human personality" (374). We could update the passage by substituting "technological" for "industrial." When instrumental means—for they are means, not final ends—are seen as the only end, then the entelechy that serves the entire human personality and the entire society will be destroyed. Young people will find the only attractive, rewarding fields of study to be those that meet one or more of the three benchmarks noted in chapter 1: fields that promise, even if the promise is illusory, high wages if pursued as a career; fields that study money; or fields that, within educational institutions, receive large grants or gifts. (For further elaboration of these three criteria, see chap. 4.)

The stress on economic competitiveness to the erosion or exclusion of other goals also ends up exacerbating serious issues of another sort. Many civic problems are simply not solved by entrepreneurship. Alexander W. Astin, in "Liberal Education and Democracy: The Case for Pragmatism," points out that "when we consider the major problems plaguing contemporary U.S. society, it is ludicrous to argue that they can all be summed up in the issue of economic competitiveness." In the marketplace, competitiveness "bears only a marginal connection to . . . issues of racial polarization, poverty, joblessness, crime, a deteriorating infrastructure, environmental degradation, political apathy, and distrust of our social institutions." As Astin recognizes, higher education does, or should, "produce graduates who possess more of the job skills required by modern business," but he cautions that "it is naive to think that this will make much of a dent in our myriad social problems. Indeed, becoming more 'competitive' economically may well be antithetical to any effort to deal constructively with problems such as the infrastructure, crime, and especially the environment" (209–10). We are more optimistic than Astin: for instance, job skills can address joblessness, and a healthy economy tends to have less crime and less overall poverty. But his basic argument stands. Economic competitiveness is no panacea. Even the best medicine for an economy is no cure for everything. In fact, it can turn into bad medicine of the literal sort. A case in point is the pharmaceutical industry's response to the alarming increase in drug-resistant bacteria: companies have reduced their R&D budgets for new antibiotics. Why? Antibiotics are no longer as profitable as many other sorts of medications (Rowland).

What if the ideal of knowledge, whether or not it serves immediate usefulness, is devalued, even lost? Several things perish with it. The possibility of ever converting such knowledge to any practical ends vanishes. Aside from examples in nuclear and genetic science, the use of thousands of chemical compounds and threatened botanical species would have remained inert if they hadn't been catalyzed by some informed and inquisitive mind. If the properties of the rosy periwinkle of Madagascar were not known, the world's most effective treatment for childhood leukemia would not exist. If the nature of the blood of horseshoe crabs were not known, there would be no effective test for certain deadly bacteria. The list is long; many technical applications are unforeseen, some serendipitous.

Another loss is idealism. The best nursery of ideals is the disinterested pursuit of knowledge and ideas and the ethical consideration of how to apply them; to tear down the idealism of learning tears down every ideal. Even freedom of choice, in particular the freedom to range among different fields, is threatened if one links the free pursuit of ideas, knowledge, and values simply to maximum economic gain. Such a loss would be devastating to any society, but particularly to a democracy, where freedom to choose and move between jobs or careers is an opportunity inherent to liberty and the pursuit of happiness. The effects of this loss won't manifest themselves right away; in fact, if everyone learns simply to become more productive, a temporary boost in productivity will result. But within a generation, premature specialization and occupational selection will deprive the citizenry of perspective, relation, and the ability to connect one field of knowledge with another. We will be forced into stereotypical ways of thinking and into predictable, discipline-bound "solutions," exactly what we have, not without reason, criticized other nations for pursuing at the expense of individual initiative and idealism.

To repeat, in an ever more competitive world, there is a danger that education pursued exclusively as an instrumental economic good will attenuate education as an associative intellectual and social good, erode it as a civic good in a free society, diminish it as a moral good, and ultimately destroy it as a final good in which knowledge is sought regardless of its perceived usefulness. Once the social, civic, and moral goods and the final good of knowledge are enfeebled—and it cannot be assumed they will thrive on their own without active help and participation—then education will be a competitive tool bereft of the ability to impart democratic, critical thinking, to transmit cultural values and inheritances, and to discover knowledge with unforeseen, multiple applications. An illustration from one of the most important professional journals in the country: In the summer of 1999, the dismissal of Dr. Jerome Kassirer, editor of the *New England Journal of Medicine,* represented, as the dean of Tufts Medical School, Dr. John Harrington, put it, "the triumph of money over medicine." Dr. Kassirer opposed the decision of the journal's board, the Massachusetts Medical Society, to endorse, for gain, unrelated products and services over which the *Journal* had no control or oversight (Tye; *CHE,* Aug. 6, 1999, A22).

The keystones in the arch containing the three instrumental goods—economic, social, and civic—are these two ends: the ethical deliberation over how knowledge should be used, and the pursuit of all knowledge and ideas, which is the final cause. These two goals do not preclude the others. Far from it; they are foundational and facilitate the others. Widely different cultures share this conviction, and every major myth about human knowledge and education expounds it: Plato's cave, the Promethean spark, Pandora's box, the Trees of Knowledge and of Good and Evil in Eden, the Faust and Frankenstein myths, or Confucius's idea of *li* and the person educated and disciplined to realize true humanity (*jen*). Knowledge discovered and values deliberated in a disinterested fashion generate and humanize the other goals (as well as being potentially complicit in any evil misapplications). The world's great moral and religious systems teach the need to enlighten general knowledge with moral commitment—even while they recognize the economic, social, and civic valences of knowledge. However, if learning pursued as the life of the mind and disinterested ethical deliberation are removed from education, then the other goals and functions will become perverted. For American education to forget this would be hubris. The instrumental goods would eventually become shills for authority without self-criticism and barkers for productivity without cultural inheritance or curiosity.

Values of economic utility are admirable. Taken alone they are insufficient. As James Madison, recognizing classes of citizens with and without property, eloquently argues in *Federalist* No. 10, such values in isolation create permanent factions with differing interests. Unregulated capitalism, capitalism left entirely to its own devices, is no guarantor of representative democracy; for without itself being regulated by the presence of a government responding to different interests of different factions, unregulated capitalism will eventually place political power in the hands of those with the most economic power. Yet, to paraphrase Churchill, capitalism may be the worst guarantor of democracy—except for all the other economic systems. Still, that leaves capitalism a far from perfect system. Some say let the markets work, but when Chrysler slid into deep trouble, government intervened. In March 2000 and again in 2001, when the markets were working perfectly well and the price of fuel and gasoline climbed sharply because supply was short and demand high, both sides of the congressional aisle proclaimed these simple, classic market forces a "problem" requiring regulation, intervention, and a change in tax policy. So did many citizens. Regulations of certain kinds are necessary. Government is inherently imperfect when it regulates, but to assume that it errs on the side of the poor or shiftless is improbable and inaccurate. In 1999, 65 percent of the taxes in America were paid by citizens earning in excess of $100,000. They reaped 71 percent of all government benefits. The broad middle class contributed 35 percent of all taxes but received only 29 percent of all benefits. As Al Hunt of the *Wall Street Journal* concluded, "Now there's income redistribution." In the ensuing five years, as college costs climbed, this income redistribution increased.

Is this entire argument moved against money and wealth creation? Not in the least. Like any form of power and exchange—oil, steam, the atom, language, statistics, or human imagination—capital in and of itself is a purely neutral force. Other things being equal, it is always better to have more of it than less. The Twain School of Money sums it up well. When anyone complains, quoting scripture for the purpose, that "Love of money is the root of all evil," think of Mark Twain's remark "Yep, all money's tainted. Trouble is, 'tain't enough." Yet, as every major moralist has affirmed for millennia, it is rather how, how far, and to the exclusion of what other goals money is pursued that counts; and, once possessed, it is what is done with it that determines its ethical worth.

The Problem with Prestige

Increasingly, institutions compete for students, money, faculty, endowments, and yield ratios. The potential benefits of competition are many, but the virtue ascribed to competition has been elevated to an unassailable article of faith, the word recurring like a mantra. The contests spin like pinwheels in a fireworks display, so intense that the mere reputation of having the best rank, the most money, is seemingly what matters, often fixed on by the media and holding astonishing sway over applicants, parents, and even counselors. Bald quantitative scores, amounts, or ranks seem what must be known. These markers possess the power of authenticated status, and measuring them becomes an end in itself. A toddler's evaluations are confined to the most general terms ("good," "bad," "fun"), but critics revert to about that level of discernment when they accept strictly numerical evaluations of colleges and universities as anything more than the crudest comparison. Such numerical evaluation, moreover, compares institutions offering very different kinds of curricula, with different settings, histories, and departmental strengths, all qualities extremely hard, if not impossible, to quantify in the first place. This obsessive striving overshadows and jeopardizes the real ends and goods—scholarly, personal, and social—of the institution. There are no algorithms for complex behavior, no ranks for distinct entelechies. Excellence cannot be measured or pursued adequately in these often trivialized forms. Boasting of its counters may mean losing sight of what, supposedly, is being counted. Longinus, echoed by the historian Sainte-Beuve, said it well: nothing so much resembles a hollow as a swelling.

It is an ironic truth that the obsessive comparison of certain measurements actually has its origin in a meritocratic approach to higher education designed to mitigate or even to negate the power of wealth and privilege. After all, enshrining SAT scores, bidding wars for students, and even scholarship aid to the gifted regardless of their families' wealth—these are mostly unwelcome results of respect for talent carried to an extreme.

Yet, even as it is remarked that they are "only" indicators, students, administrators, faculty, and parents credit *US News & World Report* rankings, yields against the nearest competitor, or gross endowment figures more than one might suspect, because they are becoming the *only* indicators in popular circulation. Though what they actually reflect is some editorial committee's judgment of present worth, those rankings directly and markedly influence mass behavior and thus become *causes* of applicant and student behaviors, behaviors themselves then measured as important factors in the next year's rankings. In other words, it's a self-fulfilling prophecy or, as James Monks, an economist with the Consortium on Financing Higher Education, puts it, "a vicious circle."

Recent studies, including one by Monks and Ronald Ehrenberg, show that these rankings actually drive (they do not simply register) significant changes at schools. Examples are the ranking criteria of how many students accept a particular school's admission offers, what their average SAT scores are, and how much financial aid the school must spend to secure their coming. At considerable expense of time, effort, and money, administrators package statistics in certain ways in an attempt to favorably influence the rankings. Claire Gaudiani, former president of Connecticut College, laments, "It's really unfortunate, because university resources could be better used educating students, rather than being devoted to working the system." Increasingly, certain colleges reject some of their very best applicants, on the theory that those students, even if accepted, will probably go elsewhere and thus will lower the "yield" ratio of applicants, making the college look less selective compared with other institutions (Golden, 2001). While Gaudiani's statement is laudable and seems sincere, the *Wall Street Journal* cites Connecticut College as an example of a college that rejects some of its best applicants. In Connecticut's case, this is apparently often because those applicants made no personal contact with administrators at the college, even though such contact is not required for admission and the student may indeed have visited the college and talked with students there. None of this can possibly be helpful for prospective students, their parents, or the larger health of higher education.

Two more college presidents, Michael McPherson, former president of Macalester, and Morton Schapiro, president of Williams, voice the larger worry: "Higher education institutions seem more than ever to be locked into a competitive framework that focuses all attention on relative standing" (2001, 59). It is as if it were a weekly poker game rather than an enterprise of years with a lifetime of effect. Gordon Winston of Williams writes forcefully in "The Positional Arms Race in Higher Education" that the whole point is to maintain your place in the pack or move up. But, this being true for everyone, it engenders "incentives to behave in ways that, collectively, may damage them all" (14). Arms races don't have a shining place in history: they eat up resources that could be used to serve important needs, they are usually precursors of war, and their final logic is mutually assured destruction.

One former editor of the *US News & World Report* ranking issue, Alvin P. Sanoff, has now decried "early-decision mania," a growing problem that is distorting the admissions process at many colleges. But Phil Buchanan, former secretary of Mount Holyoke College, finds something a bit hypocritical about Sanoff's stance. During Sanoff's tenure as editor, the decision to elevate within the ranking criteria two crucial measures— the percentage of applicants admitted and the "yield," the percentage of those admitted who actually come—helped fuel the early-decision bandwagon. Under Sanoff's editorship, such measures of "selectivity" influenced rankings even more than they do now (the method of determining rankings has not been consistent over the years). Buchanan perceptively argues that Sanoff should take some responsibility for the situation he now so bravely criticizes (*CHE,* Mar. 3, 2000, B12). But, indeed, do we really want information about a major life decision juggled in this way, only later to have the juggler decry the actions he has helped to produce? In academic year 2001–2, Yale University announced it would modify its early-action program. Some time later, Stanford, UNC, and, in 2003, Harvard followed suit. The early-admissions game needs more reform (Avery, Fairbanks, and Zeckhauser).

What does the magazine say in its defense? Peter Cary of *US News & World Report* voices a far from ringing endorsement of his own publication. The present system is "based on our best judgment," and it "isn't necessarily wrong." The magazine *Washington Monthly,* however, contends that the rankings lack "any defensible empirical or theoretical basis" (Healy). *Business Day* (Aug. 20, 2001) also criticizes the methodology of the rankings. In his book *Innumeracy,* John Allen Paulos puts the general problem succinctly: "Reducing a complex intelligence or the economy to numbers on a scale, whether I.Q. or GNP, is myopic at best and many times simply ludicrous" (91).

Many administrators and critics have groused—usually mildly, and usually when their own college drops a spot or two—about the accuracy and importance accorded rankings. But a stronger argument can be made against them: while some of the information collected on the institutions is helpful (though much is hard to interpret and of questionable relevance), the actual rankings themselves have become pernicious. They may be doing higher education, students, and parents a grave disservice. When *US News & World Report* puts its rankings on a Web site at midnight on a certain date, the site immediately gets 250 hits per second. The rankings will probably not go away as long as their publisher is making money on them. But educators and those interested in education might keep in mind that the rankings in and of themselves are inherently neither intellectual nor scholarly. They have nothing to do with the application of learning, they tend to divide rather than unite the larger community of learning, and they carry no ethical content whatsoever. Stephen R. Lewis Jr., former president of Carleton College—and he has no selfish reason to complain, since Carleton is always ranked highly—states, "What bothers me is the appearance of being scientific and quantitative, when they are not." True symbols of excellence do not rank excellence; they *are* that quality itself. Russell Edgerton, director of the Education Program at the Pew Charitable Trusts, warns, "Unless we develop measures of quality where colleges can actually provide evidence of their contribution to student learning, then this whole system [of ranking colleges] turns on resources and reputation, and reinforces the elitism of higher education" (Zernike 1999a, 2000; *CHE*, Oct. 22, 1999, A65–67, 65).

A deeply questionable addition to the rankings racket is the new system published by the *Atlantic Monthly*, a system based entirely on "selectivity," in other words, how hard it is to get into a college, a statistic as old as the hills. It is also a statistic easy to manipulate and falsify when an institution courts students whom it knows it will almost certainly then reject, a fairly common practice. If students become cynical at a young age, even about education, who can blame them? What is the cause of such tactics? "The ranking of top colleges has become a multimillion-dollar industry for magazine and book publishers, fueled by anxious parents looking for guidance, and by the institutions themselves, which spend lavishly to raise their standings in such surveys" (Steinberg).

Admittedly, it is hard to come up with reliable measures of quality. George D. Kuh and his colleagues have attempted to measure the quality of student experience through self-reporting examined rigorously and judiciously. Two clear-sighted economists, from Stanford and Northwestern, looked for exact indicators of quality in higher education and tried to develop them. Yet they concluded that neither education nor research "can be measured accurately. Educational output is measured by years of study, scores on tests, and numbers of various degrees awarded, but these measures do not adequately measure educational quality. Research is even more complex. New ideas cannot be measured or weighed. Furthermore . . . an output of research is improved capabilities and competencies in the faculty and students who perform it. As a result, providing objectively verifiable measures of a university's educational output is difficult, and objectively measuring a university's research output is essentially impossible" (Noll and Rogerson, 108). This means, in essence, that the ranking system on which the positional arms race of higher education grounds itself is simply not accurate. It is illusory. An inspector can count missiles and warheads, but how can anyone quantify what goes on in the minds of thousands of students in tens of thousands of courses over dozens of months—let alone what happens outside the classroom? Or in dozens of different labs and scores of books, whose work and ideas take years to achieve, then additional years to be recognized, tested, taught, and applied?

In "The Recovery of Moral Agency?" Alasdair MacIntyre, one of the nation's most respected moral philosophers, discusses the perils of any system obsessed with rankings. Without leading a crusade against college rankings—his point is more cogent and forceful in that context for being a disinterested examination outside that specific debate—he states: "Any kind of competitiveness that encourages egoistic thinking is . . . an enemy of good practice. So we have to learn that while it is important to care about excelling, it's corrupting to care about who is ranked higher than whom in respective excellence. Desire has to be detached from the badges of such rank ordering—prizes, fame, money—while directed toward those achievements of excellence for which, ostensibly at least, such badges are awarded" (8).

Rankings and measures of "excellence" create status and reputation as final goals or goods in themselves when at best they are shorthand signs of instrumental goods within the institution. "Prestige" is derived from *prestidigiae,* "juggler's tricks" in Latin, and even a laudatory use of the term preserves much of that meaning. True reputation comes from knowing and cultivating the thing itself, the institutional entelechy in all its interrelations over a span of time. To use a financial comparison, more of Peter Lynch's methods of research, investment, and evaluation—and less day-trading, quarterly panics, and street rumor—would serve better. Henry S. Pritchett, an astronomer, a president of MIT, and the president of the Carnegie Foundation for Teaching until 1930, in his address to the University of Michigan in 1905, "Shall the University Become a Business Corporation," praises the democratic spirit of land-grant institutions and remarks how they might vie with older institutions "in a rivalry [in] which we may well hope to see the noble rivalry of the scholar rather than a rivalry of riches, of buildings, and of numbers." The wisdom is not anachronistic.

An intensification of institutional striving for competitive goals measured by dollars, numbers, or ordinal rankings can implant heady fixations. The syndrome has the earmarks of an addiction. It intensifies itself, more and more is required to satisfy the desire, increasing resources drain into it, it distracts energy from concrete tasks and personal relations, it makes cooperation difficult, it can prevent larger community, and over time the addiction becomes a burden whose only relief is deeper addiction. Might one renounce, openly and publicly, certain commonly accepted numerical indicators of institutional worth? Or at least recall Pritchett's statement, or Einstein's: "Not everything that can be counted counts, and not everything that counts can be counted."

Some Solutions to the Problem of Prestige
Cooperation and Survival

Though each school has its unique entelechy, many schools share larger ideals and aims. As well as competing, they must exploit every chance to unite strengths, cut costs, and serve their communities better. One area where this is happening, but must happen much more, is libraries. The most common form of grant in the humanities is funding to travel to a research library. An inexorable institutional and economic Darwinism is reducing the number of research libraries in this country considered truly adequate for many fields. So, whether through J-STOR, consortia to share periodical costs (greater than book costs), digital sharing, interlibrary loan, agreements to share faculty and even student patrons, or to link up with public systems, libraries must cooperate or deteriorate. Is it a stretch to carry this to building maintenance, security, athletic facilities, health-care bargaining power, and the like? Such cooperation—with possible legal or labor ramifications—might be impractical at certain schools, but cooperative mergers of certain types can no longer be slighted and postponed. As long ago as 1986, the National Commission on the Role and Future of State Colleges and Universities stated, "Cooperation—not competition: This is the new challenge for leadership in higher education" (37). This is not a new message; its longevity underscores its importance. Since then fifty-two small schools, many devoted to the liberal arts and sciences, have shut their gates permanently (McGinn 2000b, 62). New alliances between schools in the United States, as well as between U.S. schools and international ones, will become crucial to the health of higher education. The idea is to enhance both competition and cooperation. Opposing football teams can pound each other on the field, then contribute to the same blood drive.

Leadership and Governance

Organic growth in human institutions requires planning. A coming hard freeze requires quick protection; one pervasive form of organic growth, biological evolution, proceeds at highly uneven rates and responds dramatically to rapid environmental changes or cataclysms, such as (to pick a notorious but apposite example) massive meteor impacts. Authentic organic growth encourages institutions to throw off both the addiction to mere status and the inertia of traditional rest; it permits swift executive actions, not merely reactions. These actions are ideally predicated on vertical as well as horizontal consultations genuinely frank and open. These actions entail knowing the longer histories of institutional operations, at times overlooked by peripatetic or new administrators or faculty. Presidents, schools, divisions, even departments must be ready to act, not react, to shed any false conservatism of forms and structures, among them any structures and attitudes of top governance that can thwart healthy organic change (Collis).

To balance the autocratic and consensual aspects of the university is ever a challenge. However, the new complexity and regulations that are universally agreed to have characterized the last twenty to thirty years will, if not dealt with boldly, continue to grow on their own, internally, without any new addition; this bureaucratic growth will quash both autocratic and democratic strains of governance. *Parkinson's Law,* a serious, statistical study of offices that ran aspects of the British Empire, makes instructive reading applied to universities. Leaders will feel like Gulliver tied down in Lilliput; faculty, students, and staff like pawns in a Kafka novel. No critic has ever demonstrated that all or even the majority of growth in academic administration and staff is attributable to government regulation and external requirements.

The troubling split between administration and faculty, between "advancement" (i.e., specializing in fund raising and operations) and "academic" leaders, seems to be deepening. This growing fissure endangers higher education as a whole. Fewer experienced professors seem trained or inclined to administer institutions or significant aspects of them, in part because they look to their own fields and specialties for recognition and reward. More administrators build careers by managing and making decisions about the essential undertakings and appurtenances of scholarship and teaching rather than by participating directly in them for a decade or two. The actual national median figure for the number of years that academic administrators have taught is six, but that figure includes all teaching done before the Ph.D. is received as well as after. Yet, such teaching and research participation is of "the essential essence of the academy" (*CHE* Almanac 1999, 38; Adams, 59). Suspicion breeds suspicion and soon some "advancement" administrators are reassuring each other that "unlike the academic president, you can see the forest for the trees," you have a vision (Fisher, 13). Or you get the old faculty joke that a mouse has learned to be a rat—that is, a colleague has become a dean. Why not identify, cultivate, and train faculty as administrators above the departmental level; increase the faculty willing to serve, full- or part-time, for specified periods, in administrative roles; seek career administrators with a credible span of demonstrably successful teaching or research, not just a line on a résumé? Presidents and deans still need to act as intellectual academic guardians. They cannot leave this duty entirely to their departments or internal committees. They will serve their own institution best if they consult widely with scholars and experts outside that institution.

Faculty members can feel that the layers between them and key administrators are tall barriers. These barriers—both perceived and real—block growth and change. What a difference it makes for a dean or provost to cultivate, in informal private conversations, both intelligent gossip and bedrock opinion, perhaps dispelling rumors on the way. This is not unseemly. Most professors welcome it; some crave it. With word processors and e-mail, losing the art of dictation was perhaps inevitable. But losing the art of informal conversation between administration and faculty cuts a crucial connection of an institution's sympathetic nervous system (see, e.g., Damrosch, 203–6). One potential advantage of a college or university is that it can oppose and present a counterexample to the progressive atomization of society.

The entelechy of an institution should be reflected in its trustees and governing boards. At that level, Pritchett warned against "administration of experts by [educational] experts." He goes on to say that perhaps no "wiser councilor" exists than someone in the business "of large sympathy and of real interest in intellectual problems." The last quality is paramount. Admittedly, these people "are almost as difficult to find as are great teachers" (297b). But they can be found, and they can abjure the habit of measuring the success of their chief executive officer (a title used by Pritchett as early as 1905) in purely quantitative ways—how much money raised, how many square feet added, what rank achieved. The following words from Joseph F. Kauffman, executive vice president emeritus of the University of Wisconsin system and president emeritus of Rhode Island College, are appropriate here: "Board members must understand that effective governance and management of an institution represent means to an end—and that they are not ends in themselves. The central purposes of academic institutions have to do with scholarship and learning. All of the efforts of boards, as well as faculty and administrators, are for the central purpose of having learning take place" (238). Trustees who understand economic realities are valuable. Trustees who understand those realities as means to serve the intellectual, social, and civic ends of the institution are invaluable. The whole point of giving monetary gifts to higher education is to invest the money in something other than making more money.

It is prudent to consider having on these boards at least one faculty member from a comparable institution, a member whose interest in organization and management complements the interest in intellectual problems felt by the nonacademics on the board. Intelligent variety is key. In many cases, trustees meet too infrequently and go into too little detail to be of real help. Instead, there are lapses, then lurches. Trustees need to walk the land and talk to the free yeoman farmers, the faculty. And professors need to communicate, too, not always filtered through the administration, not always prompted by frustration. If everyone feels they're on different teams, something is seriously wrong (Chait 2000). With different sets of experiences, backgrounds, and ideas, the only way to work together is frequent personal contact, not only in committee settings but also in private conversation. The concept rests in the word *trust*. If that is not manifestly evident, then everyone is responsible to make it so.

Faculty, Academic Planning, and Curriculum

Growth in an era of rapid change demands intense, strategic, long-term academic planning charted by faculty and administrators working closely together on a regular basis, not sporadically or prompted only by a crisis or an upcoming campaign. Beyond information gathered internally and reports authored at the institution, these groups benefit from applicable national data and analyses relevant to their tasks. Schools can pool resources and cooperate to provide some of these data.

It is desirable to create at the interdepartmental, even the interschool, level permanent rather than ad hoc groups whose sole task is to develop courses and programs that push academic, administrative, and disciplinary boundaries. This can be done through team teaching, through inherently interdisciplinary fields (e.g., the environment, human rights, science and public policy), or both. These groups of faculty and administrators might suggest changes in administrative structures as well as in curricula and courses.

In search procedures and hiring, faculty (and administrators too) can conduct themselves in counterproductive, amateurish, even unprofessional ways that betray the entelechy of goods that hiring the best possible person is meant to further (Stein and Trachtenberg). Every professor should be versed—through seminars, meetings, reading—on the ground rules, assignments, realistic expectations, activities, advertising, interviewing, prohibitions, and negotiations of the process. Professors in general seem not well trained in hiring. They often do not have time for this long, arduous process. Their hasty or underinformed efforts may become permanent mistakes that everyone suffers with.

The passion for celebrity and name recognition in a society of rapid change and media exposure has not exempted higher education. "Star" quality may seem obvious, but it is hard to determine and often illusory. Prizes and awards are unreliable guides. In the social sciences and humanities especially—more than ever subject to trends, factions, and fashions with short half-lifes—informed opinion varies and there is less consensus than a generation ago. To fix on a few names among scores of worthy ones rarely furthers organic growth; sometimes it catches the crest of a wave that has already broken. Some stars shamelessly milk the system; they count on administrative timidity, on fear of seeming to have failed to bag the quarry, and they end up not infrequently wasting everyone's time, and money. One of the few international studies of academic professionals concludes that careerists oriented to attaining or maintaining star quality "are sly in that they have a clear understanding of the societies in which they are living and very skillfully manipulate features of these societies for their own self-promotion. They are masters at self-advancement. Sly scholars are also the products of Western (especially U.S.) democratic society. The richness of their social fabric gives sly scholars a plethora of tactics by which to pursue, foxlike, their individual careers" (Podgórecki, 122). The free agency of professional sports might work in the academic world if, as in professional sports, real consequences occurred and sanctions were imposed, fines levied, and even contracts terminated when a star failed to show up. But this almost never happens in higher education.

The star system stems in part from economic pressures to compete, pressures squeezing universities, and from the pervasiveness of marketing in American life generally. The system copies a mentality in which being a celebrity has a skewed connection with virtue and worth. Many if not most so-called stars are productive individuals; some are charismatic teachers; some are fiercely loyal to their own institutions. But others act in ways that would make a prima donna blush. A few are extinct volcanoes. Many stars promote their friends as stars, too, and push them to be hired at their own or at another institution where they serve on an advisory committee. Offers are triggered and generally bid up the worth of their compatriots, who often do the same for them in turn. Anyone who believes that concerted, often successful efforts at jury packing the committees for certain prizes do not occur is wearing blinders. The whole system is manipulated because it easily can be. Many stars teach less than their colleagues, refuse to teach large undergraduate courses, hire teaching assistants to grade papers even in the small courses they do teach, demand and often get extra leave time, break local academic commitments on the grounds of external obligations, obligations (often paid) that they voluntarily made elsewhere after supposedly committing themselves to chores at home, and fail to perform such bread-and-butter duties as writing letters of recommendation for students, even while assuring students that those letters have been sent.

This is not a fancied list. It is hard to say whether these practices are more prevalent among stars than other faculty, but decades of teaching and observing the academic world indicate that such is the case. Every profession has moments of weakness and every profession spoils some of its members quite irrationally, elevating them above others who work as hard and possess as much talent. Until recently, however, the academic profession as a profession had always stood against such differences precisely because it was known and accepted that they were frequently invidious or inaccurate or both. No wonder many respected faculty members, such as Joyce Appleby, professor at UCLA and former president of the American Historical Association, now oppose the star system. Within the poorer humanities, a pecking order leans hard on contract teachers. Yet, the work of those contract teachers effectively subsidizes the research salaries of those who teach less (Sullivan, 87–88, 90).

Perhaps the most notable feature of the system in the humanities, where disagreement exists about judging excellence, is not that stars have higher reputations for outstanding scholarship than do many of their colleagues, but that they have a public reputation, frequently because they write about a controversial current issue or about topics that appeal to the media (Scott; Weingartner). Many times this reputation is not gained first through publishing books or scholarly articles; it is gleaned from repeated appearances on the endless circuit of conferences and lectures that now characterize academic life. It means little that one unpublished twenty-page paper often suffices for presentation at a half dozen or more such meetings. And, of course, giving such lectures and going to conferences means absenteeism from one's own institution. Some professors, seeing that an airport life brings rewards to the stars, imitate it. Indeed, conference papers can count more toward merit pay raises than do class lectures, even though a conference paper is generally half the length of one class lecture and often no more intellectually demanding. The idea is to strike a balance, but when all the tangible rewards rest on one side, that's hard to do.

Over the years, the smaller size of liberal arts and sciences colleges has made them natural laboratories for radical reform and institution-wide restructuring. Examples would be St. John's, Reed, Antioch, or, less radically, the honors program at Swarthmore. However, as a group, smaller colleges are often structured to conserve a set of values vital to the community. This can exert a braking effect on national trends and fads. For instance, star faculty are a luxury that small colleges, even wealthy ones, cannot indulge to the full: they can't afford to give up the teaching time that is usually part of the price. Their historic emphasis on teaching insulates them and their students to a considerable degree from the erosion of teaching's glamour and importance. The lower—though in many cases not negligible—publication requirement for tenure somewhat relieves the pressure on their faculty to trim their sails to the prevailing winds, especially in the humanities and social sciences. The operative word, however, is "somewhat." Demands for publication have been going up, and teachers who aspire to move to a research university must meet them. They try to publish in the most prestigious journals and aspire to get grants from the big foundations, which so often hold the key to extra leave time. Nevertheless, smaller institutions have often been able to resist the blessings of stars who get paid more and teach less.

Jonathan VanAntwerpen and David L. Kirp note that, about a century ago, "William Rainey Harper, the first president of the University of Chicago, looted the faculty of Clark University, promising to double their salaries if they jumped ship." So, has anything changed? Yes. "The audacity of Harper's raid startled his contemporaries, but in recent years such talent searches have become more commonplace and the offers have grown more outsized" (Kirp et al., 67). Institutional competition, bidding, and leveraging offers to enhance one's position are features of higher education more than a century old. At stake now is the fact that in many cases the maximum benefits of such practices have been reached. As the practices intensify—and it is in the nature of all competition to intensify—they produce damage and harm. Among other negative effects, institutions tend to avoid, as they have avoided in the past, real innovation for fear of stepping outside the closely competitive crowd and becoming an easy target for criticism (Veysey, 330–31).

Relative equity is not flashy, but organic growth requires attention. The hierarchical commodification and segmenting of the professoriat within fields and especially between fields harbor perils. If the market is followed fatalistically or constantly trumped, rather than to a significant degree resisted on principle, the market will grow tyrannical, leave no options, and make some jobs and fields so unappealing that few young talents will want to enter them.

• • •

One way to cut costs and to finance any expense other than teaching is to hire workhorse teachers who generally teach much more than the stars or than many tenured faculty, but who also earn much, much less. According to the U.S. Department of Education, the resort to adjunct and part-time faculty doubled in twenty-five years: 22 percent of faculty in 1970, 41 percent in 1995. In 2000 these faculty were teaching more than 50 percent of all classroom hours in higher education, more than tenured and tenure-track professors combined. In many community colleges, 80 percent of faculty are part-time (Nelson and Watt, 137). The Coalition on the Academic Workforce reports that tenured and tenure-track faculty teach less than half of all introductory courses (except in history and art history). In some disciplines, more than 40 percent of introductory courses are taught by graduate students. On average, only 40 percent of disciplines offer part-time teachers any benefits. Courses are taught at an average of less than $3,000 per course; a Modern Language Association report cites many institutions paying less than $2,000 per course—and a few paying as low as $450 (*CHE,* Dec. 1, 2000, A12–14; Jan. 5, 2001, A15; www.theaha.org/caw/index.htm).

The motive behind the current academic system is not intellectual and it is certainly not humane. It is economic and political. In 2003–4, the University of Virginia announced that it was "replacing [some] full-time professors and offering fewer sections of certain courses like first-year English writing courses and introductory foreign language classes" (Chaker). Basic classes, often required, are now larger, and those who teach them are paid less. This is not necessarily to blame the university administration; the whole political and economic system behind the public universities is clearly not working as envisioned. Similarly, "UMass has quietly become addicted to part-time faculty." They "are paid at a rate roughly half that of the lowest-paid full-time professor. Most make under

$20,000 a year. . . . Working 'part-time' can also mean teaching 100 percent of a full-time teaching load without full-time pay" (Nixon). This practice also holds true in the California state university system and many other public systems.

The situation is not confined to public institutions. At New York University, President John Sexton has proposed the category of "teaching professors," which might seem tautological. But it isn't. These "teaching professors" will never be eligible for tenure and will be paid less than "research professors." As Steven M. Cahn, professor of philosophy at the CUNY Graduate Center, remarks in a letter to the *New York Times* headed "Unequal Professors," all this is reminiscent of Orwell's *Animal Farm:* "All professors will be equal, but research professors will be more equal than others." And good-bye to that long-cherished ideal, so often lauded by presidents of research universities in the past, of the fruitful interplay between teaching and research in an individual faculty member.

The practice of using adjunct or part-time teachers has become increasingly bad, but it did not start out good or naive. A well-placed administrator, the vice chancellor for administrative affairs for the state university system of Florida, stated the objectives and assumptions in 1973 with a candor that today is replaced by silent "discretion": "Using part-time or temporary faculty personnel to satisfy part of the teaching workload. Such personnel do not earn tenure and normally are not seeking permanent employment. They can thus be dismissed without difficulty when reductions in faculty positions are required" (Boutwell, 47). One assumption here is that since they don't *seem* to want permanent employment, they can be fired "without difficulty." Yet, when was the last time any university sought to find out what percentage of its adjuncts and part-time teachers wanted permanent and full-time employment, and then dared to publish the results? It's just too dangerous. What university advertises how many of its classes are taught by graduate students?

The trend may now have bottomed out. It should. Tenured faculty must object to it. Institutions such as Georgia State University are showing one way to relatively saner, long-term, organic policies: create full-time posts, cultivate the young professionally, commit resources, and two academic generations from now the school should be stronger, its faculty more committed, loyal, and with higher morale. However, it remains unclear how many former part-time instructors will, even if hired for full-time jobs, achieve tenure. Their teaching loads and working conditions (no leaves, sometimes no office, no e-mail, the necessity of a second job) have made the research and publication level required for tenure hard to reach, even for the most gifted. Unless they are given, as full-time faculty, several years to devote to research and publication, they will soon be looking elsewhere, often reverting to part-time status.

Few adjuncts are pleased with their situation. *How* embittered, resentful, and desperate some part-time faculty feel is hard to gauge only because the feelings run so deep. For instance, at Georgia State, the plan to scale back on part-time faculty while creating fewer tenure-track positions elicited from one teacher this comment: "We are quite literally being used as living stepping stones both for other people's careers and for the university's projected transformation" (*CHE,* Oct. 22, 1999, A20). A disaffected teaching force cannot and will not work to help an institution grow or change. If faculty who do research teach little, and those who do teach have no time or facilities for research, this mocks any institutional avowal that teaching and research go hand in hand. They become increasingly separated, separate but unequal. Reducing reliance on piecework teaching in no way precludes strenuous, periodic reviews of tenured as well as untenured faculty. That topic is too large to consider here in the detail required, for it is precisely the details and conditions of such periodic reviews that make or break them as honest brokers of academic work. When political, economic, or personal motives drive tenure or post-tenure reviews, they degrade the intellectual motives. The complex situation of such reviews is ably and clearly summarized by Michael A. Kelley, in "Political Science and Post-Tenure Review."

The consequences of massive piecework teaching, bad now, will soon be appalling. Slowly but surely, the quality of teaching will decline. Students will be out of touch with research. It will go from a buyer's market to no market at all. Militant unionization and protest will increase. Moonlighting will increase. Tuition will increase. Administrative salaries and perks will continue to increase. Meanwhile, the quality of education suffers. The blame rests with trustees, administrators, *and* full-time faculty.

For organic growth and constructive change to occur, faculty need to cooperate among themselves in their own institutions; compromise may be required more than confrontation. This means abandoning both radical chic and a cynical aversion to any change. A chaotic "revolution" of incidental conversations and polemical books penned in highly professionalized or abstract language will not work.

Student Life, Advising, and Attitudes

Students need to know the history and missions of their own institution. Faculty, too. A few paragraphs in a handbook are not sufficient. If there is no recent, detailed account, someone in history or a keen alumnus or alumna might write one, if not as a book then as a substantial pamphlet that could also be disseminated digitally. This would be both scholarship and service. Colleges might consider offering, even requiring, a course in American higher education and its history. Of the wealth of material here, much of it recent, most students, incredibly, never read a word; they are not asked to, and only schools of education deign to pick it up. Students entering "higher education" should acquire some sense of the entire enterprise, but to most of them it is just a blur. If a course requirement seems impractical, perhaps a seminar or a series of presentations during freshman week or orientation would not. A section of the school bookstore devoted to higher education, to publications on or about the institution, and by people affiliated with it, might be a focal point. Most of all, we ourselves should remember—and help people entering the system to see—that the college or university is not a given, nor is it some predictable addition to rudimentary education. It is a fascinating and unique achievement. Requiring some basic knowledge of the history of higher education is at least as reasonable as the American history exam required of applicants for citizenship.

Students and parents may feel that they are consumers because they pay tuition, room, and board in return for a very complex product and set of services. Yet, it is important to realize that, as Rudolph Weingartner, former dean at Northwestern University and former provost of the University of Pittsburgh, remarks, "Buying an education is very different from most anything else one might purchase." What is being contracted is a set of professional obligations, not at all the same as buying a car or computer. Students are more properly professional clients than they are consumers (13). Moreover, whereas consumers have already done the work needed to earn what they buy, buying an education usually entails not only having done that work (and often borrowing against future work) but also doing a separate, unique kind of work to achieve the education itself, work that is not paid. Students do not "get" or "receive" an education passively; they must exert hard effort. This fact does not diminish—it actually underscores and enhances—the obligation of a college or university to provide the best possible professional attention and service. As with a doctor or lawyer, this means catering not to the "customer's" every whim and demand but to the client's needs and reasonable expectations as they pertain to the particular professional service offered, higher education.

Students need advising to fill out course registrations, but as young adults they need to benefit from an older adult who gets them to probe more deeply their own motives for shaping their most fundamental curricular choices and, more than that, for shaping years of their lives. This is true even, perhaps especially, if they are part-time students. It is not enough to check requirements, achieve "balance," and ponder different courses. Most students secretly desire—and always need—serious conversations about the aims and ends of their education and the direction of their lives as a whole. Once a term is not enough. Ten minutes is not enough. How a student conceives of and fits into the entelechy, pursuing both instrumental and final goods, can form one general template for these conversations. One aim of advising is for the student to develop a grounded sense of hope, the hope to be a better person for experiencing higher education, and to know why. The student may hope to contribute to some project greater than the individual self, a goal that can harness and subordinate, rather than succumb to or deny, the range of motives for personal success or gain. Instead, as Jim Sleeper, a lecturer in political science at Yale, reports, we are seeing "how bleak and burdened undergraduate life can be when competition is relentless and the bottom line is defined starkly in market terms."

There is no such thing as unmotivated learning, but discovering one's mixed motives and multiple preferences is no easy matter. Nonetheless, institutions of higher education typically give only superficial assistance to students in their curricular decision making. Requirements alone are no substitute for helping a student think through why he or she should or might want to make difficult decisions, often involving trade-offs, about their education, an education that involves more than course choices.

It is important to talk openly, directly, and publicly about student life. This is not to advocate a return to all kinds of rules. But policy statements and disciplinary procedures seem insufficient. Impersonal, they have all the force and all the impotence of abstract catechisms. The "Binge Beer" newspaper ad signed by over a hundred college presidents in summer 1999 is a welcome tactic. One of the best things any administration can do is to set a tone, an expectation. Yet a tone is set chiefly by personal acts of commission and is best set orally, or face to face, not through anonymous policies. Students come to college well aware of the cheapness of moralizing slogans. If teachers and administrators can't invest something of themselves, and can't get students to see that the institution cares about the whole entelechy of its mission, then students won't be interested.

Open forums, even debates, involving students, faculty, administrators, and guests (the mix is key) may court controversy, but they leverage the presence of the institution to expose and train students to mature deliberation, persuasion, and different points of view. (Fred Friendly's series on public television may be one model.) If controversy threatens to provoke free speech violations or intimidation, these can be adjudicated if firm rules and publicized procedures are in place.

• • •

The above strategies directed to students all fall under one larger rubric. *The important thing is learning to care, it is commitment.* It takes a lot of time, and, like most things in life pertaining to conduct rather than knowledge, one first learns such care and commitment by seeing it practiced in person. Colleges can provide this opportunity, and it is one way, a very important way, in which they distinguish themselves from suppliers simply of information, skills, or distance learning. Of the implications and actions suggested in this section, some may seem old hat, others doubtful or minor, but each stems from a vision of the whole institutional enterprise and the coordination of the constituent parts of its entelechy. Organic growth is as complex as the change that influences it. Such organic growth is far more than reactive. It is not "organic" in the sense of a social Darwinism espoused by someone like Herbert Spencer. Rather, organic here means flexible planning and activity, administration that monitors and encourages a calibration and self-correcting interrelation of parts where a set of final goods and ends are kept uppermost in mind. It will work best if it cleaves to principles and goods understood as an ontolochy whose formulation itself is not rigidly fixed and permanent but consciously self-evolving.

Rapid Change, Long Views

The presence of different goals for higher education is not new. In the 1890s "on the usual campus could be found pockets of excitement over research, islands devoted to culture, and segments of adherence to the aim of vocational service—all existing together" (Veysey, 58). More than a century later, the challenge remains to balance and merge these goals so that, to the greatest extent possible, they strengthen one another and recognize their mutual and ultimate dependence on the pursuit of knowledge and its ethical uses. Vocational service may raise practical questions that prompt research; research can lead to new vocations and improvements in established ones; and, certainly, the study and awareness of culture presents, shapes, and at times questions many of the ideals and ideas on which service and research are predicated.

There is no Golden Age good enough to want to return to. Nostalgia in that regard cheapens history. But the metamorphosis of ideals, the transformation and creation of ideas, the alliance between civic and educational arenas, and the realignment of bodies of knowledge cannot take place imaginatively without knowing how such bodies of knowledge developed and what purposes they have served, for society and for individual *Bildung*. Only by knowing the past—including the past of institutions—can one anticipate the ways in which organic change might best take place. Constitutional scholars and judges know this. Economic market analysis and risk taking exemplify it. This knowledge at times is quantitative or experimental; in human institutions it must be expressed and practiced in assimilative, complex ways, quantitatively and qualitatively, the result of which is the capacity to make decisions about people, goals, and motivations, integrating them with decisions about dollars and bytes. Jaroslav Pelikan has studied with care the history of American education. He concludes: "The most successful leaders of modern universities have been those who have come to their task from the 'business' of teaching and research, but have then learned to administer the university as 'business' without being overwhelmed by it" (72). In other words, the ends are known and practiced first, then institutional means are mastered and fitted to those ends.

In an organic model of higher education, no one discipline can claim superiority of contribution. The idea must come from the whole person, hence the continued importance of liberal education, of the liberal arts *and* sciences, as a goal and as a foundation for any professional expertise. The premise of organic change is not from "the humanities." It is humanistic in a larger sense. It does not require someone trained in the humanities. And the individuals who forget this fact most often are humanists themselves. This is especially true when they trivialize or defend themselves, well, defensively. It will prove wiser to see knowledge and reason, and the forms of them "we employ in the various 'humanities,'" as "basically a public inheritance" (Peters, 149). We are all, in David Hume's phrase, of the party of humanity.

This philosophical sense is practiced rarely and taught almost never, perhaps because such a vision of knowledge, values, and intellectual virtue is not specialized. It cannot be specialized. Anything this important is too important to leave to the specialist mind. The university is an organism with specialized parts, but it is essentially one body and it can act as such. Its different parts should not be like walls and gates that separate and imprison, but, as Francis Bacon said, like the veins and arteries that knit together and connect a larger body of knowledge and its applications.

Universities exist both within and outside the world of getting and spending. They must continue to enjoy a special status and relationship with society. An ivory tower is not built of the most robust or versatile material, but job training centers masquerading as a campus are no substitute. Let the image be that of a lighthouse permitting new commerce of ideas and knowledge while preventing the foundering and destruction of the old. And that lighthouse—or, rather, those lighthouses—should work as lighthouses do, impartially but visibly and dependably, over long periods of time for the good of all, as beacons that permit discovery of new territories. Their permeable border with immediate social and economic needs must yet be maintained as a border, a clear independence (Barber, 66; Kennedy 1997, 15). Each citizen is a tacit stakeholder in every institution of learning. No one, except a wrecker, wants to see any lighthouse fail, especially not another lightkeeper.

Long views are vital, longer even than those views demanded by financial investments. This is not for one generation alone; it is for a common, not an exclusive, posterity. For the success of this long view, the bottom line is not the best metaphor. Ending his chapter "Change from Without" in *Education's Great Amnesia,* Robert Proctor explores this metaphor and concludes starkly: "The past can have little or no meaning in a society ruled by the bottom line" (138–39). Yet that metaphor is far from the worst. Mr. Micawber is right about budgets. Income twenty pounds, expenses nineteen pounds, nineteen shillings, sixpence, result: happiness. Income twenty pounds, expenses twenty pounds and sixpence; result: misery. The yearly budget and five-year capital campaign are tools, means to crucial ends. They further the entelechy but are not the entelechy itself.

Any institution encompassing these means and ends will, by its own specific formulation of them, recognize their interplay in a society in which everyone has a stake, in which all citizens attempt to create a more perfect union. The pattern of the entelechy governing American civic polity is set down in the Constitution. With its amendments and carefully deliberated motto, *e pluribus unum,* it is a political model for organic growth. With its built-in capacity to meet change as interpreted through the generations, the Constitution aims not merely to establish government in positive terms; it also limits tyranny, balances the whole with the parts, prevents one area or region swallowing the others, and promotes the general welfare. It aims to admit change but not without check and consent. It works more slowly, thank goodness, than other institutions or corporations. Colleges and universities, like the Constitution, live on a long wavelength. They consist of, they persist in, purposes that should be grasped organically in their integration of means and ends, of goods that are instrumental and goods that are final. If institutions of higher education do not resolve to grow according to their own organic principles of change, and if they do not seek, reexamine, and strive to keep in balance their own entelechies, then accelerating external pressures will force them to become subservient organizations. Their operations and existence will be dictated from without rather than directed from within.

3

LEARNING FOR DOLLARS

Colleges . . . can only highly serve us when they aim not to drill, but to create. . . . Thought and knowledge are natures in which apparatus and pretension avail nothing. Gowns and pecuniary foundations, though of towns of gold, can never countervail the least sentence or syllable of wit. Forget this, and our American colleges will recede in their public importance, whilst they grow richer every year.

—RALPH WALDO EMERSON, "THE AMERICAN SCHOLAR," 1837

From its inception in medieval Europe, the idea of a college or university has included vital practical dimensions. It was never a monastery, a retreat, or an ivory tower. Many early universities were centers of medical and legal learning as well as of theology, and given the centrality of the church in medieval Europe, theology itself had practical implications for civic life. Nevertheless, none of these faculties or their associated disciplines—mathematics, rhetoric and grammar, philosophy—limited itself to utilitarian objectives, except in the broadest sense of utility. "Such service was *indirect,* not direct" (Nisbet, 34). Perhaps because education was a rare attainment in the Middle Ages and books precious and scarce, learning, where it was appreciated at all, was venerated as a grand communal enterprise. Neither universities nor education required an ulterior justification. Their importance was self-evident.

In some respects, that medieval reverence for the pursuit of knowledge has survived surprisingly intact into very different times. It continues to animate much of what goes on at colleges and universities in this country and abroad, and it in large part accounts for the moral authority that still attaches to a college degree. To this day, it is widely felt that engaging in the regimented life of a great center of learning has a transformative effect on a person. In the face of a spreading materialism that sets the terms for national activities and aspirations, just being a college graduate still entitles one to a measure of respect in contemporary America.

But this idealistic conception is fast being displaced by a wholly different set of assumptions. A competing and fundamentally incompatible system of values has established itself in American colleges and universities and is questioning the idealism of learning. This value system derives from time-honored American traditions of thrift, individualism, and common sense—attributes that can combine in any number of forms, from the noble to the downright antisocial. The particular configuration that has come to dominate college campuses took shape in contemporary corporate culture, above all in the domain of marketing. This value system is opportunistic and largely amoral. When it substitutes for scholarly idealism, which is precisely what it is now doing on college campuses, its cynicism becomes more pronounced. The same commonsensical cynicism—pervasive though not shared by all managers or executives—that sees profit making as the single and sufficient obligation of a business enterprise also sees the purpose of education flatly in terms of lifestyle: the function of a college degree is to secure status and lucrative employment for the graduate. The dean of the University of Virginia's School of Education, David W. Breneman, says, "We have moved during the past decade [the 1990s] to a view of education as a private good, capable of being bought and sold commercially" (54; also Aronowitz, 158–59). Or as one article in the *Chronicle of Higher Education* put it: "While some parents will send Junior to an Ivy League college just to have something to boast about at cocktail parties, most view a highly selective college as an investment. [These are the only two possible views mentioned!] They're betting that a degree that can cost more than $120,000 will lead to a successful career and, perhaps, a big salary for their son or daughter" (Jan. 14, 2000, A52).

What pass for ideals in this environment are not erudition or reasoning ability or ethical judgment but productivity and competitiveness, or even not that. It may be a mere name on a résumé: certain studies indicate that salaries and lifetime earnings correlate with the *name* of the institution where one received the degree, and *only* with the name; they have nothing to do with actual performance in school (Hoxby; Maull). This habitual rather than personal credentializing mocks the byword *excellence*. It encourages cynics, young and old, to care only about the name. Once in, it's over. Economists have published numerous papers relating college selectivity only to later earnings, nothing else. These often carry the implied message, or, as their authors admit, a message constantly inferred by parents and students, that such correlations of selectivity and later salary form a rational choice basis, even *the* rational choice basis, for deciding which college to attend. Frequent invitees on the lecture and conference circuit, such economists—Caroline Hoxby of Harvard and Alan Krueger of Princeton, to name two—have received wide media attention, often using words like "payoff" and "reward," which in the public eye magnifies the findings. (Many of the economists do not advocate the present system, they are merely reporting on it.) In these studies and the reporting of them, the word "value" inevitably means only one thing, money.

This seems increasingly true not only of motives for pursuing higher education but for administering it as well (Shils 1997a, 21). The rush to online learning has many motives, some laudable, but chief among them is money. This is brashly but accurately expressed in the formulation of Kevin Kinser, professor of higher education at Louisiana State University, when he discusses courses online: "Learning for learning's sake is noble, but it can hardly be the recipe for widespread profit making in higher education's new economy. . . . we could have a system where the precise value [read "amount of money"] of an educational activity would be clear, and a market-driven economy would function to allow entrepreneurial faculty members to earn what they are worth" (*CHE*, Jan. 14, 2000, B10).

The newly established set of attitudes is, in effect, a theory of higher education, one widely and uncritically accepted. In other words, it is a contemporary myth. And like most myths, the myth of higher education oriented exclusively to utilitarian goals did not arise overnight. Nor did the corporate world sandbag American academia with it. The predicament of higher education had its beginnings over a century ago and has come to fruition with the incremental but willing cooperation of colleges and universities. As David K. Brown convincingly argues in *Degrees of Control,* Americans created many colleges in the nineteenth century, colleges that in the 1880s suddenly found themselves precariously short of students. Necessity is the mother of invention: these hard-pressed institutions found a remedy for their plight in promoting utilitarian education. They set about convincing Americans that a college education—not a mere high-school degree—was a practical necessity for members and would-be members of the managerial class. This argument was spurious and remains so today, but it succeeded beyond all expectation. By 1930, 13 percent of college-age Americans were enrolled in some kind of college; by 1990 the number verged on 50 percent; in the late 1990s it exceeded 60 percent.

The system of higher education in America grew wealthy and powerful over the twentieth century, like the corporate economy that supported it. It also began to adopt the values of the business world. By gradual steps, American higher education entered into an implied contract with corporate America. In 1980 Thomas M. Stauffer, then director of

external relations for the American Council on Higher Education, articulated this contract, one then being redrawn in the face of a perceived
national economic decline: "Economic renewal . . . will necessitate the
most active participation by scholars in the classroom, laboratory, and
public domain. . . . higher education must contribute if economic renewal
is to succeed" (5). The private sector, says Arthur Levine, president of
Teachers College at Columbia, "views higher education . . . as a troubled
industry characterized by low productivity, high cost, poor management,
and low technology use" (2001, 60). Breneman notes that developments
in biomedicine and information technology "have emphasized a propri-
etary view of knowledge as a commodity to be bought and sold for private benefit, rather than the larger public good" (54). Indeed, there are
now whole "research" programs in higher education devoted exclusively
to commercial product testing (Nelson and Watt, 87). In two decades of
record prosperity—a prosperity, incidentally, for which few have given
credit to higher education, and during which education suffered historically harsh criticism, much coming from, of all places, corporate
America—the idea of a business-university contract has expanded and
become more entangling. Corporate America has now, as it were, claimed
part ownership and is presenting its bill.

Business and academics are not necessarily inimical. Over the years,
titans of American industry have shown an inspiring capacity for disinterested philanthropy. But in recent decades the general tendency has not
been disinterested. On the contrary, the underwriters of educational
growth have increasingly insisted on knowing that the money they supply serves some determinate purpose—that it produces something—and
they have not been content with nebulous benefits like "fostering learning" or "preserving culture." To pick one example at random, the General Electric Foundation put millions in a "Faculty of the Future" program to help women and minorities "pursue academic careers in
engineering, science, and business," but nothing else. Or another: Volvo
supports Columbia University's environmental program and gives money
for scholarships, but only for students at the environmental center. The
company also advertises itself by giving the president of Columbia a top-
of-the-line luxury car. Calling it a "freebie," denying any conflict of interest, and stating that Columbia was saving money, George Rupp accepted it. According to Rupp, it does not matter that there is "an
appearance of conflict." He and his administrative appointees decided,
perhaps without consulting Columbia's trustees, that no conflict existed.
However one judges this, and reasonable commentators may disagree,
Rupp articulates the squeeze facing institutions this way: "Universities

have to make the most of what is available—and also protect their reputations and academic freedom. We have to negotiate all the time." Presumably, he means negotiating so that such freedom will be protected. But his statement comes perilously close to endorsing a constant negotiation over the very nature of that freedom, or over how much of it should be protected if substantial temptations and side benefits accrue in not protecting all of it. As for Volvo, it receives tax breaks, a good deal of not-so-low-key advertising, and a direct line to intellectual capital that helps the company.

If corporations give universities the "gifts" of trade secrets, patents, or exclusive formulas it is usually only when those technologies are not yet commercially viable (they may never be), or when the corporation has failed to sell or license them to others. Opportunities for higher education exist here, but a university may need to shell out considerable legal and further research costs in order to reap any benefits, educational or financial. Meanwhile, the corporation gets an immediate tax write-off. Several corporations have garnered whopping tax breaks on gifts of $10 million to more than $60 million, with dollar values established by the companies themselves, not the IRS (*CHE*, Mar. 3, 2000, A36–38).

Increasingly, corporations want something back for their "gifts." "The corporate-giving world has become much more focused" is the way Roger Trull, president of the McMaster University Foundation puts it. "Now there's no interest in . . . giving unrestricted gifts" (*CHE*, Oct. 15, 1999, A42). Penn State signed a $14-million, twelve-year contract with Pepsi for exclusive rights to sell soft drinks on its campuses. The contract stipulated a minimum guarantee. When it was not met, was it incumbent on members of the university administration to exhort students to drink more Pepsi and, in effect, act as a shill for the company while trying to minimize the poor judgment shown in signing the contract? Fruit juice vendors say they are being forced out because their pockets are not as deep. Could anyone blame a professor of nutrition for questioning the whole enterprise?

It may be objected that these are anecdotes, but more than 130 institutions have such deals. For example, similar contracts were signed by Pepsi with Illinois community colleges, with John A. Logan College and Eastern Illinois, and with at least half a dozen others in that one state. The contract with John A. Logan College lasts twenty years. The Marion Pepsi-Cola Bottling Company's president, Harry L. Crisp II, signed some of these lucrative contracts worth millions, and gave $500,000 to Southern Illinois University at Carbondale in 1997 in exchange for drink concessions. The state board overseeing these deals had a quick response once the deals were uncovered: "There is no conflict of interest," said the president of the board, despite the fact that there was no bidding for these contracts with state institutions. As if the frequency of a practice guaranteed its probity, he added, "When you are looking at soft drinks or athletic equipment [or computers donated by software companies; medical labs paid for by drug companies; college ID cards with company logos provided by Citibank with a tie-in to personal accounts, private information, phone advertising, and local merchants; or environmental programs underwritten by huge automakers], these sorts of deals are made by colleges every day." That is the point exactly, and they proliferate despite warnings that the long-term effects will actually damage university budgets. One more piece of information on the Illinois soft drink deals: in 1998, at the time Mr. Crisp signed some of these contracts, he had another title besides president of a bottling company. He was chairman of the Illinois Community College Board (*CHE,* Aug. 13, 1999, A40; Sept. 17, 1999, A52; Sept. 10, 1999, A39).

The welcome exception to this trend is the long-standing corporate practice of matching employee gifts to nonprofit institutions. Mainly, however, if large corporations do not anticipate payback in research that may be helpful in producing or selling their products or in better-trained employees, then they fund only those causes that give corporate names wider exposure and buff them up with a touch of class. The academic humanities have little to offer in this regard. How many bookplates in libraries ascribe the gift of that volume to a corporation? The academic humanities usually lose out to the proven ticket sellers, lavish traveling art exhibitions and the performing arts—that is, to Monet, the Boston Symphony, or Alvin Ailey. Small fry get the crumbs. If one wonders at the lack of artistic innovation in some areas, part of the explanation rests in the never-back-a-loser-or-even-an-unknown policy of the arts' big "patrons."

Lloyd H. Elliott, former president of George Washington University, characterizes the trend: "Movement between profit and nonprofit organizations is now commonplace. . . . As the profit and nonprofit cultures mingle, they tend to rub off on each other." But Elliott, who himself has been a director of ten for-profit corporations, is not sanguine about this development. He wants to keep a valuable distinction, and for an important reason: "If we don't keep the lines between nonprofit and for-profit enterprises clear and precise, we risk doing irreparable damage to the eleemosynary sector of our society." The damage is already showing, for example, in the world of museums, where expansion and a more managerial class of curators have promoted commercial tie-ins, corporate advertising, and the use of museums for private gain. The *Wall Street*

Journal in 2002 ran a series of startling articles about these developments (Barnes; Gibson 2002a, 2002b; Grant; Mathews). A sitting college president, Joanne V. Creighton of Mount Holyoke, states: "The chief business of the American academy is not business, but education," and "maintaining some distance [between them] is," in fact, "the best way the academy can serve the commercial, political and social interests of our society."

To repeat, no one should object to the fact that higher education has a utilitarian function. In that regard, as Robert Bellah states, it possesses "its own legitimacy." Yet, as discussed in chapter 2, it is crucial to combine and integrate that function with other aims and ends, with what Bellah calls "education for the development of character, citizenship, and culture" (1999, 19–20).

What *Is* the Reward?

The most visible and, in some ways, the most insidious offspring of the utilitarian myth is the practical major. Although in actuality it is a rare occupation that necessitates years of specialized course work in order to fulfill the demands of an entry-level position, the narrowly focused occupational major has enjoyed phenomenal success. From modest origins at the end of the nineteenth century, the business major has grown stupendously, of late marginalizing all the traditional liberal arts and sciences, especially in larger public universities. Nationwide, in 2000 there were almost six business majors for each one in English.

A host of other, even narrower modifications of this basic pattern have followed. The best of the occupationally defined programs have smart, motivated students and faculty to match and can be more fundamentally academic than some nominally liberal arts curricula. A good many, however, rely on faculty who hold different full-time day jobs, teach a couple of two-hour evening classes a week, and yet receive salaries far in excess of full-time university faculty teaching history, government, or philosophy. In any case, a business curriculum alone cannot match the intellectual rigor of the liberal arts and sciences course of study. Its narrower goals preclude it. The liberal arts and sciences, in contrast, have aims too broad to define quickly and promise no specific utility: the "need" for courses in French literature, epistemology, or theoretical physics is merely the insatiable human craving to understand ourselves and our world. But as Martha Nussbaum observes, it

> now seems to many administrators (and parents and students) too costly to indulge in the apparently useless business of learning for the enrich-

ment of life. Many institutions that call themselves liberal arts colleges
have turned increasingly to vocational studies, curtailing humanities requirements and cutting back on humanities faculty—in effect giving up
on the idea of extending the benefits of a liberal education to their varied students. . . . People who have never learned to use reason and imagination to enter a broader world of cultures, groups, and ideas are
impoverished personally and politically, however successful their vocational preparation. (297)

Moreover, it remains unclear how successfully such students are prepared. What this trend harbors, as Nussbaum notes, is a threat to democracy. When vocational training replaces (rather than supplementing)
the cultivation of critical thinking required of citizens if they are to make
decisions in an increasingly complex world of policy and trade-offs, it
undercuts the vitality of democracy. When education precludes a grasp
of, and hence sympathy with, the knowledge and vocations of others,
then it weakens the fabric of social understanding and damages the political constitution of democracy.

In 2001 Douglas W. Foard, national head of Phi Beta Kappa for almost
twelve years, put the situation in stark terms: "American high schools
and community colleges, as well as four-year institutions, are under pressure to train a workforce rather than to educate a community." While
there are legitimate reasons for that pressure, it should not become the
only goal for higher education. "It's imperative to communicate to faculty and students alike that they must learn how to live a life, rather than
simply have the skill to earn a living" (1). Yet the push for competitive
"marketable skills" threatens to crowd out other motives.

Even at schools not regarded as "selective," the level of intelligence
in students and faculty in no way precludes an ample general education
or even an emphasis on the liberal arts and sciences. Many colleges have
diminished their emphasis on liberal arts and sciences because they have
felt it necessary to do so in a competitive market where peer institutions
tout an education that will provide a marketable skill and a job. The irony
is, it does not need to be this way. Learning for dollars is a hollow, if self-
reinforcing, myth, much like the emperor's new clothes. The Pennsylvania Association of Liberal Arts Schools, an organization embracing all
colleges in the state that confer liberal arts degrees, public and private,
large and small (and second in size only to its New York counterpart), reports that, compared with graduates of other schools, graduates of its
member schools five years out from college enjoy high employment, high
home ownership, and high income.

Yet, even where the practical major per se does not yet exist, the supposed utility of the B.A. is offered up to parents and students as the pretext for college study, and for this and associated reasons, academic standards have deteriorated in the last few decades. The foreign language requirement for the bachelor's degree is two years or less at most "elite" institutions, and one Ivy League school has eliminated it entirely. The C, which in modern memory was the average grade, in many humanities departments is now used only for grossly substandard work, if used at all. Ill-conceived sampler majors with names like "liberal studies" are supplanting single-discipline majors, thereby institutionalizing—often glorifying—a superficial approach to learning. Even the meritorious exceptions can reach beyond their grasp. While recognizing that "the most interesting questions increasingly crop up at the boundaries of traditional disciplines," Nannerl Keohane, president of Wellesley and then of Duke, admits that when it comes to interdisciplinary studies, "most universities talk a better game than they actually play" (56).

If students are encouraged to believe that higher education is just a compulsory formality, if they are invited to see the college experience as a literal investment designed to repay them in the form of higher lifetime earnings, and if this quantifiable goal is presented to them as the grand objective of all their class work—as it is in ways big and small by everyone from the president of the United States to their parents, from Hollywood studios to their guidance counselor—is it then any wonder that students treat their studies with increasing cynicism or even contempt? And yet the economic rationale for college education is the dominant, often the exclusive, one across the country, from the most selective campuses to the least. Lest the carrot of personal enrichment lack a corresponding stick, the promise of a pecuniary reward had better come true. A college education has become punishingly expensive, a huge financial burden to any family of moderate means, but a burden to which there seems no alternative. Parents usually want assurance of an ultimate repayment in kind. These days, tuition is viewed not so much a fee for education as a hefty initial cover charge exacted by the corporate-academic establishment, which will then provide the good life if the "right" career choices are made.

The staggering expense that college education imposes on parents and students is the clinching argument on behalf of the learning-for-dollars ethos. The adoption of this value by the academy has meant, ironically, a commitment to wasteful rather than efficient expenditures and, worse yet, often to expenditures for purposes irrelevant or deleterious to learning. It is paradoxical that a culture dedicated to ruthless efficiency of operation, as today's business culture is, would in the context of education express itself in reckless extravagance. But the meaning of waste varies according to an institution's primary functions. It would be wasteful for GM to maintain a two-million-volume library, just as it would be for Cornell to employ a large staff of automotive engineers. But major corporations are in little danger of adopting the priorities of a university, whereas the reverse cannot be said. In an age when "operated like a business" (Lennington) has become the shibboleth of organizational reform, mimicry of business activities is taken on faith to be a good thing. College administration has been the laboratory of this widespread assumption and of the unnatural hybridization of business and educational priorities. If the advancement of learning were still, practically regarded, the main objective of colleges and universities, administrative staffs and budgets would not in recent decades have been permitted to outgrow faculty at the rate they have. Nor would they have grown unchecked if colleges were, in fact, businesses aiming to make a profit. In the current climate of values, however, administrators simply by the nature of their occupation are perceived to be "productive" relative to faculty. After all, from a business point of view, administration takes care of the real work on campus: finance, development, operations, hiring, building plans, and labor negotiations—in which the faculty are at certain institutions lumped with all employees, though regarded as among the more troublesome. The wasteful luxury from this vantage point is a professor teaching dead languages to small classes, or asking students about the social pressures in Edith Wharton's *House of Mirth,* or investigating the demise of the Freedmen's Bureau. The "primarily literary curriculum of the traditional humanities"—a curriculum that the chemist and president of Harvard James Conant defended in 1948—"has little to offer any modern manager whose ideal world is one of quantification and predictability, and who therefore must play the role of seeming to make decisions on the basis of efficiency rather than virtue" (Proctor, 134).

Maintaining a surplus of administrative staff is both expensive and irrational, but it is dwarfed in both respects by universities' unthinking dedication to image. Corporations grow by increasing their market share; improving brand loyalty and name recognition is essential to attaining this goal. Thus, it makes business sense for corporations to spend huge sums of money attaching their names to sporting events, stadiums, skyscrapers, and the like. For many large companies, fame and success are inseparable. Competition is a life-or-death matter for a major business. A soft-drink—or software—manufacturer can and will, if given the chance, put a competing enterprise out of business by winning away its customers.

It is a fallacy and a mockery of higher education, however, to assume that the same situation obtains in the academic world. Nonetheless, many educators seem to make that assumption. Far from viewing education as a cooperative endeavor in which Princeton and Stanford and the University of Michigan are all on the same side, institutions of higher learning now square off against one another as if they were in mortal danger from each other's success. The aim of each competing institution is to secure for itself the maximum amount of reputation. Learning is still the ostensible objective, but when the time comes to make budgetary decisions, glory comes in first and education, especially at the undergraduate level, often a distant second.

Glory inheres—in this rather sordid contest—in having the "best" of everything: best faculty, best students, best facilities, best research, biggest endowment. The chilling catchword *excellence* is often invoked, which in this context means *reputation* used as a stand-in for excellence. And such reputations are almost always measured by crude quantitative means, by which an arbitrary (but nonetheless influential) ranking can be awarded—most notoriously, the yearly rankings published by *US News & World Report* (see chap. 2). To more and more people in ever more surprising places—for example, the faculties and administrations of the Ivy League—the satisfaction of doing a job well is insignificant compared with the reputation (or hearsay report) of doing it well. While a certain level of institutional pride is to be expected, the emotion at work here is more like conceit than pride.

All the lavish expenditures of the elite institutions can be rationalized as somehow in the service of learning. But the rationalizations ring hollow. Take faculty, for instance. The value of a good faculty was at one time predicated largely on the assumed importance of teaching. Without any disservice to research, it was felt that knowledge was sterile if not imparted. The fact that a famous researcher—a Joseph Schumpeter or an Enrico Fermi—brought more attention to a faculty than a dozen great teachers did not devalue teaching in the eyes of the institution. Teaching was simply known to be worthwhile. And, in fact, someone like Schumpeter taught a great deal, including countless individual undergraduate tutorials. But once famous scholars came to be regarded more as attributes of an institution than as contributors to its core activities, they began to become, at least for undergraduate education, more of a pedagogic liability. This unfortunate effect is unrelated to aptitude for teaching. Hired with the enticement of high salaries and light teaching duties, they end up, irrespective of their pedagogic abilities, draining resources from the institution's teaching function. Research is often the beneficiary of this allocation of resources, as is graduate education. But in the long term, scanting undergraduate education is to the detriment of all learning and, therefore, of society as well. One longtime observer of higher education, Mel Elfin, himself a former editor of the *US News & World Report College Guide,* speaks in 2003 of "a mostly losing struggle to restore teaching to pride of place on campus" (9).

Moreover, many faculty recognize that monetary rewards from outside may get them more rewards from their own institution—more leave time, perhaps, and certainly more publicity, which is rarely damaging. It simply raises one's profile. But the truth is, "Professors who have already made the jump to millionaire status admit their business ventures often encroach on their academic duties. Even if [a big if] they are able to teach a regular course load, their office hours on campus get eaten up with company business, and they often lack the time to help a student who needs special attention," and who also happens to be paying tuition for that professional service. The subtlety and power of this ethos infiltrating the academic calling is represented by John Hennessy, president of Stanford, when he says, "If you have enough financial independence, then you can do what you really love and not worry that you're missing the next dot-com" (*CHE,* Mar. 3, 2000, A16–17). This amazing statement, from a longtime professor and loyal servant of Stanford, first makes a distinction between financial independence and "enough" financial independence. Hennessy presumably means what most people would call getting rich. Next, he assumes that only then can one do what one really loves, say, teach. Finally, here, too, is the assumption that until you have "enough financial independence," you must be preoccupied with getting it and must worry so much about e-commerce and investing that you will not be able to teach or work. He might have taken a course in verbal as well as computer logic. To students, parents, and colleagues his syllogism sends this clear message: only by getting rich—and we should, indeed, worry about getting rich—can we do what we really love.

Endowments and Edifices

The scramble for trophy faculty, which some faculty now shamelessly exploit, and the increased emphasis on research and outside income have attracted criticism lately, though thus far that criticism has proven mostly ineffectual. Endowment building, however, remains almost entirely exempt from scrutiny. At the outset, it should be made clear that certain institutions are, indeed, underendowed and must continue to increase those funds. Frequently, the same institutions are desperately behind in tackling deferred maintenance and improving facilities to meet a minimum standard. The focus of this discussion is on a class of well-known institutions with a high public profile and great influence. Although famous institutions are at times resented for their great reserves of wealth, nevertheless few people inside the academy question the wisdom of continued, even endless wealth accumulation. There is, however, "growing criticism that our best universities seem to be intent upon maximizing their endowments—behaving increasingly like profit-making organizations" (Breneman, 54). The *Wall Street Journal* and many other publications now use "profit" to report university activities (e.g., Opdyke). Somehow, it would appear that endowments simply need to grow, the way birds need to sing. Why? And why are endowments so important in the first place? At some institutions, the security and liquidity they offer rarely seem crucial for actual existence, and historically the payout produced is, far more often than not, offset by a larger, at times a much larger, amount of money plowed back into principal for prudence and future growth.

In a cogent study published in 1990 by the University of Chicago, Henry Hansmann, professor of law at Yale, states that the success of trustees, and of presidents and deans, is increasingly measured by how much money is raised, how much the endowment increases under their aegis. Many trustees from business seem to understand the functioning of the college or university best in terms familiar to them from their own professional calling. Hansmann notes that the payout rate from endowment at many institutions is calculated at a blindingly conservative percentage that assumes no future gifts. During a period of five years in the late 1990s, Harvard raised an average of $1.1 million per day, seven days a week, 365 days a year. Given a five-day, eight-hour workweek, that amounts to $192,500 per hour. Nevertheless, this is a fraction of what Harvard earned in one year (FY1999–2000) investing its endowment. A return of almost 33 percent lifted the total from $14.2 to $19.2 billion. In ten years, Harvard's endowment nearly quadrupled—adjusted for inflation. Several times, twice quite dramatically, Harvard increased the payout on its endowment.

As Harvard and other institutions are beginning to realize, the institution would be very different if more of the return on endowment, along with more gifts and contributions, were used to defray current expenses. A number of attractive policy changes become feasible. Genuinely need-blind admissions (i.e., full-need aid) could rule. Tuition could be lowered, or more financial aid given. Or more regular faculty could be hired; or adjunct teachers could be paid better, even receive benefits (Harvard still has some teachers who receive no health benefits). Perhaps some mixture of all these could be instituted. However, Harvard has now decided, for a period of at least thirty years, to spend each year one-half of 1 percent of its total *capital* endowment (about 10 percent of the interest paid out to its faculties) to establish a bold expansion across the Charles River in Allston, Massachusetts. This will have multiple internal benefits, but its single greatest driving force is applied science and biotechnology with industry partnerships and commercial applications.

In 2000–2001 Williams College attracted national attention by freezing its tuition and fees (McGinn and McCormick, 28–29), a move paradoxically both modest and bold, modest because it could clearly afford to do so, bold because other institutions who also could afford it were unlikely to do so. But the move will mean little unless others take courage and follow suit, unless such unilateral action incites a national conversation that creates reforms and reins in laissez-faire market forces. As of 2004, Williams had attracted no followers. Tuition increases at private and public colleges continue to outpace inflation. Robert Bellah, writing about academic freedom, rightly remarks, "It is not only the state . . . that can coerce, but the market as well. When the market is not moderated by responsible government and other nonmarket mechanisms throughout society, then the market can become very coercive indeed, even totalitarian" (1999, 18).

The general rule has been to raise tuition and fees (above inflation) and to continue fund-raising so that each succeeding generation, in some sense, continues to pay an insurance premium for a future generation that never arrives. To a great extent, a truly large endowment is an insurance policy with no beneficiaries. But no matter how wealthy a college or university grows, its trustees fear to be overtaken in endowment, or endowment per capita student, by the nearest "competitor," a form of "endowment envy." And since any institution, no matter how rich, will always have a nearest competitor, no matter how distant—and since everyone will aspire to surpass the next one above it on the memorized rank list— there is no reason to think that current policies toward endowment accumulation will change. And many, probably most, persons involved in planning the finances of well-endowed American colleges and universities see nothing to worry about in that prospect.

But take one of the wealthiest institutions and think a little further into the future. In 1984 Harvard University's endowment stood at the then astonishing level of more than $2 billion. In 1988 it was $4.6 billion. In 2001 it stood at $19 billion. Even supposing that the U.S. economy goes into a depression, it is conceivable that Harvard's endowment could be valued around $40 billion or more by, say, 2020, calculated in 2001 dollars. At some point in the future, could Harvard (and several of its peers) earn enough income from endowment and other sources to cover all current expenses, without the need for *any* tuition income?

Editorialists in major newspapers seem to think so. Yet, it is not so simple. Just as the endowment itself is invested in any number of stocks, bonds, and financial instruments, the endowment of any institution is not one lump sum of money to be spent with complete freedom. It is more proper to speak of the endowment*s,* an older, more accurate form of the word now unfortunately sounding quaint. Any school actually has hundreds if not thousands of separate endowment accounts, many of them restricted to one particular purpose, and almost all of them divided historically among different schools, divisions, or departments. So, in effect, much of the money generated by endowments is restricted in use. It is a peculiar exception in American law that endowing a fund at a college or university permits the giver to control the use of the money in perpetuity. One could never do this in a personal will unless one set up a foundation or similar entity. Many donors hire sharp legal minds to make sure that the university can never use their money in any way other than the one dictated. It, and all the interest it generates, are locked in place. While schools are naturally timid about challenging this practice, administrators and development officers constantly and rightly ask for "unrestricted" gifts, enabling the school to make the best decisions about academic needs and priorities. However, some of the same people who urge that the university run itself "more like a business" ironically insist on giving their own gifts for very particular purposes and projects, especially if their names can be engraved on them. (Though in some cases the gift is freely given and then the school decides to do the naming.) Such generosity is always welcome, but the most generous act is to give without conditions, or where the school has greatest need. Yet, incredibly, the areas of constant national shortfall in giving are these: student scholarships, faculty salaries, and libraries, all on the short list of absolutely essential elements in higher education.

But to return to endowment building for its own sake: it remains a precept among Americans of more means than intellect that you can't be too rich or too thin. The first half of this maxim is nearly as foolish as the second, but who can pretend, straight-faced, that the most renowned institutions of learning in the nation don't effectively subscribe to it? Lani Guinier, professor at the Harvard Law School, comments on the values at her own university: "Money has become the exclusive denominator. It defines everything: prestige, excellence, competence, commitment to the public good" (Berkman, 40). Even granting some exaggeration for the sake of polemic, this is an alarming statement. No undergraduate or parent would docilely accept the news that every other penny of a huge tuition charge was going to fund work unconnected with undergraduate instruction. The rationale cannot even be (though this is close to the truth) that the market will bear it. There's a limit to how much calculation one dare make public. The ultimate justification for continuing with endowment-building policies will have to be that of caution. The economist Gordon Winston writes eloquently on this subject. "The problem," he says, "could be posed, with some risk of hyperbola [sic] this way, 'Where—as a college's savings increase—does prudence end and greed begin?'" (1998, 29). The practice of endowment building, according to some, "has now gotten out of control and left reason behind" (Nelson and Watt, 225). But you never know what might happen. In the service of this maxim, university endowments grow, and their managers often earn what they might in the private sector, or more. At Harvard Management, five such managers collectively earned more than $70 million in one year, an average of $14 million each. While theoretically justified by comparison with selected Wall Street salaries and bonuses (whether or not those are justifiable), it is nevertheless sobering to recall that for each manager this figure shakes out to almost 280 times the salary of many beginning assistant professors. Collectively it equals twice the total compensation of all the more than four hundred tenured professors in Harvard's Faculty of Arts and Sciences, a faculty that saw no increase in size from 1970 to 1999. In 2003 one Harvard money manager earned more than $35 million.

One can't know precisely what the future will bring. And what Samuel Johnson notes is true: "The future is purchased by the present; it is not possible to secure distant or permanent happiness but by the forbearance of some immediate gratification." A leader needs to be imaginative. But there is bad, falsely conservative imagination as well as good, cowardly as well as prescient. An admirer of General Grant defended him from the common charge that he "lacked imagination" with the following words: "It is true that he had not that kind of imagination that sees an enemy where none exists; that multiplies by five the number of those who happened to be in his front; that discovers obstacles impossible to overcome whenever there is a necessity to act." His "imaginative" colleagues very nearly scuttled the entire mission of the Union army through their unalterable caution, their capacity to imagine everything the army might lack in the campaign, and their utter inability to see that it had all it needed for the job it had to do. So it is with the really wealthy among American universities. The great risks are phantom risks to some spurious ranking based on criteria like the size of endowment. Leon Botstein is president of Bard College. It has a small endowment, yet each year spends a larger percentage of it than most universities. Botstein argues, "It is scandalous for institutions to be risk-averse in this environment" (Lively and Street, A50). Botstein has also stated, "We've reduced our definition of worth into fame and wealth, and it carries over into the way institutions think about themselves. . . . Learning and studying are very simple things, and the values they require are the love of learning and intellectual curiosity. Are they fostered by wealth? I don't think so. Smugness is fostered by wealth" (Berkman, 40). Bard College is doing well, and Botstein's approach will prove a worthy example. But most university presidents are far more cautious. If the institution's collective endowments lose ground to those of some wealthy rival, then the facade of prestige would be jeopardized.

Which brings up the literal facade. The last two decades have seen a tremendous building boom, especially (but not exclusively) on elite campuses. Classrooms, dormitories, student centers, administrative offices, gyms, stadiums—the sprucing up is campuswide and nationwide. A certain amount of building and restoring is necessary. And a certain amount of what is not necessary is unavoidable in any generation. But it must be remembered that, like any other expenditure, money spent on buildings is not spent elsewhere. Not on teaching, for instance. Not on tuition reduction, not on library collections.

If the current activity were just a surge in the perennial devotion to physical memorials it would not need mentioning. But the new trend is increasingly justified as a necessary survival behavior in the interinstitutional struggle. The process of thinking and teaching and discussion plays, at best, a modest role in planning on this scale. Aside from the costs of labs and libraries, the requirements of learning per se are quite spartan. But institutions seem convinced that the "best" students and their parents demand splendor, and that they are ready, or at least willing, to pay the price. Yet, as discussed in chapter 5, it is rarely the kind of splendor that promotes individual study and reading. Nevertheless, Duke, George Washington, NYU, UCLA, the Universities of Maryland, Pennsylvania, Texas, Virginia, Michigan, and Florida, as well as Yale and Washington Universities, all provide cable TV in many dorms. As if they were motels, some advertise free HBO. Rutgers offers a miniature golf course. Gyms in dorms are common. Massage services are provided, but this has nothing to do with strenuous sports or work programs. For example, to soothe those aching, twenty-year-old muscles you can call for a rub at the University of Texas or UCLA (Weinbach).

De-idealization, Selectivity

Fine buildings, evidence indicates (NYU is a good example), translate into high application numbers, which, in turn, translate into a higher yield of accepted students, all of which result in more of the "best" students at the institution and therefore more institutional prestige. Both the premises and the reasoning that support this syndrome are at best questionable, at worst subversive. Ironically, NYU paid its graduate teaching assistants so poorly that in 2000–2001 a majority voted to unionize. No free HBO for them.

The ratio of applicants to admissions can make good advertising, simple and easy to remember. But its significance is largely taken on faith. To be elite, a college or university has to be selective, and to be really selective, it has to keep its applicant-to-admission ratio high. Or so the thinking goes. But is a six-to-one ratio in actuality preferable to a four-to-one? Selecting among qualified applicants is a challenging task that is certainly not made easier by adding more applicants. Indeed, no matter what their intentions, an admissions office confronted with six or seven applicants for every place in the freshman class often begins to subtly favor the favored: aggressive savvy; charm; the accidentally "exotic" background that is, however, no product of the applicant's own energy, labor, or intelligence; the determination to succeed, whether or not success involves learning; and, above all, wealth and the packaged presentation and groomed list of extracurriculars that wealth permits—all these rise in importance, while those unforthcoming, eccentric, abrasive, critical, and nonconformist, even off-putting, qualities that often go with original minds become liabilities, as does the bad planning to have parents whose income falls below the national median.

In the 1960s B. Alden Thresher, former dean of admissions at MIT, drew attention to the inherent fallibility of the process. He cautioned that it "is entirely conceivable that some of the human types whom we reject as a matter of course would, under a different concept of life and its purpose, turn out to be the most needed. No admissions officer can ever afford to forget the Ugly Ducking, Cinderella, or 'the stone that the builders rejected'" (57). He has a worthy successor in MIT's current dean of admissions, Marilee Jones. Reacting against societal and institutional pressures that force applicants to be "human doings instead of human beings," she has crafted an admissions process that downplays lists of distinctions and activities and gives increased emphasis to personal interests and pleasures. She has also reactivated her university's traditional commitment to students who are the first in their family to attend college (Bombardieri).

For a sense of the shaky relationship to a complex reality that numbers can provide, consider the case of the University of Chicago. This excellent and individual institution, which, despite some financial difficulties, has been doing well for a long time and is still doing well, is in the process of self-transformation, apparently to resemble better its "more competitive" rivals. Stanford had 17,000 applicants in 1997 and Princeton 13,000, while Chicago had only 5,500. That is to say, only 2,000 more than the size of the entire four-year student body, and only 4,600 more than would enroll, about 900. What is more, by all accounts, Chicago's applicant pool is notably self-selecting: a higher proportion of Chicago's applicants have the intellectual and psychological qualifications to benefit from Chicago's distinctive and demanding curriculum than is the case with many other schools, even elite ones. Yet, perhaps because of that demanding curriculum and its emphasis on the life of the mind, only about three in ten who are accepted by Chicago elect finally to enroll, a relatively low yield ratio. As a result, the school actually admits more than half its applicants, with the final result being that about two out of every ten original applicants end up coming. This ratio of applicants to enrollees is comparable with many strong schools. From one point of view, Chicago's admissions office has a real problem: its "yield" ratio is low, and the overall number of applicants is not terribly high. But from another point of view, the students who do come are exceptional—they know that they are getting a rigorous intellectual experience, which the vast majority of those who come want. If they desire an easier time, they go elsewhere. (About one in six students leave before graduating, and this fact does raise serious questions.) At Chicago, if students select the institution even less often than the institution selects its students, this clearly does not seem to be because the school is weak intellectually or unattractive educationally. The reason, in fact, appears to be quite the opposite: a large and perhaps growing number of students and parents no longer want a terribly rigorous, intellectual atmosphere with minimal amenities. It is hard to tell precisely.

What is clear is that the University of Chicago has been unique. But the administration now seems ready to squander some real advantages and its undeniable uniqueness in pursuit of another, perhaps illusory competitiveness. Bedeviled by fears of their own concocting, perhaps they are like General McClellan, gazing across the James River and creating an invincible Army of Northern Virginia out of his own imagination. What is apparent is that those 5,500 applicants, no matter how well qualified, are not from families earning enough on the average to prevent a drain on the university's finances if it is to retain its admirable admission policy of need-blind financial aid. So, the object in the university's decision to get more applicants and expand the student body is chiefly or even exclusively a monetary one: seek students who are qualified enough intellectually but who come from wealthier families. These wealthier students will likely demand housing and recreational facilities more in line with what they are accustomed to, so those will be provided in the form of new dorms, new athletic and student centers that can be marketed. This makes a mockery of need-blind admissions, and it denies lower socioeconomic students an equal chance. In fact, the University of Chicago no longer has a strict need-blind admissions policy. The university is now marketed in the national neighborhoods that are better off. Aside from a wish to change the long-standing values and identity of the institution, the only rationale for this can be that the university could not survive financially otherwise. About that there are divided opinions. Meanwhile, other colleges fiddle in admissions aid offers with a category known as "merit within need" in order to boost the percentage of affluent students while still claiming the high ground of need-blind admissions.

In and of themselves, these tensions have ample precedent. "From its founding in 1892, the University of Chicago employed advertising with sophistication," writes Laurence Veysey. In fact, much of "it was designed specifically for an audience of businessmen and their sons" (326). The question is, should such practices, common in the Gilded Age, be revived now? As much as advertising was needed a few years after the founding of the university, should it now be pursued and intensified at Chicago (or anywhere) as a way to market the university to a richer clientele? In some respect, this runs against the ideal that family wealth should not dictate admission of applicants or the targeting of them as applicants in the first place.

The presidents of Macalester and Williams ominously conclude, "The system has been undermined by ad hoc manipulations of need measurement by [state] governments seeking political advantage, sowing confusion and raising doubts in parents' minds about exactly how colleges are using financial information families are required to divulge in such exhausting detail. No one institution has the power to put this crumbling system back on a sound footing" (McPherson and Schapiro 2001, 59). It has become a fierce calculating game. Professors, administrators, and public servants wonder why students approach their courses and studies, their public service résumés and personal moral lives in the same cal-

culating manner. As young people have done for millennia, they are simply following the example set by their elders. Leadership and cooperation could break this confusing and counterproductive "competition."
Bluntly, it's often more of a racket than a fair game. As colleges seek to be
more selective and provide cushier facilities, the socioeconomic differences in the nation are picked up, perpetuated, and even magnified from
generation to generation. No leveling GI bill has come around recently.
Robert Reich, former secretary of labor and now a professor at Brandeis,
has studied higher education and concludes, "The danger is that the increasing competition—to be selected and to be selective—will exacerbate
the widening inequalities that are raising the stakes in the first place."
The danger is that "the current competitive rush toward selectivity will
make it even less likely that lower-income children will gain access to
higher education. . . . Too many colleges and universities are using scarce
scholarship resources to lure student stars, who often come from advan-
taged [often rich] families and good secondary schools. . . . Across the
country, 'need-blind' admissions policies are vanishing" (B9). In addition, there is the curious fact that colleges seem more obsessed with how
accomplished and excellent their applicants are than with how much
their graduates have improved. Who publishes GRE scores of seniors to
show improvements made over their SATs? Institutions seem to have
scant faith in their own ability, despite four years, to whip even relatively
strong intellectual recruits into a crack unit.

Back in 1966 B. Alden Thresher, the former dean of admissions at
MIT, sounded a clear warning about this intensifying syndrome:

> The criteria in all this selection are based on limited values and objec-
> tives. The college will gain through the splendor of its reputation as a
> place from which leaders come. But is this kind of gain good for the sys-
> tem as a whole? . . . Centers of excellence are, indeed, essential. But not
> if they are artificially constructed by depriving others; not if tighter se-
> lection is, in effect, made a substitute for education by assembling a group
> that will perform under even the most dull and unimaginative tutelage.
> Excellence should be a product of the educational process and experi-
> ence, not a product of exclusion that may do more harm than good.
> (Thresher, 57)

If the quest for the high ratio is likely to result in a blander, more con-
ventional student body, the commitment to fine facilities is certain to.
In choosing among colleges, the "best" student who gives great weight to
expensive facilities and comfortable accommodations may, in the end, be
seduced by learning. But that student is more likely to treat the under-

graduate experience as a four-year pause on the way to a better lifestyle with strings of better cars and homes. As Alvin Kernan sums up this attitude to education, "It's just another consumable that you bought and paid for" (Mariantes). And with the increasing inroads made by grade inflation (Stanford's median grade in 1999 was A–) and the ever greater reliance on overworked part-time teachers, there should be fewer and fewer impediments to that consumerist approach. College may in time be less "higher education" than (pace Karl Marx) the expensive opiate of the well-to-do.

This attitude did not occur overnight. It took several decades, accelerating in the 1980s and 1990s. But it started earlier. In a brilliant, prescient article of 1968, Louis Kampf, then professor at MIT and author of *On Modernism: The Prospects for Literature and Freedom,* wrote that students were becoming aware that their studies made them "a more valuable piece of property," and that college was transforming each student into "an object." This, he argued, created a split or tension in the life of the student, trying on the one hand as a free agent to learn and to debate the values of civilization and society, working on the other hand to shape one's self to be sold as a commodity. In the late 1960s this commodification was kept in some kind of check, though Kampf cited John Kenneth Galbraith as already pointing out that the American government had decided "to keep the social order stable enough for business to do its business" and "to see that America's educational institutions provide the corporate machine with enough functionaries to keep it oiled" (Kampf, 311, 309). By the later 1970s, commodification was winning, and in 2004 it occupied the catbird seat.

Academic planning has grown shortsighted. Jockeying for the best image and name recognition may improve sales for a corporation and raise the price of its shares, but it has few benefits for the academic integrity of a college or university, or indeed for the "quality" that ostensibly accounts for the image. Good teaching and dedication to scholarship, if they are to be more than facades, must to a great extent be their own reward. Colleges have every reason to seek the most motivated and capable students, but they won't obtain those students with the lures of luxury and future wealth. The real mystique of higher education is not its comfort or its security. Quite the contrary: the real mystique of higher education is its rigor, its frustrations, difficulty, loneliness, failures as well as successes, its unending challenge to the mind and spirit.

Perhaps legendary institutions will recall this truth before they complete their metamorphosis from legends into brand names. Yet, reports of this transformation from the sources themselves display a curious pride. One issue of *Yale* magazine does not encourage the idealist: "In higher education these days, the talk is not always about deconstruction or recombinant DNA, the history of art or high-energy physics. Welcome to the world of academic trademarks and trinkets, of brand names and, perhaps surprisingly [to whom?], big business—a world that Yale, long a sideline player in the name game, has recently entered in a big way." The article closes with a vignette about the university's director of athletics: "Tom Beckett brought with him from Stanford a merchandising (to say nothing of a winning) tradition, and one of the most obvious results is the new bulldog logo. . . . All this talk about trademarks is part of a larger agenda as well. 'I like to call what we're doing marketing, not commercialism,' says Beckett," a distinction that may seem a little fine to persons from, say, an academic "tradition." One can argue that the university is forced by a "use it or lose it" legal bind: either exploit your publicly recognized name commercially or be willing to let others do so. But what kind of legal system forces a charitable or nonprofit corporation to commercialize its name and go into business as the only way to prevent others from using the name and doing so themselves?

The de-idealization of higher education has support, witting and unwitting, in high places. Some politicians may sincerely believe that the supreme and single objective of postsecondary institutions is improved economic performance. Others have a more elevated and more complex conception of what colleges and universities do, but generally they also promote the economic rationale. In the present cultural climate, it is thankless to approach voters with any but the crudest prudential arguments on behalf of higher education. A leading American educator cited by Jaroslav Pelikan warned of such false friends back in 1943: "Industry and government will control education, and it is evident that these customers will have little use for many of the wares which the institutions of higher learning value exceedingly" (Pelikan, 73). One of the goals of higher education should be to shape constituencies who demand more from their elected leaders and representatives than the one-track idea that the only thing education is really for is a boost in the leading economic indicators. Education should produce an electorate who will lead, who will correct the politicians when they become glib about being an "education" president or governor. Politics, of course, erects special obstacles to taking the high road, at least when money is involved. It may be more reasonable to hope that politicians will follow reformers out of the current situation than to expect them to lead any such reforms themselves.

Who knows the academy better than the president of a major university? Presidents and ex-presidents have produced abundant books and articles. The writings of James Conant or Robert Maynard Hutchins show that it is possible to use the insights gained in high office with candor. These pioneers of the modern university are impressive figures, yet it must be admitted that they had an easier job than fell to their successors. Colleges and universities, and the educational system as a whole, have grown steadily in size, wealth, and complexity since World War II. A president now oversees more activities and is answerable to more constituencies. A major university is a daunting entity to characterize, especially when one has been in charge of it and is personally acquainted with hundreds of eminent people ready to take offense.

Is caution, then, responsible for the subtle but pervasive Panglossian flavor that suffuses many presidential writings? The faint of heart do not, as a rule, become presidents of universities. The presidential habit of circumspection is born not of personal familiarity and good breeding but of a very understandable and in many—but not all—respects a laudable sense of identification. The president of a university becomes identified with that institution and with what that institution represents: American higher education. Not that these writers eschew or palliate all grave problems, not even those connected with their own policies. Most people capable of performing the job of president are big enough (or, at any rate, sensible enough) to admit to some mistakes of their own, and objective enough to see significant—even scandalous—flaws in the larger system. Few, however, have the stomach to go further and contemplate the possibility of a slow systemic decay. Problems there may be, according to presidential writings, but problems big enough to eat into the heart of the whole educational enterprise are simply disallowed. They do not exist because . . . because they can't exist. To say they do would be to act like scientists warning about global warming in the mid-1980s, and to incur the label slapped on those imprudently candid scholars, "mere alarmists." It seems wise to be wary of presidential assurances, and they are plentiful, that higher education is fundamentally hale and hearty. Those assurances are the product of a curious perversion of Sherlock Holmes's maxim on the art of deduction: eliminate at the start the "impossible"—what cannot be accepted—and whatever remains, however improbable, must be the truth. Real evidence can then be safely ignored.

4

HUMANITIES AND THE MARKET-MODEL UNIVERSITY

I look forward to an America which will reward achievement in the arts as we reward achievement in business or statecraft.

—JOHN F. KENNEDY, AT AMHERST COLLEGE, 1963

Economic pressures and rewards have transformed American higher education: from 1965 to 2005 budgets grew, campuses grew, and tuitions grew appallingly—even after adjusting for inflation. Advanced degrees and centers for special studies, "usually peripheral in location, personnel, and mission," multiplied (Geiger, 75). Administrative personnel multiplied faster still. After a slight downturn in the early 1970s, research funding resumed its climb and dispersed itself over a larger number of institutions. Faculty salaries eventually outstripped inflation, with a few "stars"—and quite a few administrators—earning sums unimagined in the early 1960s. The Age of Money had arrived, and happy days were here again, for some.

For others, these decades seemed like the winter of discontent. At lower pay scales, more teaching was assigned to part-time faculty. For financial, not pedagogic reasons, graduate students assumed a growing portion of the enlarged part-time labor force, a trend with obvious implications for untenured full-time faculty as well as adjuncts. Eventually, even tenured professors at many institutions feared for their jobs. The environment is tough from top to bottom. The current median term of college and university presidents—more than 70 percent of whom are imported from another institution—has increased recently but is only six years, less than that for presidents of research universities (*CHE,* Apr. 10, 1998, A49–50; Aug. 27, 1999, 38). Accountability, strategic planning, and downsizing came in vogue. The basic raison d'être of colleges and universities could no longer be assumed—or was forgotten. And—in our opinion, not coincidentally—during the Age of Money of the last forty years, American colleges and universities systematically disinvested in the humanities. Consider the data.

Vital Signs

The humanities represent a sharply declining proportion of all undergraduate degrees. For 1970–94, the number of B.A.'s conferred in the United States rose 39 percent. Among all bachelor's degrees in higher education, three majors increased five- to tenfold: computer and information sciences, protective services, and transportation and material moving. Two majors, already large, tripled: health professions and public administration. Already popular, business management more than doubled. In 1971, 78 percent more degrees were granted in business than in English. By 1994 business enjoyed a fourfold advantage, in 1996 business remained, by far, the largest major with a four-and-a-half times superiority over English. In 2000 the ratio was close to six to one. In master's degrees, business and marketing outrank English and the visual and performing arts combined by more than five to one. English, foreign languages, philosophy, and religion all declined. History fell, too. Some fields plummeted. Library science shrank to near extinction, from 1,013 B.A.'s to 58 in 1996 (*Fact Book;* Kernan 1997). On the PSAT, only 9 percent of students now indicate interest in the humanities.

Measured by faculty salaries—a clear sign of prestige and clout—the humanities fare dismally. On a national average, humanists receive the lowest faculty salaries by thousands or tens of thousands of dollars; the gap affects the whole teaching population, regardless of rank, in both colleges and universities. Nationally, in 1976 a newly hired assistant professor teaching literature earned $3,000 less than a new assistant professor in business. In 1984 that gap had grown to $10,000. In 1990 it was $20,000; by 1996 the gap exceeded $25,000. Beginning assistant professors in economics, law, engineering, and computer sciences enjoy a hefty advantage, too. In 1990 their salaries averaged $10,000 a year higher than peers in literature, by 1996 more than $15,000. Nor is English literature the runt of the litter. Fine arts, foreign languages, and education are lower yet. Salary figures at four-year institutions for 1999–2000, compiled by the College and University Personnel Association and reported by the *Chronicle of Higher Education* (May 12, 2000, A20), confirm that the growing disparities continue unabated. The spread between disciplines, in constant dollars, persists in widening. That year, beginning assistant professors in financial management averaged $69,470 in public colleges and $76,685 in private ones (colleges, not business schools, where they would generally earn much more). In English literature, the average for all ranks combined, including full and associate professors, public and private, was $51,500. Writing in 2004, Ronald G. Ehrenberg, labor economist at Cornell, reported, "It is striking how large the differentials are at the new assistant professor level between the salaries in the highest-paying disciplines and English language and literature." On average nationally, in 2001–2, new assistant professors in business were paid more than twice that of new assistant professors in any humanistic field, those in computer science or legal studies 70 percent more, and those in economics or engineering 50 percent more (Ehrenberg 2004, 27).

In 2002–3, the average salary for all ranks in financial management was $87,699 in public and $91,184 in private four-year institutions. For English literature the same pair of figures was $52,894 and $56,810 (*CHE Almanac* 2003, 22). The prize for the lowest paid teaching job in higher education—28 percent below the average of all salaries—goes for conducting a course so vitally important that almost every college in the country requires it: composition, how to write effectively. It is mistakenly called a basic skill. It is, in fact, a sophisticated skill hard to teach and difficult to learn. Composition also happens to be one of the most time-consuming of all courses to teach. Anyone who thinks anyone can teach it obviously hasn't taught it.

Salary figures don't tell the whole story, not even for faculty compensation. Consulting fees and second jobs substantially boost incomes in many disciplines—except the humanities, where outside income represents less than one-third the average earned by all disciplines (National Center for Education Statistics). The kicker is that professors in other fields, already more highly paid by the institution, spend more time on outside ventures and less on duties at the institution itself. Humanists' teaching loads are highest, with the least amount of release and research time, yet they are now expected, far more than they were three decades ago, to publish in order to secure professorial posts (Seth Katz).

Humanists are also, more than others, increasingly compelled to settle for adjunct, part-time, nontenured appointments, lower in pay, with little or no job security, and carrying reduced benefits, or none: no health care, no life insurance, no disability, often no office or e-mail account, nothing more than a year-by-year contract at low salary. When the cloth is threadbare there are no fringes. Many adjuncts teach writing, the one course administrators ironically (the kindest adverb that can be used) give the emphatic endorsement of making it a near-universal requirement.

Consider, too, the health of graduate programs. From 1975 to 1992 the elite top quarter of Ph.D. programs in English cut their yearly output by more than 29 students per program; equivalent programs in chemistry increased on average by 38, computer science by 47. On the other hand, a number of humanities programs with the lowest reputations have expanded (Goldberger, Maher, and Flattau; Maher).

In 1960 one out of every six faculty members in the country professed the liberal arts and sciences; in 1988 one in thirteen. According to the U.S. Department of Education, 50 percent of students attended predominantly liberal arts and sciences colleges in 1960; by 2000 the figure had dwindled to one-third of that, 17 percent. While one can argue that this is a return to the norm of the first half of the twentieth century, such a contention is hard to document. The truth is, there was slow slippage in the liberal arts and sciences beginning as early as 1900, interrupted in the 1950s and early '60s (Bowen and Schuster; National Science Foundation). But in the last forty years, the downward trend didn't just resume, the erosion accelerated, cutting into a base now much weaker.

The weakened condition of the humanities within higher education is also reflected in the caliber of students pursuing the disciplines.

By all available measures, national performance in the humanities has declined. SAT verbal scores have fallen. Even making every allowance for the undisputed complexity of the causes, the key fact is that they've dropped far more than SAT math scores, both reported for exactly the same population. Moreover, the number of top performers (scoring 750 or higher) in math have climbed; in language they've plunged. In 1995 the College Board "recentered" verbal scores: starting in 1996 anyone previously scoring 424 would now automatically make 500; a "perfect" 800 would be given to anyone who under the old regime would have scored as low as 730. No historical statistics now published by the College Board can be trusted unless it is noted that in publishing them the board now "recenters" all scores on tests taken since 1972! This, it is stated, is for the sake of comparison, but what it actually does is erase true comparison and obfuscate the sense of lowered scores by moving the goalposts. If the decline in ability were small, there would be no need to "recenter." It is hard not to conclude that such a word is a euphemism for "make easier" or, to use the publishing term, "dumb down." One reason given for lowered verbal scores is that more test takers speak English as a second language. But the real decline began in the early 1970s when that factor was far less significant.

Equally disturbing is the fact that SAT scores, verbal and math, correlate directly with the student's family income (*CHE,* Sept. 10, 1999, A56). If society cannot find ways to minimize the effect of personal wealth on education at the primary and secondary levels, then wealth will become the chief object of all education. The two will be seen as mutually dependent values so closely and strongly related that, with each seen as the way to the other, they will together exclude the consideration of other values.

A more select population takes the GREs. But again, the verbal slide remains unmatched in math or analytical sections. In addition, in subject tests, from 1965 to 1992 scores for chemistry and biology remain virtually unchanged. English literature scores drop by some 60 points.

Teaching and mastery of languages other than English have declined. An educationally intensive skill that might really make a positive impact for students who will work in a global economy—namely, ability in a foreign language—is neglected. Across the country, language requirements, for entrance and graduation, have been eased, even dropped. In 1960, for every 100 students in college, 16 enrolled in foreign languages. In 1970 it was 12, and by 1995, with the global economy in full swing, fewer than 8 (E. Boyer; LaFleur; Huber; Brod and Huber 1996, 1997). From 1995 to 1998 the total number of foreign-language class enrollments rose somewhat, about 4.1 percent, attributable chiefly to Spanish (*MLA Newsletter,* Winter 1999, 1–2), but this represented no gain—even a slight loss—calculated as a percentage of all class enrollments.

Past declines of the humanities were by degree. In 2004 a dangerous change in kind is occurring. Society and higher education seem to accept that the more students who enroll in college, the less important it is for any of them to study the humanities.

The Credentials Culture

Even in terms of securing future employment, does this make sense for the students themselves?

As the fate of liberal education darkens, occupational majors have largely replaced the humanities. Ironically, these courses of study fail to demonstrate that they're better preparation for their respective occupations and professions than the liberal arts and sciences. Medical schools do not prefer particular majors, not even biology, as long as basic premed courses are taken successfully. The Association of American Law Schools recommends courses that stress reading, writing, speaking, critical and logical thinking. Law schools report that by the yardsticks of law review and grades, their top students come from math, classics, and literature, with political science, economics, "pre-law," and "legal studies" ranking lower.

The idea that students are in college to prepare for full participation in society—including participation that won't advance their careers or enlarge their bank accounts—no longer has much sway in higher education. More than ever before, policies, curricula, and salaries do not follow what an institution thinks students and citizens need in order to prepare for life, work, judgments, and complex decisions requiring a social context of several kinds of knowledge; rather, policies and budgets follow, increasingly, the voting feet of students from class to class, although students' grasp of what training eventually helps to secure good jobs or a meaningful life, likely punctuated with several career changes, is often naive and unformed. If you do not believe us, take the word of a dean at Harvard Business School. Linda S. Doyle, former president and CEO of Harvard Business School publishing states, "Certain kinds of knowledge get outdated so fast now, particularly application-focused training for a job. . . . I certainly see that in business education. In the long run, that might get people to understand the value of a general, liberal-arts education" ("Future," 49). Stanley Aronowitz puts the situation this way: "Students are ill-served by educational regimes that tailor their learning to a rapidly changing workplace whose technological shifts belie the assumptions driving many specialist curricula." In a world of accelerating change, "the best preparation . . . might be to cultivate knowledge of the broadest possible kind" (161).

Following student and parental pressures for job training can be rationalized as respect for student opinion or meeting consumer demand. In the market-model university or college, what is prudent prevails. In 1998 Hugo Sonnenschein, then president of the University of Chicago, put it this way: "The commodification and marketing of higher education are unmistakable today, and we can't jolly dance along and not pay attention to them. One hears constantly from parents and students: 'We are the consumer. We pay the tuition.'" His vice president Michael Behnke, hired to improve marketing and recruitment, made college sound a little like a '60s happening: "We are in a culture of choice, of doing your own thing" (Bronner; Kirp 2001). A few months later, Sonnenschein chose to leave Chicago. His successor has kept most of the new policies in place. The situation at Chicago is complex (see chap. 3), but it is clear that in expanding the undergraduate population and in marketing the college nationally, the motive was money. In the minds of some, the financial situation of the institution had become so precarious that it simply had to generate more tuition income in order to maintain its excellence. For others, this represented a selling out of the very excellence it was meant to save. As Robert Maynard Hutchins, the great president of Chicago, once said, "When an institution determines to do something in order to get money it must lose its soul" (Kirp 2001).

Serious education often entails unpopular decisions on the part of administrators or faculty. When students don't get the education they deserve, that affects their wisdom and judgment more than their intelligence. Narrow-minded doesn't mean completely unobservant, and students can tell which way the wind blows. As one American Association of University Professors report demonstrates, undergraduates at one school became keenly aware which professors were getting paid more, and this strongly affected their choice of majors and classes. "News of these developments reached undergraduates quickly, with the result that enrollments in these fields began to increase rapidly, further accentuating the demand for faculty members in these disciplines" (Hansen, 6). For two decades the self-fulfilling prophecy has continued to unfold.

If the priorities guiding today's educational establishment paid off in practical economic benefits that could be gained no other way, they would at least have a kind of plausibility. They become questionable, however, in the face of some national and global studies that cast doubt on a direct correlation between higher education and a country's economic productivity. Other studies adjust that conclusion, but it remains unclear exactly how much higher education boosts economic productivity (see chap. 10).

Another reason students and parents choose as they do is that the United States has become the most rigidly credentialized society in the world. A B.A. is required for jobs that by no stretch of imagination need two years of full-time training, let alone four. Why do Americans think this a good requirement, or at least a necessary one? Because they think so. We've left the realm of reason and entered that of faith and mass conformity—mighty forces in human behavior. College credentializing has also lowered pressure on secondary schools to keep up their standards, so low to begin with that they prompted college credentializing in the first place. Over the past two decades, a sharply increased number of classes in four-year and especially two-year colleges must be categorized "remedial"; they teach what was once mastered in high school—or junior high. Secondary schools no longer guarantee basic skills needed for middle-income employment. But there's no reason they can't. Richard Murnane and Frank Levy argue that if high schools produced graduates who knew ninth-grade math, could read well, wrote correct simple sentences, engaged in problem solving, and possessed basic computer skills along with the ability to work in small groups, then a high school education would suffice for middle-income jobs. Yet, collectively, high schools can no longer guarantee these minimum skills. So, even if some of their graduates greatly exceed them, they must still obtain the credential of a B.A.

The Contemporary College

Because they are more segmented, more market driven, colleges and universities avidly pursue—and then advertise—trophies: star faculty, plush facilities, and the reputation of excellence, often while neglecting undergraduate teaching. Not to teach has become a *reward*. Professorial salaries correlate with teaching load *negatively*. One does not risk overstatement by concluding that the primary task of higher education now is *not* to educate, certainly not to educate undergraduates. Higher education now reserves all its highest rewards for published research. In the last thirty years the average number of maximum classroom teaching hours has remained steady, but the minimum—that is, the amount performed by those already teaching less, predominantly outside the humanities—has dropped. This trend started in the mid-1950s (Caplow and McGee). In 1965 Harry Huntt Ransom, head of the Texas higher education system, worried that "larger budgets invited larger numbers of the faculty to do less teaching in order to do more research" (37). In 1971 Robert Nisbet of UC Riverside spoke of this rising phenomenon: "Ordinary research was not enough. It had to be made conspicuous . . . through one's conspicuous exemption from all ordinary academic activities. One must first be exempted from teaching, or from a significant share of teaching" (109). This pattern is not confined to particular institutions or regions. Research can and should inform and improve teaching. But a primary emphasis on research doesn't foster that improvement. Nor does it involve faculty in consideration of the curriculum—quite the opposite. Sadly, of all data available on the subject, only one study is able to conclude that research correlates positively with teaching quality, but then only at four-year colleges, not at doctoral or research institutions.

While 80 to 90 percent of colleges and universities are not traditionally called "research institutions," the 10 to 20 percent with that reputation perform a great deal of research. Abundant anecdotal and statistical evidence connects a skewed emphasis on research with scant attention to teaching. For example, the former president of Princeton remarked that "many faculty members 'suggest that undergraduate teaching "gets in the way" of frontline and increasingly complex research . . . [while other faculty members] argue that blockbuster grants for research centers . . . siphon internal funds away from teaching.'" Hard data from the late 1960s have recently been reconfirmed: "The academic department's legitimation of, and emphasis on, research specialization made reduced teaching loads not only acceptable as a professorial goal but indeed a demarcator of status on campus" (Hearn, 26, 23). In the mid-1980s, one study reported, "only 15 percent of the faculty members at high-quality research institutions said that they were very heavily interested in teaching" (Yuker, 34–35). From 1983 to 1991 in public institutions the increase in spending for research was 40 percent greater than that for instruction (Slaughter and Leslie, 234). In 1994 William Massy, then vice president for business and finance at Stanford, and Robert Zemsky, of the Research Institute on Higher Education at the University of Pennsylvania, concluded, "The tendency to subordinate teaching to research seems to have spread from the major research universities, where it might conceivably be justified . . . to the much larger number of four- and even two-year institutions" (49). The most recent, exhaustive study, in 1997, reached a statistically unambiguous conclusion: "Our findings clearly indicate that research is rewarded more than teaching" (Fairweather, 86). In most cases, "Nothing . . . convinces faculty members that the quality of their teaching matters to their careers, especially as compared with other demands made of them, such as producing publications" (Weingartner, 55). As Nicholas Steneck, director of the Historical Center for Health Sciences at the University of Michigan, observes, "The ideal faculty position, it seems, is one that demands very little in terms of on-campus commitments and maximizes the opportunities to work with colleagues in specialized fields of research" (Steneck, 15) In the mid-1990s David Smith, president of Wolfson College, Oxford, was quoted as saying, "If you have a post open these days, you say: 'Let's find someone who can build a good research center and hope he can teach well, too.' Since research brings in the money, teaching is losing out" (Slaughter and Leslie, 225).

The erosion in teaching is not uniform. Partly this is because most smaller liberal arts and sciences colleges keep alive the respect for teaching traditionally attached to their curricula. The education practiced at these colleges brings home the value of intensive, small-classroom teaching to teacher and student alike. When people who have gone through this regimen step out into the world, whether as graduate students, parents, teachers at larger institutions, or simply as citizens concerned with the health of the culture they inhabit, they carry the memories of their own college experiences both in and out of the classroom. They carry high pedagogical expectations, too—not just for themselves but for their children, their own students, and for children and students in general—and they do not abandon those expectations when they see them frustrated or disappointed elsewhere.

The erosion in teaching is not uniform also in part because faculty in the humanities teach differently and teach more, especially faculty in the languages and composition. They teach more because by tradition and by virtue of the areas they encompass, the humanities have charge of literacy in undergraduate education. Their basic mission is to ensure that recipients of the bachelor's degree can read and write critically, can reason in language (often more than one language), can argue, can persuade and be open to persuasion. Teachers in other disciplines assist humanities faculty in this task, and not infrequently surpass them. But the bulk of this job—much of it the hardest, most time-consuming and least rewarded—belongs to the humanities. Yet why, for example, are first-year graduate students, some barely three months from the B.A., often assigned freshman composition, a required course central to writing, critical thought, and the logic of argument? Because it's far cheaper for the institution. The money saved is spent elsewhere.

Given that professors in the humanities are paid much less than those in other fields, and given that the tuition paid by humanities majors usually equals the tuition paid by students in other fields, parents and students associated with the humanities actually subsidize the parents and students associated with other fields. In blunt terms, the poorer fields are required to enrich the richer, a lesson not without implications for national life at large.

There is no question about the benefits to the life of the mind and to the well-being of society which result from robust programs in the natural sciences. Everyone stands to gain by keeping them healthy. Yet, modern science is and will always be capital intensive. Near the beginning of the new Age of Money, in the single decade of the 1970s, start-up costs in chemistry, for example, increased on average more than 20 percent per year for ten years in a row (Association of American Universities, 20). In 2000 it could cost $3 million or more just to set up a lab for a single junior faculty member. In a competitive atmosphere, such capital-intensive fields demand large sums.

In short, test what you will—majors, salaries, graduate programs, cross-subsidies, teaching loads, requirements, languages, aims of education, standardized test scores, capital investment—the results come back the same. The humanities' vital signs are poor. There are pockets of health dotted about, but nationally the patient is not well. Since the late 1960s the humanities have been neglected, downgraded, and forced to retrench, all at a time when other areas of higher education have grown in numbers, wealth, and influence. To term the last thirty years the Age of Money refers in part to the dollar influx of research grants, higher tuitions, and grander capital improvements. But there's another, more symbolic aspect to the Age of Money, and one no less powerful for being more symbolic. The mere concept of money turns out to be the secret key to prestige, influence, and power in the American academic world. Here's how.

The Three Criteria

The starved logic that sees money as the most desirable result of education—that knowledge is money or should be directly convertible to it—has produced what we call the three criteria, mentioned already in chapters 1 and 2. Their rule is remarkably potent, uniform, and verifiable. Academic fields that offer one (or more) of the three criteria thrive; any field lacking all three languishes. This effect can be measured by any one or combination of indices—relative proportion of degrees earned, faculty salaries, time allotted for research, new numbers of faculty appointed, graduate or professional populations, capital investment in facilities, support staff, and alumni giving. As outlined in chapter 1, in the Age of Money the royal road to success is to meet at least one of the following:

> *A Promise of Money.* The field is popularly linked, even if erroneously, to improved chances of securing an occupation or profession that promises above-average lifetime earnings.
> *A Knowledge of Money.* The field itself studies money—fiscal, business, financial, or economic matters and markets—whether practically or more theoretically.
> *A Source of Money.* The field receives significant external money, that is, research contracts, federal grants or funding support, drug company checks, or corporate underwriting.

The humanities, apart from a few superstar professors and high-profile performing arts programs, satisfy none of the three criteria. They've been penalized accordingly with a steady loss of respect, students, and, yes, money. Fields that study money, receive external money, or are associated—rightly or wrongly—with monetary rewards are precisely those that have fared best in American higher education in the last thirty years. (Theoretical physics is an interesting anomaly among the sciences. It's met the third criterion to some degree but produces little of immediate utility and is often now cut off from high-paying jobs and funding, such as that for the Super Conducting Super Collider.) Psychology falls in the middle of all fields, sociology and anthropology slightly below. Health and computer sciences, law, business, engineering, and applied sciences: they're all higher. The fine arts, languages, literature, history, religion, and philosophy: all lower.

Administrations and administrators of higher education nicely fit every one of the three criteria. Administration has been a booming industry, for decades outpacing, at times hugely, the growth, if any, in size of faculty. More administrative and middle-level management jobs at higher pay are created, even as support staff positions that directly help faculty members are often cut. Administration is the leading growth sector of higher education. Despite alarms sounded in the 1980s, this trend continues unabated at many institutions (Nicklin and Blumenstyk). From 1980 to 2000, overall administrative costs of most institutions jumped from 5 percent of total budget to 10 percent. And this while total budgets were themselves growing, often quite rapidly (C. Smith, 79). Some administrative growth was required to meet increased governmental regulations and a changed student body with new needs for support, including increased technology and enhanced library resources. But no one pretends that these factors explain more than half of the increase. From 1976 to 1989, nonfaculty professionals in higher education created new jobs in their own ranks: they more than doubled them (a 123 percent increase); during the same thirteen years, professional administrators permitted their faculty members to increase only 30 percent (Nelson and Watt, 40).

The bitter humor of Parkinson's Law is not that it's a good joke but that his analysis of bureaucracy is remarkably accurate: "An official wants to multiply subordinates, not rivals. . . . Officials make work for each other." This nicely predicts, for example, that if administrative and executive personnel grow by x percent, then their subordinates will grow by $2x$ percent. In a large organization you cannot have one subordinate, that's a rival; you must have at least two of them (Parkinson, 1–4, 13). This is exactly what happened in more than three thousand U.S. colleges and universities from 1985 to 1990. While full-time faculty grew only 8.6 percent, administrative personnel rose by 14.1 percent, and their subordinates, "other professionals," increased by double that, or 28.1 percent (Grassmuck; Nicklin and Blumenstyk, A43). It is virtually a law—resisted successfully at few institutions, most of them small—that central administrations tend to expand even when there is less work to do. Of course, universities initiate worthy academic and nonacademic programs to serve students, faculty, staff, alumni, and community. However laudable (though not all are), these programs accumulate. A new one rarely replaces an old one. It's an add-on. Edward Shils observes, "These activities all increase the size of the administrative staffs of the universities; they bring into the universities a larger number of persons who have no primary interest in intellectual matters and who in the course of time possess vested interests in their own activities and offices" (1997a, 23).

Many central administrations take a portion of overhead on research money to fund their own operations, including their own expansion, typically without any faculty oversight. And increasingly, administrators spend little or no time teaching or conducting research. Administrators, particularly at institutions with a large research mission, have professionalized, becoming more of a distinct class. Little by little, historical ties between faculty and administration have loosened or broken altogether. Exceptions exist, but nationwide, many administrations and faculties square off as "us" versus "them," an employer/employee pose. Faculties unionize. Power over personnel and budgets—hence over curriculum and policies—shifts away from faculties toward administrative bodies, presumably because faculty members would botch the task. Most observers believe that the already diminished faculty role in governance will further wane. Shared governance has its problems: gridlock and overly cautious players—whether faculty, administrators, or trustees—who fear to rock the boat. But overcoming the problems of shared governance is preferable to facing the trench warfare of permanent splits between faculty and administration or, equally as bad, between the humanities and sciences.

If the vast realignment we have been discussing has any justification beyond the imperatives of power and realpolitik, it must be that administrations are supposed the sounder judges of the needs and nature of higher education, research, teaching, and knowledge than are faculties themselves. A remarkable proposition, to be sure, but not by any means the oddest feature of higher education's odd predicament. It is sometimes hard, often impossible, for faculties to obtain a transparent budget, or to know beforehand of important decisions that affect their teaching, their students, their place in the institution, even their professional future. At the extreme, departments or schools are cashiered out of existence. Perhaps some should be, but who should judge? Should it not be a cooperative endeavor of faculty and administrators in which they both freely communicate and draw on each other's experience?

These developments and the money culture of higher education prompted the late Bill Readings, associate professor of comparative literature at the University of Montreal, to claim in 1996 that "the University is becoming a transnational bureaucratic corporation. . . . The University . . . no longer participates in . . . the historical project of culture" (3, 5). Four years earlier, Robert Zemsky saw the trend. Universities, he said, were becoming "more like holding companies" (Nicklin and Blumenstyk, A46). The more that colleges and universities act as purely utilitarian operations, the more these forces intensify, and the more harshly the three criteria come into play. When humanists raise these issues, they're often told, or scolded with, the Feel-Good Funding Myth.

The Feel-Good Funding Myth

Administrators and scientists have long claimed or implied that federal or external funding for research benefits not only the funded fields but all fields in the university. According to this pleasing and serviceable conjecture, funds delivered to one part of an institution are reallocated internally to benefit other parts of the institution—libraries or perhaps the humanities and the poorer social sciences (history, anthropology, and sociology). Any such claim should be expressed, if at all, in a far more circumspect, complex way: When universities first receive outside research funds for science or other fields, they are able to support those fields in a new, expanded way. As funding continues, universities can sustain or expand those fields without siphoning funds from other departments.

But accepting outside funds entails a Faustian bargain. For if those funds are later cut, universities must either retrench (perhaps drastically) in those fields, or cut elsewhere. The choice is almost always the latter. As Donald Kennedy admits—although he attempts to mollify his statement with "probably," "may," and "almost"—cutting funds that directly benefit one field will strand "all the disciplinary boats: the pinch felt in the English Department probably comes later than that in Biochemistry, but in the end it may hurt almost as much" (1997, 29). External funding increases the amount of scientific research and often the size of science faculties, a good thing. But there is no hard evidence to confirm any direct or indirect financial benefit to fields not receiving external support. To top it off, as noted below, certain studies conclude that universities end up *paying* an overall unreimbursed cost for some support. A few administrators even pursue grants that will land the university with a net cost and do so not for intellectual reasons, which could be defended, but because to have bagged such a grant looks good on their own résumés. The details of the price paid are not mentioned (C. Smith, 75). Overall, the three-criteria programs pocket the vast bulk of external funding; when it comes time to make up for funding cuts, it's share and share alike.

If debunking the Feel-Good Funding Myth seems controversial, evidence to do so is overwhelming. William Massy, echoing what Alice Rivlin had published thirty years earlier with the Brookings Institution, came to the belated, obvious conclusion that "there is a very real question of whether research is in fact being subsidized by undergraduate education." He warned that federal funding cuts will place "even greater pressure on research universities to cross-subsidize sponsored programs from all available sources" (79). "To cross-subsidize sponsored programs from all available sources" is a genteel circumlocution. It translates into: raid the already diminished funds available to the humanities and social sciences, ask alumni to support "the college" or "the university," and, in all likelihood, hike undergraduate tuition again, to underwrite the research of "sponsored" programs.

• • •

The motives and efficiency of the system are, to say the least, not clear. Two economists from major research universities report that because government grants are supposed to pay indirect costs of research, usually about 30 percent, "the main response to the indirect cost controversy has been for government and universities to devote more and more resources to calculating and auditing overhead [indirect] costs." But "this process itself is a major cause of the increase in overhead expenses because administering the accounting system is itself treated as an overhead cost!" (Noll and Rogerson, 107). More problems arise. Evidence suggests that "increased spending on research" also increases the escalation of the costs of higher education and the price tag of tuition. When institutions prepare to get in the hunt for funding, they direct "resources away from instruction." These effects seem "particularly pernicious at public institutions" (Losco and Fife, 68).

Absent a more specific rationalization of the current system, "prestige" is often offered up as the intangible benefit that accrues to the whole institution when some segments are fattened with more staff or better facilities while others make do. "Prestige" is a concept that, like a gravel pit, grows more empty with use. To be sure, there seems a gain in prestige and perhaps, in certain areas, in quality for universities that enjoy external research support; these institutions may generate a "product mix" that attracts bright students, especially undergraduates, in many fields, arguably including the humanities. But that explanation begs the question whether it's good policy or even honest to lure students with institutional prestige while chopping away at the very basis of that prestige (Garvin). Self-beguiled, many universities and even some colleges have in effect decided that their real business is golden eggs; the goose will just have to fend for itself.

None of the foregoing is intended as an assault on the sciences, nor indeed on any funded field. Any cut in funding to science represents a grave danger to research universities and to society. Scientific research is indispensable to national intellectual and economic life, as well as to its health care. It has proven a wise collective investment. Not only should it continue, it should continue to expand. Yet, the trickle-down fiction that the prosperity of programs externally funded will find its way to undergraduate instruction and to the humanities needs to be exposed for the fairy tale it is. Moreover, to spend federal grant money on anything other than its specifically designated purpose and related overhead costs violates federal law.

Consequences of Growing Inequalities

When inequities between academic areas are pointed out, the last advice that humanists should accept is to be silent because speaking up would precipitate a Kulturkampf against what "brings money in." While pretty pieces of rhetoric produced by high-ranking officials of some research universities promulgate the notion that all boats are lifted by a rising tide—and that the humanities prosper at the hands of the far more heavily funded sciences—these speeches and articles are devoid of hard figures, local or global. (For the benefit to administrators of having others know only "incomplete and ambiguous" information and figures, see Hoenack, 143–45.) Even without going in for hard sciences with heavy external funding to the extent that many other institutions do, the University of Virginia still generates humanities programs and library collections of the first water. And smaller liberal arts and sciences schools give the lie to any presumed financial dependence of the humanities on the funded "useful" disciplines. They produce humanities undergraduates the equals of their college peers at research universities, and their faculties rival and are a source for humanities faculties of those universities. As new federal guidelines for financial accounting in higher education go into effect, it might well be seen—if it's not kept under wraps— that humanities and unfunded social science programs have been cross-subsidizing so-called externally funded programs all along.

To pay markedly and, by comparison, increasingly lower salaries to professors in certain fields, using the "rationale" of the marketplace, actively denigrates and will destroy those fields treated as poor inferiors. It degrades them in the eyes of students, parents, alumni, and graduate trainees. It immediately provides a strong disincentive to enter those poorer academic fields, especially for people who have the talent and ability to enter several fields—and those people are often the most talented. It sabotages any sense of academic equality. Administrators who worship a so-called market like a golden calf actually help create it, and they will need soon to take personal responsibility for contributing to the degradation of the very fields they are supposed to nurture and cultivate.

Here one might speak not only in defense of the humanities but in defense of every field treated with growing inequity. As two naturalists attest, this affects fields in the sciences, too: "The traditional natural historian has been pushed to the margins of academe. Moreover, the institutions that finance scientific research . . . government or private . . . may wrongly assume that the natural historian has comparatively little to contribute. Unable to obtain support for their research, the natural historians drop even lower in the academic pecking order" (Wilcove and Eisner). Natural history does not meet any of the three criteria. It is all so shortsighted. Destroy natural history and an important dimension of environmental studies suffers. Disciplines cannot be treated with exact equality. But neither can genuine interdisciplinary work flourish if disciplines are treated institutionally with growing inequity.

In May of 2000 the digest standard of higher learning and its "industry," the *Chronicle of Higher Education*, published a tragic story. Scott Heller's "The Lessons of a Lost Career" is about Harold J. Overton, an ordained minister, a linguist who studied ten languages, taught twenty-seven years, and chaired his department, but at his death "was still making substantially under $40,000 a year." Overton worried constantly about debt, took on other jobs, taught extra courses at about $2,000 each, and had not been promoted to full professor at Charleston Southern University (where some new business professors earn more than long-serving humanities professors). An associate professor, Robert Rhodes, pointed all this out publicly, just the facts. Two weeks later, the president fired Rhodes on the pretext that he had "irrevocably broken the collegial bond that joins us." People who accuse others of starting class warfare are usually the ones who have already reaped the benefits of prosecuting the very conflict they accuse others of instigating. Heller has the candor to relate "the story of a bargain broken: the disintegration of an informal pact between colleges and generations of academics. The professors knew they would not get rich. But they expected to feel that the life of the mind was indeed valued, that their compensations—financial and otherwise—would sustain them." It is only one instance, but sands make the mountain. To assume it is isolated would be foolish and false. Near the end of his article, Heller concludes: "The distance between the haves and the have-nots is widening throughout higher education, not just at Charleston Southern University."

As noted above, the differences happen mainly between fields. "The cumulative advantages accruing to some disciplines," observes Cary Nelson, "are astonishing: higher salaries, supplemental summer salaries, research support that is not only substantially higher but also much easier to obtain, reduced teaching loads, extensive service from assistants and secretarial staff, constantly updated computer equipment, unlimited travel and expenses" (Nelson and Watt, 267). In higher education today, something not true before in the history of American higher education to nearly the same degree, academics are now passengers on a *Titanic:* first-class, second-class comfortable enough not to grumble until kept from the lifeboats, third-class forced below decks without leave, and low-wage labor, often with no benefits, told to shovel coal to increase speed and make profit. They drown first. It is a scandal that the enormous, and growing, discrepancies are not more of an open scandal.

"Those Milder Studies of Humanity"

Knowledge has changed and proliferated. It has changed, too, in what John Dryden calls "those milder studies of humanity." But no such changes can explain why universities and colleges have sharply disinvested in the humanities, which continue to ask what all those changes mean for us as human beings individually and socially—how such changes affect our lives and values. In 1963 Clark Kerr may have judged that the role of the humanities "was clearly a subordinate one" (Aronowitz, 32). However, forty years later, our most difficult problems remain precisely those that do not admit of solutions by quantitative or technical means alone, or, if they do, the political or social will to carry them out can't be mustered. Nor are they susceptible to solution by one traditionally defined profession working alone. Ethical debates in medicine, environmental crises, legal issues involving the history of race relations—on these questions and more we require eloquent language, hard analysis and persuasion in words, and the combined insights of science, history, religion, business, medicine, and ethical traditions.

This is something that business itself understands. Each year 150,000 people apply to Southwest Airlines, ranked by *Fortune* as the number one company to work for in America. Of these, 5,000 are hired; the company can take its pick. CEO Herb Kelleher describes his work culture not as corporate but as "humanistic," where "intangibles," not specific credentials, count the most. Similarly, Marvin Bower, the former leader of McKinsey & Co., one of the most successful and respected of management consulting firms, said he "built McKinsey into a global consulting powerhouse by insisting that values mattered more than money" (Byrne, 38). Bower's view was that consulting is a profession, not a business, and that it serves clients, not consumers. The same distinction would help set the gyroscope of higher education on a better course.

However, humanists of the last three decades responded to the three criteria with near-complete ineptitude. They yielded ground in various ways on nearly all fronts. Many of their tactical and strategic failures can be traced to their apologetic attitude to other disciplines, itself arising from self-doubt about the value and relevance of their own activities. Humanists began speaking—and arguing—more and more only with themselves, and then wondered where the audience went. Their acquiescence in the role of grateful pensioner of the implicitly "useful" three-criteria disciplines and administrations was tacit acceptance of their low rank in the academic hierarchy of a new era.

It must be admitted, in fairness, that humanists have been maneuvered into a false position where any response seems like an endorsement of the pecuniary ethos. To insist on their fair share of funding, if only for equal salaries and library collections, is, in appearance, to accept the false proposition that money is the measure of everything. Yet if they endure without protest their Cinderella status vis-à-vis the three-criteria disciplines, they end up conveying the same message: what is, is right.

No such problem would exist if humanists were not embarrassed to proclaim their traditional eminence in the academy. Humanists willing to stand up for their high relevance have only to say both "Yes, we too need money—and more than we're getting—to support our activities" and "No, that doesn't mean we accept the status of wealth as the paramount human and educational value." Not having done so, humanists and the humanities have come to be construed as useless, an expensive and dispensable luxury. This sort of idea could, in a different climate, be laughed off as academic slander. The scandal is that, collectively, by silence in general, as well as in faculty meetings and administrative posts, humanists have acquiesced.

The humanities inform every deliberative body from the U.S. Congress down to the local PTA. The fact is that no matter what is happening in higher education, no one ever stops dealing with ethics and aesthetics, with language and rhetoric and religion and the arts, with the legacy of our past. We're human—we couldn't stop being that if we wanted to. What can be done, evidently, is to pretend that we can cope with these matters just as well if no one studies them. A peculiarity of American society is the capacity to question, with apparent sincerity, the desirability of producing and supporting minds trained in the study of such matters. In this capacity the nation seems unique. In Germany, after all, it was the humanities and not the sciences that first introduced, in the earlier nineteenth century, rigorous empirical methods. These sharpened the search for editorial and linguistic knowledge of written texts.

And, in turn, knowledge and awareness of these systematic methods in the humanities prepared the way for concerted scientific research in German and American universities in the mid- and later nineteenth century (Ashby, 22–23). The American tradition of anti-intellectualism is all the more amazing in light of the nation's history, since it counts among the Founding Fathers some of the most distinguished and learned humanists ever to engage in political life: Madison, Franklin, Jefferson, John Adams, John Quincy Adams, Marshall, and Jay, to name a few. This is a country that spends more to advertise beer and shaving cream on one Super Bowl Sunday (not to mention tax subsidies to build the stadiums) than its government spends on music and art and theater in a year. As Richard Hofstadter quipped in 1963, "In the United States the play of the mind is perhaps the only form of play that is not looked upon with the most tender indulgence" (33).

Remarkably, humanists have been active participants in their own subversion. A few stuck their heads in the sand and waited for change to go away. Others fell upon each other in accusations of right and left, traditional and trendy. Inner political and theoretical bickering in the humanities, prevalent for two decades, has contributed little wisdom to the political life of the country or local communities, a point underscored recently by Richard Rorty. Just as the cult of money was laying siege to the culture of learning, many beleaguered exponents of humanistic study divided into parties and embarked on a series of unedifying public disputes, including ones that degraded the name "humanist." To say that no one can be disinterested or pursue a disciplined search for objective knowledge became so common that it became cant. Then, astonishingly, in many quarters, such cant became regarded as—what else—objective knowledge! (Happily, the self-contradictions of this scheme prevented its implementation, if not its promulgation.) New subjects were worthy enough: the nature of language and gender, the roles of politics and race and non-Western culture. And these received fresh, welcome attention. The disputes produced positive curricular changes and aired some cultural questions long ignored or suppressed. But such gains were often squandered through endemic pettiness, bad faith, bitterness, and guilt by association. Tolerance, inclusiveness, and original thinking were touted, but the practice was frequently obscurantist and arrogant. Most serious, the debates were often not responsible in scholarly terms. Humanists developed their own cult of personalities, their own politically motivated games of name recognition. And nowadays few people, understandably, want to write the way many professors of literature do. The humanities exerted little impact on the way individuals viewed higher education or governed it. In the mid-1980s Northrop Frye warned that humanists, like Fortinbras in *Hamlet*, were starting to fight wars over territories barely large enough to hold the contending armies.

Troubling, too, was one general failure—might it be called ignorance?—of humanists who "discovered" being "interdisciplinary" or, conversely, pursued hyperspecialization. Both groups failed to grasp that, historically (no matter what narrowing had occurred since the 1940s), the humanities had always sought results emanating from other areas of endeavor in order to incorporate those results into judgments of human value, relevance, and historical significance. This is one aspect of Matthew Arnold's apologia: the humanities absorb and interpret the results of science, knowledge, and technology for inner lives, values, and ideals. The humanities help direct their uses in light of what is inherited in cultures, in light of what we cherish yet also criticize, in light of what we must change in order to continue to cherish.

If recent internecine wranglings are impoverished and their appeal diminished by rebarbative jargon, by name-calling, by narrow specialization, and by the dull, predictable accusations of being on the wrong side of a polarized "war" (where an intelligent middle ground is regarded as "solid" but not "sexy" enough), then it's all the more sobering to realize that humanists have picked an especially bad time to fall upon each other. In his 1994 book *Dogmatic Wisdom,* Russell Jacoby warned humanists to recognize that the real division to cause concern is not in the canon debates or culture wars but in the "narrow practicality" that increasingly marks higher education. In 1997 Earl Shorris put it this way: "The division should come between market-driven culture and the humanities, not between the beauty of an Asian poem and a European poem" (1997a, 343).

• • •

The humanities can better fulfill their functions and impart skills if they teach rhetoric and prose argument again, not simply as the correction of mechanical faults in composition, but as logic, dialectic, and sound as well as persuasive argument. Language is that great instrumentality serving all nonquantitative disciplines. To teach it requires using first-rate models of intellectual prose, the majority of which are not contemporary. Teaching composition as autobiography is not teaching composition at all.

What always in the Western tradition accompanied rhetoric (partly because some philosophers had a dim view of rhetoric)—that is, moral philosophy—needs to be taught prior to any professional ethics, when it is too late to start. It is legitimate and useful to require students to investigate ethical questions and issues; it is futile and counterproductive to dictate the results (see chaps. 6 through 8).

Seeking relevance from the past can be accomplished not by forcing Austen or Shakespeare to be "our contemporary," but by challenging everyone to ask why certain texts and arts persist, why their ideas and visions do not die and are not mired in the prejudices of their own times. "Relevance," tainted by its use in the 1960s, has always been one goal of the humanities: to affect action and conduct. As Alfred North Whitehead remarks, the danger of academic study is inert knowledge; Edmund Burke argues that, accounting for changed circumstances but not jettisoning wisdom, past models should not be directly imitated but imaginatively applied.

Genuine interdisciplinary study rather than mere talk about it is needed. Only one Ph.D. program in English requires formal study in even one of the following: history, history of science, philosophy, art, music, government, law, or religion. Required languages have slipped from three to, sometimes, one. It is important to revitalize *litterae humaniores,* the articulated spine of many disciplines that form the backbone of the humanities—plural.

In teaching, publication, and promotions, it should be asked how specialization serves a broader understanding beyond the immediate topic, and how it serves general humanistic ends such as tolerance, critical thinking, judgment of motives, aesthetics, and a sense of the relationship of knowledge to experience and conduct.

There are now available more of past and present expressions of human experience than ever before. There is the potential to produce educated individuals who are the least provincial in history. Technology is an added boon. Information systems, sophisticated enough to benefit the humanities, are revolutionizing libraries and can spread humanistic learning as nothing else since the rise of the printed book and mass literacy. Vast collections are literally at our fingertips (all English poetry and much prose, 800–1900, for example). Without sacrificing print collections, conversation and personal contact, incorporation of technology enhances and advances the humanities, too.

A caveat: Since 1650—Milton being the most recent plausible candidate to have read virtually all of importance that was printed in his own day—there have always existed more key texts and scholarship in the humanities (now even in a single subfield) than any one person can consult, let alone master. The crucial issue is actual time spent in hard reading, careful listening, and painstaking revision. Only 15 percent of college papers are rewritten. New technologies have not made writing demonstrably better, nor the teaching of writing either better or easier (Strauss). The technology having the greatest impact on American society since 1950 may still well be TV. Studies cited by *Time* magazine provide sobering statistics: the average American child views thirty thousand TV commercials per year, estimated conservatively at thirty-five minutes each day; the average child aged six to twelve reads 63.7 hours per year at home, eleven minutes each day, one-third the time spent viewing commercials, let alone the actual programs ("Numbers"). Recall the halcyon predictions from education experts in the early 1950s about the virtually limitless, positive effects of TV? The sad irony is, they had good reasons, in terms of technical potential, to make them.

Because much of their subject matter was written in, or deals with, times before the present generation, it is often assumed that the humanities look essentially backward, concerned with the human condition as it has been rather than as it is or might be. Even someone as sophisticated as Harold Shapiro, former president of Princeton, can regard humanistic education as having stressed mere "indoctrination," "some specified set of moral claims" (78–79), a judgment that would have disturbed not a few thinkers venerated in older pantheons: Socrates, for instance, or Erasmus, Mary Wollstonecraft, Voltaire, John Quincy Adams, George Eliot, or Frederick Douglass. The humanities preserve in order to reform. They pay attention, even homage, to the past, but they also criticize whatever is inherited and calibrate the fact that social and individual lives change in the present in order to serve the future. The humanities pursue the education of character and the shaping of society in order to balance what has been known with the pressure of what is being discovered. The humanities openly cherish and brazenly criticize and see no contradiction in the two. Human thought and communication are always both deeply traditional and of the moment. The only choice is whether to live in ignorance of the culture and history we rely on, or try to understand and use them to better and enrich our lives.

What Do We Want?

For three millennia in East and West the humanities have been associated not only with imaginative art but with the world of affairs and professions—law, medicine, trade, government. Apollo is the patron god of healers *and* poets. Solzhenitsyn's chapter on the family doctor in *Cancer Ward* might be put before medical school students and their teachers. Law has ancient, deep connections with rhetoric and composition. Solon wrote his legal code in verse. Behind the Iron Curtain—in fact, wherever there was or is repression and intolerance—poets and physicists alike to-gether kept the faith of humane action and human rights. The environ-mental movement unites sciences, social sciences, and humanities, busi-ness, economics, and religion. John Muir and Rachel Carson: scientists? humanists?

There is no faster way to guarantee the shattering of a societal mosaic than to assume that higher education should be the sum of a series of sep-arate professional specializations, supplemented in the humanities pri-marily by arguments over the study of various cultures constrained to serve present political goals and social agendas. Are we ready to jettison three thousand years of collective experience in higher education? In his eloquent book *The Idea of Higher Education,* Ronald Barnett concludes with a pertinent question: will higher education be forced to settle for "the narrowness of an industry-led competence-bound curriculum?" (199).

Is the disinvestment in the humanities—what might be called the de-humanization of higher education—a legitimate response to desirable market factors? Or is this disinvestment more accurately one core symp-tom of a national loss of faith in whole areas of human endeavor as they're treated in the academic world—areas not quantifiable, not driven primarily by economics, areas representing a quality of life we call cul-ture? Whatever the answer, the systematic devaluing of humanistic study in higher education makes it suicidal for humanists to trivialize them-selves, producing specialized studies few care to read, or to knuckle under to demands for more publication at the expense of more and bet-ter teaching and better, not more, publications.

An economic social Darwinism can apply itself to higher education. Society seems bent on distancing itself from pursuits and learning that take considerable time and don't pay immediate cash dividends. Eco-nomic competitiveness is responsible for much good and prosperity. But when visited on every segment of society, and on higher education as an exclusive goal, it may contribute to a social breakup. Do we want it in-creasingly applied to colleges and universities?

It has been avowed that "the discovery and transmission of truth is the distinctive task of the academic profession" (Shils 1997a, 3). Neil Rudenstine, who led Harvard for a decade, contends that "the only in-stitutions charged with trying to keep, as fully and accurately as possible, what we might call 'the human record,' the record of civilization," are colleges and universities. "And that includes constantly interpreting the record as we know it." Responding to this, Ethan Bronner echoes that universities "serve the function of being honest brokers of information and knowledge. At a time when public discourse is shot through with branding, and the use of the information is sometimes suspect if it comes from the private sector, the research university offers itself as an arbiter of knowledge" ("Future of the Research University," 47–48). But do we care any more whether colleges and universities are custodians of collective, diverse cultures; whether they record, teach, and transmit traditions; whether they provide the linguistic and symbolic tools to express our veneration, criticism, and contribution to culture; whether they make connections within its variety and examine its checkered past and imagine its possible future? If institutions of higher education don't do this, who will? For intelligent young people, should careers in the humanities be obviously much less attractive, and increasingly so, than other options open to them? Should market forces thoroughly work their will on the very set of institutions that we once, after careful deliberation, decided should be largely protected from them?

It all boils down to one question: Does it matter? The nation cannot steer the best course through exciting but complex and perilous times without the aid and leadership of men and women who have mastered language, who can put together a sound argument and blow a specious one to bits, who have learned from the past, and who have witnessed the treacheries and glories of human experience profoundly revealed by writers and artists. The humanities can and should be broadly instrumental, as well as existing for pleasure and aesthetic pursuits. Their functions are multiple. Especially with regard to the uses of language, history, and ethical reflection—as well as alerting everyone to their abuses—the humanities can keep our collective capacities for thinking flexible, adaptable, inquisitive, tolerant, and open, and not only open to reasoned discourse but actively involved in shaping the best expression of that discourse. Narrowly conceived instrumentality is an enemy of this spirit, and this spirit is necessary for a free society.

But if nothing changes, society will soon face a difficult world and the formidable complexities of an endlessly complicated future without new generations trained in that spirit. We will soon be looking at, not a weakened tradition of humanistic learning and education, but a defunct one.

5

THE DESTRUCTION OF READING

When you see my face in libraries on a poster that says READ, you know that I've been a lover of that passing fad, literacy. I've spent many years encouraging young people to go to books instead of the mall. However, I am afraid that one day soon, young people won't be reading much more than BANANA REPUBLIC and EXIT. And the incredible thing is that this dumbing down is being led by our colleges, *where cell phones and beepers are sounding instead of an alarm.*

—BILL COSBY, "SHOULD YOU HAVE TAKEN
THE *CONSERVATIVE* ARTS?" 1999

This book deals with the inversion of priorities on college and university campuses, and this chapter presents one such inversion, both glaring and subtle. It is also an inversion directly related to how time and money are spent. On the contemporary campus, reading, arguably *the* constitutive activity of higher education, is frequently treated as a wasteful and dispensable luxury, while entirely dispensable luxuries—cable television, fast-food courts, the latest gym equipment—are purchased as necessities. This reconfiguration of values, though obvious once noticed, does not grab attention because the activity it affects, reading, is by its very nature reclusive, quiet, and generally practiced in hours of solitude.

The complexities of language and the full scope of written texts form the backbone of whole bodies of knowledge. Profoundly and perpetually challenging books, documents, and essays in politics, philosophy, history, theology, and literature shape and define those modern disciplines. Expressive spirits, such as Thucydides, Mencius, Galileo, Li Po, Spinoza, Kant, Jefferson, Wollstonecraft, Douglass, Keynes, DuBois, Wittgenstein, and Holmes, do not bequeath sets of strict procedures to follow or facts to plug in, but restless, complex works that defy substitute summaries. The life and power of such texts rest in their study, interpretation, and application. They give rise to other texts of varying but often great or even greater value. Taken together, these diverse writings and the teaching of them fill many college curricula. Discussions about curriculum—what to teach—are constant. Disputes on this single topic have the potential to disrupt institutions. Curricular matters and the associated debate over a literary or cultural "canon" command public attention, too. While not the main subject here, that debate is important. Unfortunately, it generates constant heat but sporadic light, and it often produces the false rhetoric of pseudopolitical polarization. Even some better-informed commentators on education, ones with thoughtful ideas to offer (Shapiro and Kennedy, for example) fall into ways of writing that reinforce the common notion that the situation can be accurately depicted as a two-party system of educational philosophy and practice: one is either a "traditionalist" or a "challenger," a "conservative" or a "liberal," either a "gentleman" (i.e., a bigoted supporter of the status quo ante) or a "progressive" thinker with no prejudices (i.e., a trendy, shallow, politically correct ideologue). After a while, this reductive analysis creates and reinforces the polarized reality it posits. Acceptance of this schema leaves little room for what Susan Haack calls a "passionate moderate," let alone for an eccentric thinker whose ideas toe no particular ideological or political line.

But the argument here is not about those divisions. It is about something more fundamental. Every one of these issues assumes the untroubled continuance of certain essential conditions that receive scant attention. Despite very large sums pumped into buildings and information technology, and despite seemingly endless debates over what should be taught, the actual conditions for learning, and, above all, for learning to love the inheritance of human thought expressed and preserved in language, are not improving. They are deteriorating. Reading-intensive fields in the social sciences and humanities generally do not meet any of the three criteria of money: its promise, its direct study, or its receipt (see chap. 4). Moreover, there is another kind of erosion especially evident in institutions of higher learning pressed for space and enmeshed in urban environments that restrict growth or improvement. More and more faculty commute. Student housing is frequently squeezed to the extent that Virginia Woolf's minimal condition for productive literary activity, "a room of one's own," is now denied to women and men alike and instead allotted to the rich, the lucky, or a few seniors who win the housing lottery. The changing physical environment of American higher education is, for the purpose of intensive reading, changing for the worse.

This does not mean reading just novels, plays, poems, and their associated criticism. It means reading what David Hume, Cardinal Newman, and Raymond Williams mean by literature: the written record, in language, of human thought and experience; whatever in knowledge and values can be expressed only by exploiting fully the resources of language. Over and above what is now conventionally regarded as history or literature, much in political science, economics, psychology, anthropology, religion, ethnic studies, and even the physical sciences is, in this broader sense, literature—what used to be called "letters"—and it requires hard, intensive reading.

The effect of this subtle, far-reaching deterioration is deleterious and cannot be underestimated. As college populations increase and admissions applications set record highs at many schools, not only has the study of written texts changed—it always will—and not only have new questions been raised and new methods devised in every field, but something else, unprecedented though usually ignored, has set in: a decline in the conditions provided for the study and learning of knowledge conveyed by language in complex written texts.

"Conditions" here does not mean the conditions of the faculty—leave time, schedules, tenure decisions, course loads, compensation, grants and fellowships, or support staff. These play a crucial role in teaching and scholarship, but they receive constant attention and lobbying. Here, "conditions" means, first of all, the social and intellectual conditions of what Northrop Frye calls this "post-literate" age, a society deluged in visual images and one not very productive of avid readers: more than half of young Americans attend college, yet one-fifth of the adult population is functionally illiterate. An even larger percentage fails to attain what E. D. Hirsch identifies as "cultural literacy." Digitization has changed written and visual materials. It has transformed their storage, retrieval, and availability. There is now more at fingertips' end than many previous scholars might have obtained in days or months. This is good and desirable. Yet, this availability guarantees opportunity, nothing more. It does nothing to perform the tasks of reading, absorbing, disputing, comparing, interpreting, and judging that material. The desiderata and goals of many digital advances are evident, as every advertised improvement in personal computing indicates: speed, visualization, more memory, multiple, quickly changed applications, the interface of media, immediacy, and ease. This reduces effort and saves time. Saves it for what? More television and more time-saving? It is an irony that the most time-consuming preoccupation in the United States is saving time itself. So, increased productivity has produced the overworked American, a harried life amply documented, quantitatively as well as qualitatively. It is more pressured than that of any previous generation, more rushed than any other society.

Television and video streaming impress on young psyches that the natural, even best medium for information, knowledge, and ideas is fast if not instantaneous. More damaging, this presentation should be "fun"; it should entertain. Neil Postman states, "The problem is not that television presents us with entertaining subject matter"—although it fails to do that frequently, despite scores of channels—"but that all subject matter is presented as entertaining, which is another issue altogether." How a student experiences life and how the student views that experience and learns from it—and that means, in large part, in what medium the student demands both experience and learning—form a large part of *what* the student learns. This in turn determines how difficult and complex are the ideas mastered; how adept the pupil becomes at unmasking faulty logic, pandering, or control of information by vested interests; and how much the student can strengthen powers of analysis, make proper generalizations, and come to reasonable inferences. This is a lesson about lessons taught first not by Marshall McLuhan but by John Dewey and, long before Dewey, by Athenians, who required youths to read and perform in the choruses of the plays (Postman 1985, 87, 51, 144).

Paradoxically, the culpability of television in the de-educating, deculturing, and decivilizing of contemporary society is so obvious that it gets neglected and, in a way, forgotten. To make matters worse, its most ardent opponents come off a bit cranky. Nonetheless, critics such as Jerry Mander, in *Four Arguments for the Elimination of Television* (1978), present a good clinical case based on extensive studies: TV encourages a passive, zombielike mental state, one neither creative nor truly relaxing. Television prepares its viewers to reduce life to a screen, for example, to prefer a computer game about a walk in the forest to a walk in one, or to prefer communication via computer over less mediated forms, like conversation. Research in the early twenty-first century, a national study by the Henry J. Kaiser Family Foundation, confirms, in a chilling way, the pernicious effects of TV on children. Many boys and girls under the age of six, and many as early as six months old, are spending two or more hours on screen time daily. A TV with remote control is now common in many children's bedrooms, a practice the American Academy of Pediatrics explicitly decries. Exposure to screens at this early age literally shuts down neural circuits otherwise dedicated to social interaction and deductive reasoning. Learning becomes passive, and the need to be entertained, rather than to learn or to imagine, grows like the addiction it is (Meltz).

Most features of popular technology militate against long periods of concentrated mental effort. They militate against reading longer, complex texts. Even Bill Gates, advocating digital tools to enhance large-scale corporate and group activities, and right to do so, admits that when anything runs over four or five pages, he prefers reading it as hard copy. Much has been written and published, electronically and in print, about the merging of paper and photons. That merger holds great opportunities (see chap. 6). Less has been said, however, about the overall effect of electronic media on attention span and on the willingness to spend long hours grappling with and comparing multiple sets of tens of thousands of words. And it is a grappling, a struggle, and an agony to read difficult texts well. If a book is written with care, a critical intelligence has poured countless hours into its composition and shape, in most cases supplemented by the aid, observation, and criticisms of others, before it appears in print or electronic transmission. Reading well—receiving and criticizing well—the complex, considered thought of another human being on a subject of mutual importance is one of the hardest things to learn to do. Writing cogent, crafted prose also takes years to develop. No important writer in English writes his or her best prose, or in most cases even a noticeably strong prose style, before the age of thirty. To cultivate that skill is the product not of a few but of many years of frustration, trial and error, rejection, correction, and self-criticism.

This kind of education, it should be stressed, is not comforting. It is uncomfortable. As the famed Williams College professor of political science Robert L. Gaudino put it, "Isn't education . . . one big upset stomach?" He spoke directly: "Pain. That's the philosophy of higher education that we work on." Yet he was no intellectual sadist in the way a few misguided teachers can become. He did not relish embarrassing students, only demanding of them that they do their best. He had the audacity to insist that students show up on time, address each other formally, speak in complete sentences, and finish assigned readings before class. He asked uncomfortable questions, and he didn't just let them float over the assembled group. He would turn to ask one particular student the tough query. He would push and could be witty in his pushing. The now former president of Carleton College, Stephen R. Lewis Jr., engaged Gaudino in conversation in 1960. Lewis mentioned that he might like to become a college administrator. Gaudino replied, "But, Mr. Lewis, I thought you were interested in education!" Gaudino earned a reputation at Williams that places him in the forefront of all its teachers. His students became excellent lawyers, educators, businessmen, and public servants. They so admire his legacy that they—among them Lewis—keep up a fund in his honor (Zernike 1999b).

Roughly since the advent of television and its impact on a generation now middle-aged, and in stark contrast to teachers like Gaudino, publishers have consistently dumbed down textbooks. Editors assigned specifically for that purpose take the language of leaders in the field and simplify it. This is not editing intended to clear away obfuscation, jargon, needlessly dense terminology, or just plain bad writing. Too much of that remains in other publications, a good deal of it in scholarly monographs issued by presses that have occasionally abdicated editorial responsibilities. Real dumbing down takes perfectly good language and prunes its vocabulary, reduces its syntactic range, shortens its sentences, and simplifies its ideas. The earlier in school this lowering of verbal expectations begins, the more it seems (or becomes) necessary later on. It starts in elementary- and secondary-school textbooks and proceeds through college- and even, in some cases, graduate-level readings. Things that get dumbed get dumber—and people too.

Discussing textbooks of American history, one Macmillan/McGraw-Hill editor, who did not want to be identified, said, "In trying to avoid anything that might be offensive to either the left or the right, we were reduced to producing totally bland . . . pabulum." The whole process, states Byron Hollinshead, former president of American Heritage and Oxford University Press, "is destined to produce a dumbed-down product." More pictures, more snippets, more sidebars, more graphics: it's not as if the books were designed for young readers with attention deficit disorder, it's as if the books were designed to *create* that disorder. And historical substance? Houghton Mifflin's *Build Our Nation* gives the student thirty-three lines on the Great Depression and the whole of FDR's administration combined (thirteen years). Then it devotes more than two entire pages to Cal Ripken Jr., a baseball player who holds the record for appearing in most consecutive games (Stille 1998, 15, 16, 18). This is the old case of lowered expectations writ large. Invoke them and you get lower performance. Teaching and reading "down" achieve what they cater to: something lower. In a fundamental sense, it's a kind of cheat.

Increasingly, students who use online services such as Campus Pipeline are, while "reading," bombarded with flickering or "flash" ad messages as part of that medium of learning. This supposedly saves the school money; what it really does is buy distraction at the price of integrity. It inextricably connects the life of the mind with commercialism. Andrew Hagelshaw, executive director of the Center for Commercial Free Public Education, warns, "We've gotten to the point where students don't mind being used. . . . There's advertising in the hallways, in lunchrooms, in the curriculum. After a while, it becomes invisible: you don't understand how it's happening or how they're using you" (Zernike 2001). "In short," as Thomas Ehrlich of the Carnegie Foundation remarks, "the use of advertising says to the student that the institution can be bought. Even student learning can be bought" (*CHE,* Sept. 24, 1999, A76). Moreover, many schools, including MIT, Brown, and Duke, pipe college TV networks such as Burly Bear directly into dorm rooms. Freely distributed programming includes *The SexTalk Show* and is in no way educational. David Owen, who manages the TV system at Michigan State, is unabashed about the reason for this: "That is the key word—'free,'" he explains. "It's a way to enhance the resident life. . . . It's what they're talking about anyway" (Rutenberg).

Out in the commercial world, the average American newspaper publishes at the reading level of a twelve-year-old. In Europe and Japan that level is sixteen and eighteen, respectively. If reading can be understood without much attention, if it quaffs like some insipid liquid, there's not much to it. The writer William H. Gass, who teaches at Washington University, remarks about his early reading encounters: "Joyce, [H. G.] Wells, Carlyle. Well, Wells I could understand. That, I would realize later, was what was the matter with him" (48). Late in life, Goethe confided to his friend Eckermann, "Folks don't realize what time and effort it takes to *learn to read*. I've needed eighty years for it and still can't say that I've got it down pat."

A book of testimonials could be compiled on the joys of reading, and another book of advice on its usefulness. Such books have been published, but what good are they unless read? In *Idealism and Liberal Education,* James Freedman, former president of the University of Iowa and Dartmouth, cites two compelling passages. Judge Learned Hand avowed, "It is as important to a judge called upon to pass on a question of constitutional law, to have at least a bowing acquaintance with Acton and Maitland, with Thucydides, Gibbon and Carlyle, with Homer, Dante, Shakespeare and Milton, with Machiavelli, Montaigne and Rabelais, with Plato, Bacon, Hume and Kant, as with the books which have been specifically written on the subject." Justice Felix Frankfurter advised a boy with dreams of a law career: "The best way to prepare for the law is to come to the study of the law as a well-read person. Thus alone can one acquire the capacity to use the English language on paper and in speech and with the habits of clear thinking which only a truly liberal education can give" (16).

Yet, what is the situation now? Deanna Marcum of the Council on Library and Information Resources and Clifford Lynch from the Coalition for Networked Information note that two studies—the first by the Pew Charitable Trust, "Internet and American Life," conducted at two- and four-year institutions, and the second by Outsell, Inc., conducted at universities and liberal arts and sciences colleges—both confirm that three-quarters of all students surveyed use the Internet more frequently than the library. This is true even though the library also offers the Internet, of course, as well as many other electronic resources and the traditional print collections. Undergraduates, especially, rely on the Internet and go to the library only as a last resort, like war in diplomacy. The Internet is an incredible tool for all fields, but to use it as a default setting in reading-intensive fields raises serious questions.

Eroded Conditions for Reading

What are the basic conditions of reading-intensive study for students in day-to-day college life? These conditions are not hard to characterize but, like many simple, important things, they do not have the glamour or shock value to merit attention from the press. They are not delineated when *US News & World Report* ranks colleges. Yet every serious student, eager to learn, soon becomes concerned about these conditions not only in the classroom but also *outside* it, where, after all, the majority of students' time is spent and where they do virtually all their reading, writing, and much of their talking about what is read. The conditions necessary for learning fall into four main types: a room of one's own (privacy); secure blocks of time without hourly pressures, deadlines, or activities; well-run, well-designed libraries; and the opportunity and comfortable space for conversation with faculty and peers.

Whatever individual interests, opinions, or methods students favor, as a group they rarely enjoy the privacy and undisturbed time needed to read and digest a significant body of writing, to agonize over texts whose reward is in direct proportion to the hours devoted, or to write and rewrite with care. Even when compared with their predecessors of only twenty years ago, fewer students now "find the time" to read any books not specifically assigned. Yet, most teachers swear—and surveys and research support the assertion—that reading lists today are shorter than a generation ago. Before assigning blame to secondary schools, the stereo amplifier, economic realities of work-study, or the students' own bad planning, it is worth examining what other developments in the structure of campuses and campus life have proven hostile to the conditions that make intensive reading possible.

This problem is more pressing in some institutions than in others, and generally poses less of a threat to small, well-endowed colleges. When presidents of major research universities and MacArthur fellows in the humanities and social sciences complain that they cannot write where they teach or work, and cannot devise their best ideas except by getting away from a hectic pace and cramped quarters, then students who voice similar complaints deserve attention. "Shakespeare's plays," writes

Virginia Woolf in her famous essay *A Room of One's Own,* "seem to hang there complete by themselves. But when the web is pulled askew, hooked up at the edge, torn in the middle, one remembers that these webs are not spun in midair by incorporeal creatures, but are the work of suffering human beings, and are attached to grossly material things, like health and money and the houses we live in" (43–44). The study and love of those plays and of other complex written works, fictional and nonfictional, depend on similar conditions.

Students frequently do not have a room to call their own. They are thrown back on those conditions Woolf relates with irony and anger as she describes efforts to raise money for a women's college: "We cannot have . . . separate rooms" (21). At present, many colleges, even comparatively wealthy ones, resort to housing overflow students in local hotels or condos, squeezing two or three in a single room. What James O'Donnell of the provost's office at the University of Pennsylvania calls the "summer camp" aspect of college—an aspect with certain social benefits—becomes insidious when it impinges on or even precludes the ability to isolate one's self in order to read and think. As in summer camp, bunk beds and noise are hallmarks of the dorm experience.

Less than sixty years ago, the House system at Harvard was designed to break the power of the clubs dominated by wealthy undergraduates, but also to provide a private room for each student. The latter motivation acted as the guiding principle of architectural design, which also provided faculty office space in those Houses, so that professors and students would, rather than could, meet daily. This office space has all but vanished in order to accommodate more students. The desire originally was not luxury but an environment with minimal distraction and maximum faculty-student conversation. But as at many other colleges, two or three rooms originally intended for two students now house four, five, or six, along with several telephones, answering machines, stereos, radios, disk players, television sets, and computers. The trend to luxury dorms (see chap. 3) is not for the sake of quiet study but generally for amenities, TV rooms, kitchenettes, and diversions. For many students it is impossible to sit privately in a small room and read or write for even a few undisturbed hours.

Driven out of housing in search of quiet and privacy, students do not always find a better environment. In many college libraries, chatting and the stage whisper are tolerated. The library is often regarded as a second—or sometimes the only—social center. Some libraries provide superb study space and quiet; others are uncomfortable, poorly furnished, poorly lit, large and barnlike, with no one monitoring or enforcing any semblance of silence. Other problems arise. For instance, students should *hear* poetry and public speaking; they should read or recite aloud, but the library is hardly the place for that, and without some privacy, the practice of reading poetry and speeches to hear their music and rhythms is discouraged. In urban settings, most rooms, dining halls, offices, and buildings are, when not scheduled for regular use by groups, kept locked to prevent theft or damage. On some campuses, there is little place for privacy and quiet. As in T. S. Eliot's line from *Burnt Norton,* students are "Distracted from distraction by distraction." Neurophysiological studies verify that constant short visual bursts, distractions, and disconnected details have two strong effects: first, they create an addiction where neurons crave repeated stimulation of the same kind; second, they corrupt the cognitive ability to grasp essentials and to identify causes and effects in complex situations, whether intellectual or social.

There are still lonely thinkers. But it's hard to be one, and getting harder. The quiet time to encounter books and ideas demands this: a mind, the texts, time, and silence. But without the last two we soon won't have the first. Norman Mailer, a physics major in college, an old left liberal, and not by any stretch of the imagination a "conservative" or member of the "gentlemanly" class, comments on the situation:

Culture's worth huge, huge risks. Without culture we're all totalitarian beasts. After all, what technology promises is that . . . the world is ours to dominate. The only thing that stands up against that is culture. And culture is more than just being able to get it on CD-ROM. Culture is going into the library, and finding an old book on an old shelf, and opening it, and it has the patina of the past and maybe hasn't been taken out in five years, and that's part of its virtue at this point. There's a small communion that takes place between the book and yourself, and that's what's disappearing.

And when it disappears, the young cannot know that it existed in the first place. Teachers, especially teachers of writing, remark that computers place more in front of students and permit them to produce a greater volume of words. But despite the chance for endless revisions without endless retyping, poor quality often results. "They read more casually," says Sven Birkerts, who teaches at Mount Holyoke. "They strip-mine what they read." Because students "do not enter very deeply into either the syntax or the ideas" of what they scan, they generate their own "casual prose." The presence of e-mail and the possibility of endless, visually enticing images just one keystroke away mean that some teachers, too, by their own anxious admission, are reading less and, it would follow, writing less well, too (*CHE,* Nov. 26, 1999, A67–68; Mar. 3, 2000, A64).

Library Costs Soar, Their Budgets Flatten

Libraries face enormous pressures. They are suffering a ruthless form of institutional Darwinism. Adding digital resources and information technology increases, not reduces, the cost of keeping up adequate college teaching collections, let alone decent research libraries. Even when electronic materials do replace print ones, they often cost more, and frequently, electronic and digital resources are add-ons, not replacements. But in cutting up the campus pie, libraries often receive a small piece or even crumbs. They have no interested constituency save the faculty as a whole, which is hard to mobilize. As a result, most college and many university libraries are lagging behind, collecting less and less of what is available (in both print and digital formats), and relying more and more on interlibrary loan, or on the fact that professors will travel elsewhere to do research. And in the bizarre logic of destroying reading, universities and colleges almost seem to want to drive out those very individuals who know how to preserve and develop libraries, many of whom now practice advanced technological skills. Institutions offer professors of library science the lowest of all faculty salaries in higher education—the lowest, that is, save the job of teaching students how to write well (*CHE,* May 12, 2000, A20).

Alvin Kernan, whose experience as a scholar includes using the best libraries in the nation, worries that they "may be a dying institution, the ziggurats of the old universities" (1999, 290). Many college libraries once considered adequate for research no longer are. The most common form of grant in the humanities is now designed to enable travel to a distant research library or archive. Why? Few libraries can keep up with costs that constantly outstrip inflation. Libraries as a whole "are purchasing a continually decreasing portion of the world's knowledge products" (Whildin, Ware, St. Clair, 124). In 1989, in a short article that became infamous, a well-placed university administrator called libraries "bottomless pits" (Munn, 636). One Ivy League president, miffed at budgetary and space demands, let fall that his library was a "white elephant." The Association of Research Libraries confirms that not long ago, 50 percent or more of the nondigital acquisition budget of most libraries went for books; at many it is now 30 percent, at some as low as 20 percent, and at a few less than 10 percent. The rest is eaten up by a growing number of periodicals. The quality of many is questionable, and their cost is high. According to the Association of Research Libraries, scientific journals hiked their rates, on average, 10 to 15 percent per year above inflation each year from 1989 to 2000, a stunning compound increase. A single subscription can exceed $10,000 per year. From 1986 to 2000 the consumer price index rose about 55 percent while health-care costs jumped about 125 percent, but the cost of all scholarly journals soared 226 percent! In 2001 the average cost for a single journal subscription in the sciences reached $800. Commercial publishers of these journals have no interest in education.

Digital resources help libraries keep up with the information explosion and create greater access to materials, but digital resources are not cheap. Many are very expensive and require updates. One recent study concludes, "The digital library is an even more bottomless pit of the 21st century information landscape." There is no evidence that the information and digital revolution has produced cost savings in libraries, quite the opposite. In other words, "Creating the digital library is expensive" (Whildin et al., 141, 124, 134, 150).

Digital materials promise—and are delivering—a rich array of resources, and their availability online has a potentially democratizing effect. Yet, the "digital library" raises new questions of long-term storage; moreover, electronic records and sources must be integrated with print collections. Vendors of electronic catalogs or storage systems are sometimes ephemeral or missing in action when needed most. Institutional budgets may keep up with a low rate of inflation, but the cost of buying books and periodicals, and storing them in accessible locations, always exceeds inflation, so many collections tread water or slowly drown, especially when faced with the added costs of the digital. For destruction, says Robert Frost, fire is as good as ice. Print collections of 1840–1940 (and later), in which rests much glory of American culture, are going up in slow smoke, their wood fiber oxidizing. Left environmentally unprotected, half those publications are now brittle: dog-ear a corner and it snaps off. In a few more years, the whole page will crumble into powder. This is not just true of pulp fiction but of all fiction and all fact. Those books and magazines were almost all printed on acidic pulp paper, and once gone, it's gone. Worse yet, many materials around the world continue to be printed on acidic paper. Projects are preserving, digitizing, and microfilming American newspapers and selected book titles, but losses overwhelm the rescuers. And once a library falls behind in or loses a collection area, whether from decay, neglect, or lack of money, it is either impossible or absolutely prohibitive in cost to go back and buy what was missed.

University presses could once count on library sales of 1,200 to 1,500 volumes for their titles; this figure has dropped in many fields to 400 or fewer, driving costs up further. In the meantime, many universities have cut subsidies to their presses and encourage them instead to enhance revenues. There "the corporate ethos continues to spread" (Schiffrin; see also Nelson and Watt, 226–32).

A generation ago one Canadian study accurately remarked that there is almost always some self-interest attached to corporate giving. However welcome, it is not, therefore, true philanthropy (Axelrod, 40–41). If it goes to fields associated with reading, it is typically not for reading but for exhibitions or performances, which display the corporate name and carry the corporate image to the public. A sinister interpretation placed on this last trend, one voiced by George Grant, is that the humanities will become an opiate to a society dominated by material means. He fears that the central role of the humanities "will be increasingly as handmaiden to the performing arts." With universities beholden to a small number of individuals who control corporate giving and governmental funding, Grant foresees that the idea of "purpose for the majority will be found in the subsidiary ethos of the fun culture." Indeed, majors in colleges aimed at leisure management or at a recreational, consumer culture continue their sharp rise. Grant is gloomy. The performing arts will "provide the entertainment and release which technological society requires" (Niblett, 30–31). Reading-intensive fields will transform into fields of quasi performance, film, television, and media communications. Hard reading—and the hard meanings it presents—will fade.

Performance can, of course, raise many of the ethical issues that reading does (Winn). In writing and teaching, humanists could use more of the spirit of adept performers, who know that, despite the difficulties of what they are presenting, they must capture, even captivate an audience, not rely on a captive one. But performance can also become what Aristotle calls the least important of all elements of drama, spectacle, Juvenal's "bread and circuses" in the stadium. This possibility is a pessimistic one, implying a devaluation of the performing arts, themselves often in need of help. The processes described here also have the unhappy effect of reducing the performing arts to a small list of approved spectacles or blockbusters. The worry is that as reading wanes and as the visible, "popularized humanities" and performing arts become identified as a replacement for those fields once associated with intensive reading, then the culture of learning and the nature of culture will have lost a vital organ. The operation will entail some gain but huge loss.

Information or entertainment will replace reading and thinking, a trend stressed, even welcomed, by someone like Eli Noam, director of Columbia's Institute for Tele-Information and professor of finance and economics. It is hard not to hear glee in his blanket pronouncements that "books will cease to be the mainstay of knowledge in academia, and . . . will become primarily . . . entertainment. Culturally, books will descend to secondary status. . . . Printed text books will become secondary. . . . Books are yesterday's technology . . . slow to produce, slow to write, and slow to read" (85, 87). Taking time is obviously a bad thing. Chapter 6, below, argues that the medium of reading, whether electronic or print, makes far less difference than taking the time to read in the first place.

Crowded Out

The American university is curiously structured and highly fragmented in its scheduling. Few, if any, students or faculty in any given institution enjoy the same daily schedule. Schedules are usually filled, often with conflicts. Many terms are brutally short for the proper assimilation of literary material. In faculty debates over calendars, humanists usually argue against shorter terms, trimesters, and quarters. Weeks and days are segmented, scheduled, and filled up with a rigor that often makes four or five consecutive free hours an event so unusual that it is, understandably, used as a refuge to recover from the previous forty-eight. Time is sliced too thin for the mind to form itself. Most students take a full load of courses, lab work, and scheduled activities that together perforate the week. While only part of their time is scheduled, it is scattered so thoroughly that any remaining time is even more scattered—the leavings only. Add to this in many four-year schools, especially select institutions, a healthy interest in community service, voluntary activities, music, theater, and sports (some requiring travel), and a student may be fortunate to have three hours clear at a stretch. Moreover, even at those elite institutions, some students also work several hours or more each week to help pay tuition. Under conditions of sliced and diced hours and days, some subjects can survive and even flourish. Many closely structured or quantitative forms of knowledge can be absorbed in short segments; it is sometimes preferable. Lab work, even of long duration, is appropriately, even rigidly scheduled, and the laboratory contains few distractions.

But material that does not require weekly problem sets, memorization, and procedural mastery suffers under timetables geared to serve those forms of learning and teaching. The need for faculty to commute because proximate housing is hard to afford places further strictures on meetings with students. The expanding administrative network that manages university activities and personnel makes demands of its own. The more complex and larger administrations become, the more time and energy students and faculty must devote to bureaucratic requirements, directly or indirectly. Professors and students become enmeshed in forms, reports, questionnaires, metaprocedures, and more forms for exceptions. The federal government realized this trap and passed its own Paperwork Reduction Act. Few institutions of higher learning have followed suit.

The changes transforming the American university, beneficial in revolutionizing the means and conditions of study in many other fields, have so far exerted a limited positive impact on reading and writing, perhaps even a negative one. Word processing, microfilm, and computer library or database searches are indeed improved tools, but they are not the final products of scholarship and learning. Word processing and automated searches are time-saving devices whose function is to allow more time for writing, rewriting, and thinking. Yet these searches, highly useful for some tasks, also erect new and rigid barriers, especially for the inexperienced, and by their seeming thoroughness create false confidence in the unwary. Even without word processors and computerized library files, one could still rewrite or research, or make a concordance or index—it would simply take more time. Gibbon managed to write *The Decline and Fall* and Balzac his *Comédie humaine* without benefit even of a typewriter. (And their publishers got the books out on the market much faster, too!) In contrast, in many other fields, computers perform calculations, data analyses, or simulations that would otherwise be literally impossible in length and time consumed. But in branches of knowledge expressed through language, there exist few instances of this expansion. The job of authorial attribution on evidence of stylistic and syntactic patterns may be one humanistic activity revolutionized by technology, but even there it is easier, and usually of limited value, to establish that a particular author did not write a work in question than to prove who actually did. Computer-aided study of stylistics is, in any case, a specialized area. Searchable digital texts make it easy to determine how many times a given phrase or word is used by whom and in what contexts, but elevating to scholarship such searches without an accompanying idea or explanation produces what Swift, almost three hundred years ago, derided as "index learning." There is no substitute in sight for doing the reading and reflecting on what has been read.

Three other corrosive trends should be mentioned. First, grade inflation is not just worse but the *worst* in reading-intensive fields, in the humanities and soft social sciences. We do not propose here to analyze a complex situation that many others have already treated. A few analysts find the origin of grade inflation in the Vietnam War because some professors wanted to keep students out of the draft. Others see the causes in more-competitive admissions policies, lowered expectations in college, the teacher's as well as the student's desire for a class that takes less time, pressures for professional popularity and high teaching evaluations, and the cost of tuition: as a "consumer," you simply can't pay a lot and then be told you're doing poorly (Rojstaczer, 18–20). Another cause rests in automatic GPA cutoffs at graduate schools. And how many professors, let alone adjuncts up for a one-year renewal, will alienate, with grades lower than those other teachers give, the very "customers" who then evaluate their teaching? Nor are poorly designed or crudely interpreted evaluations the only popularity ordeal. It is hard to grade on a curve without quantitative measures. Teachers who grade stiffly end up with smaller classes and then are penalized for that in all kinds of ways. But since the causes of grade inflation are numerous and the phenomenon itself lavishly documented, not disputed, we focus on one practical result: grade inflation—as noted, worst in reading-intensive fields—means that less gets read and it gets read less well. Occasionally, a respected professor who gives grades lower than the mean is so good that students continue to seek out that teacher. In those cases it becomes clear that students can and will do the hard reading. Students may not always read diligently, but they know what it is to do so, and, after the fact, many feel cheated if it has not been demanded. But after graduation it's too late. Those special years and that unique opportunity are over. Habits have been formed and reinforced. And as William James notes, "Habit is twice Nature."

The second trend is more elusive but equally important. If a college admits one in three applicants, or possibly, as at a few highly selective institutions, only one in ten, it is easier to spot talent in quantitative and scientific fields. There are more types of national recognition for such skills, more contests, more awards, and clearer, more verifiable test scores. And talent in reading-intensive fields emerges, on the whole, later. If a committee must pick just one student and not the other two, five, or nine, more often than not the student in the humanities, in literature or history, will simply not shine with the clear magnitude of someone whose scientific and quantitative skills are above the ordinary. Institutions know this and in various ways compensate. Yet, it is hard to argue against the bird-in-the-hand attitude. It minimizes taking the risk of admitting someone who seems to show early promise, but in areas where large amounts of reading and writing yet to come must confirm that promise. It is safer to admit someone who clearly has and who will—where the predictors are strong and reliable—continue to shine in fields in which extensive reading and writing mean less.

David Bromwich sums up the third trend. He discusses the "inherited trust" of humanistic disciplines "to teach reading at a high level."

He argues that it is these very disciplines, including history and philosophy, that have often abandoned such a task. The teaching of reading at a high level has become "insufficiently professional or rewarding . . . and probably [for some] unrelated to real knowledge" (1988, 11). That's the real rub. Teaching this skill is supposed to be a large part of one's profession. But it is hard to fashion into an enticing item for the résumé, hard to export a reputation for it beyond one's own institution. So to teach students how to read very well has no professional cachet whatsoever. It fails to lift a professor—or the professor's institution—into the buzzword categories of heavyweight, distinguished, or prestigious.

Some teachers of literature have become so bollixed up in arcane theories, so worried about expanding or defending the canon, so concerned with who's where or obsessed with what can be done on the lecture circuit that they have forgotten that something fundamental underpins all these sophisticated, professionalized questions. As Robert Scholes says, "The one thing . . . English *must* do . . . is to lead students to a position of justified confidence in their own competence as textual consumers and their own eloquence as producers of texts." But even in this formulation, notes Andrew Delbanco, "It is a symptom of the current state of English that Scholes cannot bring himself to say, 'to teach students to read and write.'" Delbanco makes a claim as simple as it is necessary: those who teach literature need again to regard it as a calling (1999, 38). They need to profess the practice and passing on of a skill and a use of time—reading and writing—that honors the large number of books, speeches, and publications that, if read with effort and intellectual vigilance, repay their reading by changing permanently our experience. Such reading deepens our complexity and compassion as human beings. It changes society and inner lives in ways that entertainment and information cannot. More reading will not produce anything as grand as Truth with a capital T. Yet, such reading and the writing it fosters guarantee that the search for truth remains open to the scrutiny of others; its complex nature can be expressed, tested, and extended (Givler).

Reading History

The prospect of hundreds of pages of history often conjures a distant world of sterile dates, inert realities, and dead actors. The study of history has declined in prestige and popularity. It is thought to have scant practical value. But civic leadership without historical acuity fosters an inability to understand the structure of social institutions, their purposes, possibilities, and limitations, and a failure to discern what reforms are needed, or even that any reform is needed at all. Commercial leadership without historical imagination produces inefficiency, repetition of failed strategies, lack of situational awareness, and strategic miscalculation of long-term behaviors. When people successful in business have amassed fortunes and are prepared to aid society through philanthropy, a historical perspective helps ensure effective, meaningful gifts of lasting impact. Scientific leadership without historical imagination encourages the easiest rather than the best social and commercial applications of science to cultural and social life. Scientific leadership without knowledge of the history of science risks unethical applications. Political leadership without historical consciousness results, at best, in blunders and ineffectiveness, at worst in fiasco and tragedy. Harry Truman, who was not even a college graduate, remarked, "No one ever loses by reading history, great literature. . . . Readers of good books, particularly books of biography and history, are preparing themselves for leadership." Intellectual leadership without historical passion gives rise to an insidious form of anti-intellectualism.

In general, the reading of history sharpens an awareness of societal developments; it nurtures a grasp of the nature of cause and effect in human activities; it heightens, too, an awareness of the impact of accident (never to be underestimated); and it promotes moral and ethical judgment. In higher education itself, little can be done in thinking about curriculum without a sense of its history (Bell, 169–71, 208, 213, 223, 257). "Yet the truth is," states David McCullough, biographer of Harry Truman and John Adams and a leading and popular American historian, "we are raising a generation that is to an alarming degree historically illiterate. The problem has been coming on for a long time, like a disease eating away at the national memory." McCullough reports in 2002 that four out of five seniors from leading colleges fail a basic high school history test. None of the nation's top fifty colleges require any American history, and only a few require history of any kind (88). Yet, if "change" is a key factor in modern life—and in modern higher education—then it would be helpful to recognize that knowledge of history is the only way to appreciate and to judge change.

"Lincoln was . . . a very lazy man"

To advocate student privacy, quiet study conditions, sane scheduling, and freedom from unwanted distractions, may secure a temporary, secular cloister. This protection is not sought out of the misguided belief that early exposure to the world of political, mercantile, and professional interests is detrimental. Such exposure, along with its responsibilities, choices, and pressures, is inevitable and healthy: it arrives soon and stays for life. But many colleges and universities often fail to guarantee the indispensable, minimal conditions for intellectual activity based on written texts. They need to create and protect the spaces and daily habits in the university landscape and structure that are the most conducive to reading and writing. Their inspiration might be found in Wordsworth's *Prelude,* where he speaks of his college room as "my abiding-place, a nook obscure," and of times when he would read there "For a whole day together" or contemplate "The hemisphere / Of magic fiction" alone, "Through hours of silence."

Not all intellectual subjects and problems require lonely contemplation. For some it is a detriment. Studies conducted by Richard Light and others demonstrate that mastery of certain subjects—for instance, college calculus—benefits from group study. It seems true to some extent of law, and it is true in collaborative, experimental science. Teams are the most effective means of production and decision making in many businesses, and the most effective units of learning in some academic subjects. In the humanities, not enough credit accrues to collaborative work. As humanistic projects become more complex, such as those on the diversity of American religious life headed by Diana Eck, or the *Encyclopedia Africana* written by a team headed by Anthony Appiah and Henry Louis Gates Jr., it will become more important to support and cultivate them.

Yet notwithstanding the importance of collaborative projects, in many areas of inquiry there remains no substitute for the individual, private encounter with the written word. In the communal babble rising from Lincoln's one-room schoolhouse, each student still met the words one on one. Lincoln himself exemplifies this excruciating, individual wrestle with language. He read carefully and would often recite by heart. He quotes in his correspondence the political writings and orations of Jefferson, Clay, Webster, Madison, and Washington; poems by Gray, Burns, Shakespeare, Herrick, Knox, Halleck, Trumbull, and Pope; sermons by Wesley and hymns by Watts; the Bible; the stories of lone pilgrimages by Defoe and Bunyan; and legal texts by Blackstone, Chitty, and Greenleaf. Lincoln studied dense books of grammar, rhetoric, and elocution. He read poetry and politics equally, until the differently constituted Dennis Hanks was moved to remark, "Lincoln was lazy—a very lazy man—He was always reading—scribbling—writing—Ciphering—writing Poetry &c. &c." Henry McHenry told William Herndon, Lincoln's law partner, that Lincoln "read so much—was so studious . . . was so laborious in his studies that he became Emaciated." His "habits of study . . . were incessant." Asked by John Brockman in 1860 the "best mode of obtaining a thorough knowledge of the law," Lincoln replied, "The mode is very simple, though laborious, and tedious. It is only to get the books, and read, and study them carefully. . . . Work, work, work, is the main thing."

As Lincoln knew, what is read remains inert unless discussed, debated, and applied. Most reading implies a social activity and an eventual social use; even solitary study requires two participants, author and reader. Many institutions provide smaller classes to encourage discussions. There is also the question of conversation outside the classroom. The best faculty-student ratio does little good if the two parties do not, as a matter of routine, engage each other regularly in a setting conducive to conversation and advising, whether that be the dining hall, gym, or departmental corridors. This ideal of conversation is found in all civilized societies and cultures. It marks ancient academies, Renaissance courts, Enlightenment salons, debating societies, and scientific laboratories.

In a democracy, it is crucial that the experience of intensive reading remain open to all, that it be carefully taught and encouraged. The study, assimilation, and formation of values communicated by written texts—the shaping of democratic character, decision, and dissent—are not guaranteed by machines. These qualities are guaranteed only by the continuing activity of thoughtful, independent individuals, reading and acting on personal initiative. Informed decisions often require a background in, and an immediate act of, reading, something more demanding than thirty-second TV spots or attack ads. Important public issues rarely resolve themselves with a picture or numerical chart alone. Again, history enters in. "History is—or should be—the bedrock of patriotism," concludes David McCullough, "not the chest-pounding kind of patriotism but the real thing, love of country" (89).

In the end, the requirements for reading-intensive learning, for the conversations that enliven and apply it, and for the decisions that put it to the test in a democratic republic are, broadly stated, space and time—in other words, necessities that require investment. Yet, in the teaching and study of what is written, the results of such investment rarely look impressive to the unpracticed eye or development office brochure. They are almost intangible: rooms devoted to reading and writing with little, if any equipment, perhaps a wired network in the wall or a wireless one in the air; schedules that ensure intellectual conversations among peers and between faculty and students outside the classroom. To argue effectively for improvement in conditions for reading-intensive study and conversation is hard for teachers in disciplines constantly identified as ones that "bring in no money." The irony is that the very disciplines now so disparaged—philosophy, history, the study of languages, and theology—

originally created both the idea and the fact of the modern university. What we are not advocating, and the last thing needed, is a curtailment of student and university activities or a jealous, competitive attitude toward other disciplines. However, teachers and students living and working in institutions require nothing more, and nothing less, than the ability to escape the conditions necessarily provided for certain other studies or those suitable only for recreation, and to find solitary time in a room of one's own.

This is not an escape into escapism, it is an escape from the exclusively specialized and the predominantly selfish. Reading, as Mario Vargas Llosa affirms, "has been, and will continue to be, as long as it exists, one of the common denominators of human experience through which human beings may recognize themselves and converse with each other, no matter how different their professions, their life plans, their geographical and cultural locations, their personal circumstances" (32). Reading intensively is a profound entry into both the collective and the diverse aspects of society. A world without intensive reading will ensure more conformists. It will be less free. It may be materially rich, but it will be intellectually and spiritually poor.

In American higher education, the destruction of teaching, learning, and loving texts that require long and careful attention, and the destruction of the rational discourse that can be built only on that reading, stem from a strange institutional evolution. That evolution, without intending to hamper reading-intensive studies, now threatens to prohibit them precisely where those studies must take root for students, and where they must survive in their adult lives—outside the classroom. There is no sudden apocalypse, just slow erosion until—as with pollution that mounts by increments unnoticeably—all at once, at a cusp, conditions change completely, often with little hope of recovering what is lost. The college or university may even look physically better, more comfortable, with newer, snazzier buildings. There may even be more books in the libraries, and countless books online. But what transpires inside the buildings will be the transfer of more information yet the exchange of fewer ideas, the generation of more data yet the degradation of judgment. Together, parents and students, donors, teachers, chairs of departments, administrators, committee chairs, and committee members can secure an environment and establish an attitude in which reading-intensive study will thrive. If these open conditions and simple values—which, in actuality, are costly and elusive—become unavailable, then their absence will frustrate teaching, militate against the formation of values, and destroy the cornerstone skills of democracy.

6

MEANS AND ENDS, SIGNS AND SYMBOLS

Some men, in science and other fields, conceive of their ideas in words, and others find their intellectual stimulation in, and can work better with, mathematical symbols. The experimentalist deals as much in symbols as the literary and mathematical thinker.

—HAROLD SHARLIN, *THE CONVERGENT CENTURY,* 1966

The master economist must possess a rare combination of gifts. He must be mathematician, historian, statesman, philosopher—in some degree. He must understand symbols and speak in words.

—JOHN MAYNARD KEYNES, "SIR ALFRED MARSHALL," 1925

To the degree that the ethos of money ascendant in higher education detracts from or disregards ethical considerations, it is damaging. Signers of the republic's first declaration mutually pledged to risk their fortunes but also their lives and sacred honor. This resolve and the sacrifices of later generations secured for free people the inalienable rights of life, liberty, and the pursuit of happiness. Change has come fitfully, and progress has not been equal but often discriminatory, including in the history of higher education. Yet, while not gone, discrimination has diminished. Higher education has tried to address it vigorously, if variously. Haltingly the nation has honored the vision of the Founding Fathers. Their "more perfect union" continues as a national objective, however distant it may seem at times.

Jefferson did not write "the pursuit of luxury" or "the pursuit of money." Those alternatives would never have occurred to him. He wrote "the pursuit of happiness," an object harder to obtain, harder to conceive. The continuing life of the Declaration of Independence has taken root in America's educational system and the American people's identification with it. American schools are the subject of controversy, at the national and local levels, largely because they are the unifying symbol of the United States as a democratic, single people. Whatever motivates the nation's best endeavors, whatever gives citizens a will to continue, and whatever keeps alive conscience, a sense of purpose, and the pursuit of happiness is understood to rank high among the concerns of American schools.

Increasingly, technical advances created by the advancement of learning enhance abilities to manipulate matter, store and move information, harness natural laws, and—with polls, demographics, and market analysis—calculate and interpret mass behavior. The material, market economy and its consumerism drive two-thirds of the economy. The progress of higher learning is deeply implicated in that economy. American universities excel at "endogenous" activities; that is, more than universities abroad, they are able to set the stage for economically useful knowledge, they turn raw knowledge into useful knowledge very well, and they produce prototypes that other sectors of society can then develop and market (Rosenberg, 36–42, 49–57). Computers, the Internet, and biotechnology are but a few of many examples. Progress is dazzling, even to the skeptical eye. Gains in medicine, satellite mapping, anthropology, genetics, mathematics, telecommunications, biophysics, agriculture, meteorology, computing, and mesoscale and nanotechnologies emerge not as distinct points but as planes of knowledge that intersect at unexpected levels to form new lines of inquiry, ideas, and products. Many serve the public good and increase national prosperity. Many also exert a democratizing effect, especially advances that foil the concentration of knowledge, power, or capital in a small or secret set of hands. The real issue is not to accept or reject all "the available and often competing technologies" made possible by the advancement of learning, but as Leo Marx urged a generation ago, "to find an effective way to assign priorities among them" (8).

Far from being crass, one of materialism's less flattering epithets, its advances can be heroic. In his study *Civilisation,* Kenneth Clark uses "heroic materialism" as shorthand for one way to gauge human progress and well-being. It is heroic because it demands sacrifice and ingenuity in the service of ends that benefit more than a few. Yet, having reached an unprecedented level of material culture erected on the labor and ingenuity of generations, and foreseeing further acceleration of technologies and information, the human spirit still remains, as Wordsworth described Isaac Newton, "Voyaging through strange seas of Thought, alone." How much is the pursuit of happiness being furthered? Is it happiness that is still pursued? David Ehrenfeld, professor of biology at Rutgers, cautions against easy optimism: "Our world is one of models, of analyses based on models, and of expert predictions based on analyses. Our entire civilization is predicated on the assumption that we, the ultimate managers, can isolate all the important variables from the chaotic events now happening, make sense of them, and act accordingly. That this assumption is usually not true occurs to few people" (109).

All knowledge and the power bestowed by knowledge filter through the condition of being human. Pandora's box remains open: for every advance, a dilemma, whether nuclear power or SDI, urban redevelopment or carcinogenic solvents leaching into ground water. Humans now have the capacity to destroy all life. In a few generations, we have destroyed one-quarter of the species we cohabited with for tens of thousands of years. Yet—such is the Faustian nature of progress—the only way out or up is not back but through. And it is good to remember that in Pandora's myth, one thing always remains at the bottom of her box, and that is hope.

Ironically, though, one "need" can create another, and the constant improvement of all technological means becomes expected. As Robert K. Merton notes in a salient aside to his study of early modern science, "Need is an elliptical term which in this context always implies realization or consciousness of need. . . . an observer from a culture which has an established tradition of attempts to improve material welfare and to control nature" will see such needs everywhere and always, but "in another society, that need *may not exist*" (1970, 157). For example, in one society a microwave-heated ice cream scoop becomes a need, but billions of people in thousands of societies would hardly recognize it as one. Yet, because of "an unending flow of achievement" established since the seventeenth century and especially since about 1800, "the instrumental" nature of new knowledge "was transformed into the terminal, the means into the end" (1973, 268). Once techniques are established, they often ask no questions about ends. More broadly, identifying the pursuit of happiness as the accumulation of wealth and the fulfillment of synthetic needs cannot guarantee, or in many cases even obtain, happiness.

Norbert Wiener, godfather of modern computer technology, wrote a valuable little book called *Cybernetics* (1950), and four years later revised it as *The Human Use of Human Beings*. Wiener argues that humankind has, in a very few centuries, entered a radically new phase, one in which mastery over nature is common and moves at "a still increasing pace." Yet, he advises that "the more we get out of the world the less we leave, and in the long run we shall have to pay our debts at a time that may be very inconvenient for our own survival. We are the slaves of our technical improvement and we can no more return a New Hampshire farm to the self-contained state in which it was maintained in 1800" than we can think ourselves taller or shorter in stature and make that happen. "Progress," he states, "imposes not only new possibilities for the future but new restrictions." However, Wiener is not glum or pessimistic. Why not? He believes that "the new means of meeting these [new] needs" may be within our grasp but only if we do not act blindly, ignoring ultimate ends. It is this larger awareness that higher education itself needs to cultivate if it is to be complete. As Wiener notes of anything less, "The simple faith in progress is not a conviction belonging to strength, but one belonging to acquiescence and hence to weakness" (46–47).

Leaders and educators must embrace and advance useful new means, but the pursuit and management of these without judging the relative worth of what ends they serve will only put society on "the downhill path we are trying to escape" (Wiener, 47). Education devoted solely to such means is insufficient. This is affirmed by other figures, older ones as diverse as Samuel Johnson, Mary Shelley, and Sigmund Freud. More recently, many scientists share this view, including J. Robert Oppenheimer, Werner Heisenberg, Steven Weinberg, and E. O. Wilson. As Swift defined the species, a human being is *capax rationis,* a beast endowed not with reason but only with a *capacity* for it.

Higher learning serves new needs and new means and spends on them an increasingly large share of its budgets, personnel, and energies. The success is manifest. So are the perils of regarding it as the only kind, or even the best kind, of success. One crucial function of higher learning is to examine vigilantly the motives that direct the uses of knowledge. It should test the choice of ends, not just means, and foster humane values in the use of knowledge for the pursuit of happiness that Jefferson and the other signers held a self-evident right.

How to define those ends produces debate, disagreement, consensus, policy, statute, and dissent. An essential function of higher learning is to encourage those activities as intrinsic to learning itself. In some cases, the advancement of knowledge registers with solid, indisputable evidence. Yet, the hardest questions and choices are precisely those that remain impervious to purely technical or quantifiable solutions. If technical solutions exist, they're often unacceptable. Many modes of thought necessarily come into play in dealing with judgment and the expression of those values, explicit or implicit, by which members of a society employ each other, hire or draft youth for wars, treat the infirm and aging, set and spend taxes, and vote.

To succeed in education is not to succeed in what one sets out to do, or even to succeed in doing whatever is within the realm of possibility; success means to succeed in doing something worth doing. Yet, the freedom to decide that worth independently and then to pursue it is in jeopardy. The commercial world wants access to the intellectual capital found in colleges and universities and should have it, but obtaining it should not take priority over the more fundamental purposes and commitments of the entelechy—the set of collective goals—proper to higher education (see chap. 2). What need nurturing and protection are its more disinterested, fragile, and long-term functions.

In addition, the university is or should be a place to question and to criticize the means and ends that seem dominant or exclusive. As Jerome Bruner puts it in *Acts of Meaning,* "Intellectuals in a democratic society constitute a community of cultural critics" (32). Seventy-five years earlier, in 1914, Henry Adams warned that universities were starting to turn into quasi businesses that trained specialized scholars and professionals blind to any sense of "relation." These scholars fail to see connections between different fields of knowledge—or, if they are able to see them, they fail to grasp the relevance of such connections to larger problems of public policy and social life. Those knotty social problems demand solutions that synthesize knowledge and articulate judgment drawn from many fields. Thorstein Veblen, in *The Higher Learning in America* (1918), saw educational institutions becoming enmeshed in, and too cozy with, the prevailing economic system. If the nature of higher learning is no longer first predicated on love of knowledge or love of virtue—on neither the intellectual nor the moral virtues—then it will eventually consist entirely of preparatory training and research for regulated professions and applied technologies.

The more general case might be put this way. Scanning what humans have done and created in various societies, present and past, and not forgetting that, as far back as history records, every society has exercised a language of great subtlety and complexity, there is ample justification for regarding humans as preeminently "idea creatures." Perpetually engaged in observing the world and expressing their observations, they use what they find to make more and different things, always trying to make sense of their situation and of whatever and whomever they encounter. From this point of view, the organized search for learning and knowledge in a modern, complex society would seem self-justifying. If making sense of many different things is a need, just like food or sleep or companionship, then meeting that need constitutes a large part of higher education's special utility.

However, it is also possible to see humans as creatures that simply get things done. Looking at it from this somewhat different perspective, and leaving aside the objection that any ability to get things done grows out of a need to name, investigate, and explain, then "utility" becomes whatever aids people in getting done whatever they do. From this second point of view, any accomplishment and the means to accomplish it constitute utility, and nothing else does. This second perspective is the more reductive.

In its entelechy (see chap. 2), higher education serves both perspectives, and it must. Yet, if the second gets the upper hand and begins to displace the first, then something corrosive occurs. What observers from Tocqueville to Walter Lippmann to Lewis Lapham repeatedly confirm, from 1840 to 2000, is that American society tends to translate "doing things" into making money. It designates—it is the sign of—status in the boardroom, in Hollywood, and in the neighborhood. Money has the capacity to become the lingua franca of all means, the one that mediates all efforts to supply any need. If through this process it becomes the epitome of needs themselves, then it symbolizes all imagined accomplishments.

The Debate about Common Ends

The modern university justifies and defines itself largely in terms of the pursuit of knowledge. Knowledge has become increasingly specialized and often identified with particular professions. It is not uncommon for students to begin preparation for entrance into graduate school during freshman orientation week or earlier, whether aiming for law, literature, medicine, engineering, or economics. Often with an exaggerated sense of what graduate schools prefer, some college curricula stress what seem like prerequisites for professional study. The pressure to specialize is fed by the success of the pursuit of knowledge; subfields chipped off existing fields become fields themselves.

There naturally has arisen a concern with what, if anything, remains a body of common knowledge. For many, this concept is obsolete. According to an extensive study by Alexander Astin, only 2 percent of colleges in the United States have a true core where all students study, for any length of time, the same subjects and methods. As an outflanking maneuver, some programs attempt to establish a common acquaintance with various methods of pursuing knowledge, the theory being that knowledge of method serves as a legitimate substitute for actual knowledge—knowing how one discovers knowledge without actually going through the paces. This approach of common method reacts to the justified fear that as knowledge expands, common knowledge must erode. But no one masters anything in this manner. It is good that this model of education by method alone is not applied to surgery or civil engineering.

Both the approach of "method" and its earlier—and for some dis-credited—counterpart of a core body of books or facts arise out of a be-lief in the value of common method or knowledge and, usually, a wish to transmit culture as well as information. But this version of higher learn-ing, evidenced in what is too loosely termed liberal education, stems from a partial and nostalgic view of what was previously taught and, more pointedly, from a partial sense of why it was taught.

What, then, if anything, was ever common to higher learning, and es-pecially to liberal education? Not a single core of knowledge or of meth-ods—in fact, these have both always changed—but a sharpened, disci-plined sense of the habits of learning and the debates over motives and values: the acquisition, uses, and limits of knowledge in individual and social affairs. For centuries, religion acted as a moving force behind Western education. In certain eras, organized religion could stymie the pursuit of knowledge. It can still do so. Yet, it has always been an indis-pensable participant in the conversation about values. A century and a half ago, university education seemed based on Greek and Latin. In a sense it was, but not because memorizing declensions made one edu-cated; rather, because real mastery of a foreign tongue (even of a "dead" one) is itself a mind-expanding experience, and because what was writ-ten in Greek and Latin embodied varied, often competing, philosophi-cal approaches to life and values. Those texts were taught side by side with the Hebrew and Christian scriptures. Yet, even elements (religion, the classics) that dominated for long stretches have not been the same at all times. They are not the essence of liberal education. While rejecting those approaches because of their age is foolish, liberal education does something far more than inculcate them, or anything else. Education ("to lead out") is the opposite, in spirit and etymology, of inculcation ("to trample in").

The end of higher education was not seen simply as the achievement of stable, common knowledge. The final consideration, the optimal con-dition or *eudaemonia* of education, did not stop at the pursuit and preservation of knowledge. It included the *stewardship* of knowledge—the active consideration of its potential for human good. It is unfortunate to hear Cardinal Newman's idea of the university—with its ideal of knowledge for its own sake—dismissed as piously anachronistic. But what is constantly forgotten is that although he does promote the pursuit of knowledge for its own sake, he actually sets a higher, final goal: all knowledge, whether applied or relished alone, is to be considered in light of ethical conduct and human good. He consciously maintains a hard standard, an ideal not hazy and fuzzy but hammered out with strife between different kinds of knowledge, methods, and specialties. The reason that his book is still read is that his ideas and the debates he engages remain stubbornly contemporary.

The larger point is that beyond knowledge of a common language, higher learning was rarely conceived or intended primarily to provide a common core of knowledge or of method. It was intended to amass knowledge—bricks can't be made without straw—but, above all, the university, and liberal education especially, provided a common, learned discourse about the *use* and *value* of various kinds of knowledge, knowledge to which the university contributed. At its best, that common discourse never relied on agreement or conformity. That would betray academic freedom. Instead, such education is liberal, not as a political or ideological label, but in being capacious, generous, extensive, tolerant, intellectually free, an aid to choices for individual and social conduct.

Thus, whatever unity once existed in the university and in higher learning should not be reconstructed on the hypothesis of one long-lasting core of common knowledge or method. Any beneficial unity comes from accepting and protecting an environment favorable not only to the pursuit of knowledge but also to the debate over the applied value of many different kinds of knowledge and their relevance in human affairs. This recognizes the pursuit of knowledge for its own sake as a good but also recognizes that knowledge is applied in various ways, with varied benefits and liabilities. John Quincy Adams, in his 1810 course of lectures on rhetoric and oratory, remarked of that subject what might be said of the object of liberal learning in general. It is lifelong. Some think, he says, that all knowledge

> is to be acquired at the university. According to this estimate of things a liberal education means no more, than the acquisition of a degree; and the pursuit of the sciences here taught is regularly laid aside with the square cap and the collegiate gown. But . . . the student . . . must consider himself as able to acquire here nothing more, than the elements of useful knowledge, a mere introduction to the porches of science. These fountains . . . are destined not to quench but to provoke his thirst. Here he can only learn to be his own teacher hereafter. (360–61)

Higher education has traditionally served civic and ethical purposes, providing skills of complex thinking, interpretation, writing, and judgment for the application of knowledge. To animate a body of otherwise inert facts or technical information means to call on ethical, spiritual, and aesthetic values. This is why John Kennedy, at a college commencement address delivered in 1956, said it is more important for politicians to know poetry than for poets to know politics. He remarked, "If, in the effective use of language, style is the man, style is the nation too; men, countries, and entire civilizations have been tested and judged by their literary tone." Such a tone is no cheap effect but the result of judgment domesticated into habitual expression.

At the end of an exhaustive historical analysis of moral education in American colleges and universities, Julie A. Reuben writes that even if universities "no longer have a basis from which to judge moral claims," the "separation of fact and value" remains problematic. She adds, "The notion of value-free scholarship has been challenged from its inception," and concludes, "Since it has proved impossible to completely separate fact and value, we should begin to explore ways to reintegrate them" (268–69).

Higher education should keep intact Kenneth Burke's dynamic equipoise of perpetuating and transmitting the mainstream culture of society while criticizing and proposing alternatives to the status quo. Either one without the collaborative inflection of the other is dangerous. Untutored, constant change disrupts social good faith and leads to demagoguery, even tyranny. But education without the express purpose of change suffocates reform and thwarts efforts to seek a more perfect union. Education without the purpose of *selectively* changing values by critical thought and communal consensus serves only to perpetuate existing inequalities. Decisions that direct the use of products are not at all identical with the technical knowledge required to invent and produce them. To abstain from judgment, to let the impersonal energy of "progress" or "the market" do all the thinking, is flying blind.

The physicist Werner Heisenberg is usually invoked in intellectual arguments by employing his "uncertainty principle" as an analogy. Here he speaks for himself on the topic under discussion: "Modern science is yielding knowledge whose correctness cannot, on the whole, be doubted; and the technology springing from it allows this knowledge to be harnessed also to the realization of wide-ranging goals. But that by no means settles the question whether the progress thus attained is of any value. This question can be decided only in light of the value concepts that men choose to be guided by in setting the goals. But these ideas of value cannot come from science itself; at all events, that is not where they come from meanwhile" (131). In the same vein, Nobel laureate in physics Steven Weinberg noted in 2001 that "although we may learn how we have come to have the values we have, and scientific knowledge will doubtless continue to improve our ability to get the things we value, nothing in science can ever tell us what we ought to value" (62).

In that sense, education never stops dealing with original sin, with the human, maddening skill to remain imperfect, and to incorporate imperfections into ever more advanced societies. To expect the humanities to provide practical solutions to specialized problems misconstrues their purpose. Jacques Barzun, in "The Misbehavioral Sciences," says, "The humanities will not rout the world's evils and were never meant to cure individual troubles; they are entirely compatible with those evils and troubles. Nor are the humanities a substitute for medicine or psychiatry; they will not heal diseased minds or broken hearts, any more than they will foster political democracy or settle international disputes. All the evidence goes the other way. The so-called humanities have meaning chiefly because of the inhumanity of life; what they depict and discuss is strife and disaster." As Samuel Johnson noted, the cure for most human ills is palliative, not radical. The humanities can reveal an active repository and source of conscience, memory, remorse, laughter, and hope. Without these and similar qualities, knowledge in time grows humorless, boring, historically naive, and at last venal and dangerous.

Education of Motive

Higher learning is for an elite, not the product of class or wealth, birth or privilege, and not determined by gender, race, creed, sexual orientation, religion, or politics, but based in an inalienable equality of opportunity to be elite, to be picked out, which historically has been synonymous with the ability to read. Higher education is, or should be, meritocratic. It is clear that Americans, desperately and rightly, want to believe that (Kirn). Since the mid-twentieth century, much has been done to make higher learning more meritocratic where once it had rarely been so. Higher learning means permitting and encouraging the unusual, lonely, groping souls. William James wrote in 1903, in a commencement address given at Harvard University, "The old notion that book learning can be a panacea for the vices of society lies pretty well shattered today. . . . vice will never cease. Every level of culture breeds its own particular brand of it as surely as one soil breeds sugar-cane, and another soil breeds cranberries. . . . The true [university] . . . is the invisible [university] . . . in the souls of her more truth-seeking and independent and often very solitary sons." Were he alive today he would include daughters as well. He goes on, "*Thoughts* are the precious seeds of which our universities should be the botanical gardens. Beware when God lets loose a thinker on the world—either Carlyle or Emerson [it is Emerson, in "Circles"] said that—for all things then have to rearrange themselves. . . . The university

most worthy of rational admiration is that one in which your lonely
thinker can feel . . . least lonely, most positively furthered, and most
richly fed."

The curricula of most schools and universities develop as a set of
compromises or truces between faculty groups and vested institutional
interests, sometimes in answer to the dictates of administrators, sometimes as responses to vocational pressures, real and imagined, and sometimes in recognition of new fields. But curricula imply certain ends: what
makes a person educated, what qualities of character does such a person possess, not just what knowledge or methods. Character here is no
code word for a particular background. Class, race, religion, and gender
are important to study, but individual strength, "the content of our character," is, as Martin Luther King Jr. knew, more than the sum of those attributes. Character requires an autonomous moral will and a critical mind
that can self-correct. The highest product of education is not knowledge
but people of character who possess and use knowledge. David Mamet's
discussion of the nature of acting subsumes these aims:

> And so we might ask ourselves . . . what is character? Someone says char-
> acter is the external life of the person onstage . . . . But that person onstage
> is *you.* It is not a construct you are free to amend or mold. It's you. It is
> *your* character which you take onstage.
>
> The ability to act, to resist, to assent, to assert, to proclaim, to support,
> to deny, to bear. These are the components of character onstage or off.
>
> Your character, onstage or off, is molded by the decisions you make:
> which play you do, whether or not to pursue employment in commer-
> cials, in sex films or pseudo-sex films, in violent or demeaning films . . .
> whether or not to treat yourself with sufficient respect . . . whether or not
> to conduct your business affairs circumspectly. The ideas, organizations,
> actions, and people you support and dedicate yourself to, mold and fi-
> nally *are* your character. Any other definition is the jabbering of the un-
> committed. (39)

The humanities educate for an active as well as a contemplative life.
Alongside Mamet's definition of character it's worth setting Philip Sidney's survey of knowledge from his *Apology for Poetry,* which itself casts
an eye back to Aristotle's *Politics* (8.5). All knowledge, remarks Sidney,
should be "directed to the highest end of . . . knowledge, by the Greeks
called *Architectonike,* which stands . . . in the knowledge of a man's self,
in the ethic and politic consideration, with the end of well doing and not
of well knowing only."

In a recent formulation, John Kenneth Galbraith puts the case this way: "The growth and influence of college and university communities are in response to the needs of the industrial system. But this does not necessarily create a primary obligation to the needs of the industrial system. Gratitude and debt do not exist as between social institutions. The only reality is the right social purpose" (378). However, it is easy to lose sight of that purpose. It is easy to take the signs and symbols of knowledge, its means, for its ends. Why? Knowledge relies on those signs and symbols, and their power seems limitless.

The Parable of the Signs

In 1837, when Emerson spoke of the "American Scholar" in his Phi Beta Kappa address, he did not mean a specialized academic or antiquarian, nor someone who necessarily worked at a school or college. He meant an American intellectual, any person who thinks and cares about the mental and moral life of the nation. For "scholar" or "intellectual" Emerson could have said "signworker," what business guru Peter Drucker calls a "knowledge worker." For signs are—regardless of the discipline—the scholar's materials and tools, and signs convey knowledge. Signs are as numerous as summer flies, so examples are in order. To begin: the Harry Elkins Widener Memorial Room in Widener Library, the calculation of the U.S. Census, and an anonymous Greek slave. Put another way, consider Johannes Gutenberg, IBM, and video games. The appropriateness of these choices will become clear.

On a conceptual plane the topics are words, numbers, and images, all three as media for information and values. Each mode of signs or symbols communicates knowledge but is also used to create it. Moreover, any American Scholar, any sign or knowledge worker, depends on a community. All three modes—words, numbers, images—require a human collective that has, over time, established the conventions of sign systems, a community that teaches, memorizes, regulates, and records them. Words, numbers, and images are attempts to represent reality, in the broad sense of *represent*. Certain provinces of knowledge may seem in the domain of words, others of numbers, others of images. But these divisions are matters of convenience. The borders prove porous and the signs themselves transformable, free of categorical loyalties. Spoken words, for instance, become written ones, roughly translatable into different languages and—if they are alphabetic—precisely translatable into Morse code, the brainchild of an American inventor who also was an expert in images, a portrait painter of renown. As Edward Sapir notes in the

"Introductory" to his study *Language,* "The letter of the telegraph code is thus a symbol of a symbol of a symbol" (20). Numbers can represent words, too, as word processors demonstrate by the binaries of 1 and 0. At a high level of complexity, images of the solar system captured by interplanetary probes are converted into code, transmitted as electromagnetic waves, received, and reconverted by computer and computer enhancement from numbers into visual images. By virtue of the yet more complex biochemistry and neurotransmission of retina, optic nerves, and visual cortex, we see these images, perhaps on TV or in a newspaper, after several more complicated transformations. It is possible, too, to describe that vision in words, a shattered asteroid or a rough, red storm on Jupiter.

Images become words and words become images. Figures of speech such as metaphor and synecdoche are built of images, and those figures in turn are integral components of the time-honored study of rhetoric. Rhetoric is the oldest chair in many universities and fundamental to liberal education, though these days the word is colloquially misused as a synonym for loose talk or ideological obfuscation. In the mind's eye and in the imagination, words or memories summon up mental pictures. This idea of the mind's eye, which Shakespeare delights to mention, has a neurological origin in a second visual "screen" located at the anterior of the brain. Words, to enlist a grander vocabulary, can also give birth to visions, such as justice or equality.

In short, every field of endeavor deals with semiotics or the study of signs, which John Locke more than three centuries ago identified as one of the basic branches of all knowledge. He noted that while it was basic, it had yet to undergo systematic study. The term itself goes back to the ancient Greek *semeotikos.* At times the internal logic of signs—these numbers, symbols, words—seems aligned with the operations of nature itself, and we use them to express what are called natural laws, whether of quantum mechanics or of evolution. Many distinct semiotic modes exist, such as musical notation or the composite mode of chemical formulas, which combines numbers, words in shorthand, and even a visual schema of molecular structure. Choreographers have developed their own notation and machines to record it. Nowhere is humanity's fertility of invention better displayed than in the ability to devise and manipulate sign systems of special application, often translatable one to another.

In turn, words, numbers, and images fertilize the root of every society's civilization or culture. There has never existed a civilization without them. The more active, complex, and refined the three modes of symbolic representation, and the more perfected each in its own sphere, then the more active the civilization is. This does not mean necessarily good or just, but advanced in its ability to express, to understand, and to shape nature. A civilization of semiotic sophistication may, in fact, be depraved and inhumane, coveting knowledge more than wisdom, order more than compassion. Yet every field of knowledge depends, to varying degrees, on one or more of the three modes; many regions of thought are open only to the semiotically sophisticated. Literature uses words, but words enter the sciences too, if only to describe what numbers and images cannot—a common circumstance in biology, biochemistry, and physics. Depending on approach and taste, economics and other social sciences can be pursued largely with numbers or largely with words. Architecture combines the three modes, with words usually in third place. Historians may be statisticians, as may literary analysts. If we consider that health is inevitably holistic, it is not surprising that medicine, in diagnosing and treating the whole patient, should rely on words, numbers, touch, sound, and images in its efforts to determine how bodily, mental, and psychosomatic processes follow natural laws, psychological patterns, and environmental pressures. Poetry is often an equation in words—a metaphor—between the human and the natural. Aristotle says metaphor humanizes the natural world, as we hear in the Song of Songs:

> Behold, thou art fair
> Thy lips are like a thread of scarlet
>   and thy speech is comely: thy temples
> are like a piece of a pomegranate within thy locks.
> Thy neck is like the tower of David builded
>   for an armoury.

And as Morris Cohen notes, "Metaphors are not merely artificial devices for making discourse more vivid and poetical." They "are also necessary for the apprehension and communication of new ideas" in every field (83, 85; see also chap. 9).

What can be said about those first particulars? Widener Library's Memorial Room, the Harry Elkins Widener Room, named after a young book collector, owes its existence, as does the building surrounding it, to a series of accidents or failures in semiotic systems that in their day everyone regarded as the most advanced, foolproof, and sophisticated. The *Titanic* was engineered, by blueprint and equation, by image and number, to be the largest, safest ship afloat. Built and protected in its maiden voyage with the aid of the most advanced semiotic reasoning and communication, the *Titanic* was described by one writer as "unsinkable." But sophistication in deploying signs is not the same as maturity in judgment. In the event, various normally reliable semiotic systems could not in their combination guarantee reliable interpretations or outcomes. First, numbers failed; the imagination wielding them did not anticipate a gash so long under the water line. Then, the image failed: when the iceberg—the possibility of which was considered but minimized, and which was sighted visually but too late—ripped the hull and the ship began to sink, her captain ordered new-style distress flares shot high into the dark sky. But the nearest ship, the *California*, apparently misunderstood these eye-catchers and interpreted them as rich people partying with fireworks. Though operational and spectacular, this visual sign misfired owing to faulty interpretation. Error in deciphering was not the only culprit, though. The iceberg alert, transmitted in plain English, was not heeded with due caution. By some accounts the warning was lost amid the stack of well-wishing telegrams and stock quotations that passengers sent and received by wireless, a new technology that made instant communication across the ocean a common reality. But no technology, new or old, can determine what, for its users, is most important. Judgment was lacking all around. The owners of *Titanic,* desiring to outstrip competition, stoked the boilers, perhaps for a record crossing, a kind of semiotic trump card measured in hours and minutes. The last SOS or Mayday from the paralyzed giant cut through the ether of the night too late. In other words, words—in wireless Morse code—also failed. In April of his twenty-seventh year, Mr. Widener and more than a thousand others died in the loss of *Titanic.*

One of the books Harry Elkins Widener collected was the Gutenberg Bible, the first book printed in the Western world. Though Gutenberg's productions are now valued in part for their painstaking craftsmanship, he inaugurated the age of books on a mass scale. New styles of knowledge and education followed, and they transformed societies. The Enlightenment fortified and nourished the Gutenberg Age with ideals of democratic education and a mass reading public. The hegemony of the printed book wanes imperceptibly but steadily. Still, it would be unwise to confuse that waning with the waning of language, reading, or composition. There are myriad means of processing and reproducing words, and new means often serve as well as the old. It is nice to hold a book in our hands, but it is better to hold it in the head and heart, places where words must eventually reside if they have life and effect. How words get to head and heart—by voice, linotype, dot printer, screen, Braille, or digitized photons—is only a means. Although means have their own allure and, as Gutenberg showed, can influence ends, they do not supplant them. As Thoreau says of the victory of the mere capacity to do: we do not ride on the railroad, after a while it rides on us. There are also at times detrimental, unforeseen results (at least unforeseen by the majority). One can genetically engineer—"modify" or "manipulate," according to the slant of the user—crops and eat them, although unintended effects can appear. Some genetically modified corn kills monarch butterflies. It is hard to know where the links in the chain end.

The next particular on the list is the U.S. census, a shelf of words and statistics amassed every decade to tell us who we are, how many of us there are, and what we do. (The census report is now produced on CD-ROM.) The census is a bone of political contention because its numbers dictate federal funding and congressional representation. A recent Supreme Court ruling held that the count must be literal, person by person in the flesh, and cannot rely on statistical sampling, in spite of statisticians' assurances that sampling would in most cases be more accurate. Back in the later nineteenth century, the onerous task already struck fear in the heart of Washington, long before programs and revenue sharing hinged on it. So the federal government sponsored a competition for a machine to tabulate the growing returns. It awarded the prize to a man whose computational machines and the company formed around them became the corporate ancestor of IBM.

Computers, and the revolution computing brings, were thus from the beginning part and parcel of a mass democratic society. All ways of processing symbols or images are products of human ingenuity and subject to human imperfection, for they are all used and manipulated by human motives. When Socrates drew lines in the sand and asked a nameless slave about geometry, the untutored boy replied correctly. Images may symbolize and indeed encourage intuition, "seeing into a thing," adding something concrete to what before was only abstract. The thought experiments of Einstein and Galileo employ visual images and gifted forms of intuition transferred to a communicable form, to symbolic and mathematical equations. In a letter to President Franklin Roosevelt, Einstein suggested one application of his most famous equation, which eventually led another physicist, J. Robert Oppenheimer, to apply words from the Bhagavad Gita to the newly revealed role of scientists, himself included: "I am become death, the destroyer of worlds."

• • •

What, then, does the new American Scholar find? It is not the age of the book, nor is it the age of the computer, video tape, digital disc, or e-book. It is, as it really always has been, an age of word, number, and idea, where the means of processing, transmitting, and displaying these modes—voice, book, screen, chip, optic fiber, and printout—are intermeshed and sped up. They grow more interrelated as they grow faster. The new

American Scholar must be conversant in—or at least familiar with—all symbolic modes, especially if that intellectual or knowledge worker wishes to be more than a mere custodian of the past or a transparent source of data for others to use.

The new intellectual, the new knowledge worker and knowledge consumer, will also need to guard against being carried away by methods and hypnotized by techniques to the extent that ends and values become incidental. Calculation is not thought; display is not intuition or conception; word processing is not rhetorical skill; copying is the opposite of invention. It's the old axiom of programmers: GIGO, garbage in, garbage out. In the early 1990s Neil Postman warned that, having "solved the problem of information scarcity, the disadvantages of which were obvious," society was unprepared for the ensuing "information glut." Without interruption or respite, "through every possible channel and medium—light waves, airwaves, ticker tapes, computer banks, telephone wires, television cables, satellites, printing presses—information pours in. Behind it, in every imaginable form of storage—on paper, on video and audio tape, on discs, film, and silicon chips—is an even greater volume of information waiting to be retrieved." In massive, usually undigested quantities, "information has become a form of garbage, not only incapable of answering the most fundamental human questions but barely useful in providing coherent direction to the solution of even mundane problems." Under these "advanced" conditions, "the tie between information and human purposes has been severed, i.e., information appears indiscriminately, directed at no one in particular, in enormous volume and at high speeds, and disconnected from theory, meaning, or purpose" (1993, 60, 69–70).

As symbol-making creatures, human beings, including even poets, can become so enamored of semiotic systems that the system, rather than anything it might be used to represent, consumes all their energies. Late in his career, W. B. Yeats wrote, "Players and painted stage took all my love, / And not those things that they were emblems of." Scholars have treated some theories of semiotics with such sophistication that they end up doubting whether the signs represent anything but their own "play": everything in language becomes equally suspect or ambiguous in its communication, equally worth interpreting, and infinitely interpretable. Considering ethics in the act of reading is then not about ethics itself but only about the ethics of reading. To this brand of sophistry Hume's rejoinder is still the best: one can maintain this detachment in the closet, in the study, but not in the world. In his tonic good sense, Oscar Wilde comes a close second when he describes the cynic (like the auctioneer), as one who "knows the price of everything and the value of nothing." In science, one danger of manipulation that destroys value is the fabrication of data, the creation of results that are false, and such fabrication is on the rise (see chap. 7). Or, one may appropriate the words or numbers of someone else and claim them as one's own. These perversions of signs, too, have infected the American Scholar in the last generation.

Means and techniques count; they are half the story, or almost half. If one fails to learn to use power, then someone unscrupulous or evil who has learned to harness powerful means will become master. This is one lesson in Arthur C. Clarke's *2001,* both when the computer HAL (= IBM in elementary code) usurps the space expedition and kills the crew, save one survivor, and also at the beginning of the film adaptation, when primitive man learns to use a piece of bone as a tool and, almost simultaneously, as a weapon. As the hominid throws it up into the air, the camera transforms it into a spaceship.

But if, in the pursuit of scholarship, means become ends, if visual images exceed the capacity for vision, then the prophet's warning is apt, "Where there is no vision the people perish." Take, for example, the poor Krell civilization in another film, *Forbidden Planet,* an early effort in science fiction, somewhere between art and corn, and loosely based on Shakespeare's *Tempest.* In this story, a civilization has developed vast sources of nuclear power that are self-maintaining and controlled by a kind of telepathy. Just imagine your work—and behold!—the nuclear machines do it. Here, at last, machines have created true leisure. The problem is, the Krell citizens, like any decent people, go to sleep each night. And in their sleep of reason, in a series of Goyaesque episodes, their nuclear reactors carry out, not the benevolent designs of the wakeful Krell superegos, but the destructive impulses of their restless ids and never-sleeping desires. In the end, the overworked reactors melt down and destroy the planet.

The inversion of means and ends is not a new impulse, but it seems now a particularly tempting one, fostered by a rapid acceleration in the acquisition of knowledge and ways to apply it. Among the first to grasp the implications of this, Shelley put the paradoxical results clearly:

> We have more moral, political and historical [knowledge], than we know how to reduce into practice; we have more scientific and economical knowledge than can be accommodated to the just distribution of the produce which it multiplies. . . . We want [i.e., lack] the creative faculty to imagine that which we know; we want the generous impulse to act that which we imagine. . . . The cultivation of those sciences which have en-

larged the limits of the empire of man over the external world, has . . .
proportionally circumscribed those of the internal world; and man, having enslaved the elements, remains himself a slave. (*Defense of Poetry*)

Shelley underestimated how great the benefits of material progress could
be, and consequently he was too pessimistic. Common life today, for
many, is longer, healthier, and richer than when he wrote these words
in 1821. But the environment is arguably more degraded, more species
are gone, the general means of destruction greater. As knowledge mounts
and disparities among people and populations widen, his protest, as prescient as it is pessimistic, remains apt.

Semiotic systems also give an ability to reconstruct the past. That reconstruction is never perfectly objective, but without skills to make and
decipher signs, we would have only objects: the pots, skeletons, foundations, and shards of archaeology and paleontology. These, it is true, reveal what nothing else can, but without numbers, words, and images, the
reconstruction of the past would be terribly hampered, much like the
"conversations" that the rigid philosophers hold in Swift's *Gulliver's
Travels*. In their belief that words deceive and should be reduced to
things, they mutely hand each other objects from portable stores they
carry on their backs. Yet, while diligent research and new knowledge
make the past richer and more layered, society seems dominated increasingly by the present. No matter how much of the past we know or
record, it is inert if it cannot affect and change us. For society, as for a person, to rely only on short-term memory is to never grow up. This is what
Emerson aims to say in his essay "History." He makes the astonishing
claim that "Man is explicable by nothing less than all his history. . . . A
man is the whole encyclopedia of facts." This insight is usually tagged
with something trite, such as "learning the lessons of history," or Santayana's remark that those who do not know the past are condemned to
repeat it. The past will unlock itself but only through meditation, reflection, imaginative sympathy, and humane reconstruction. The past may
be stored in books and paintings and measurements, but it does not live
there. It lives only in each individual who learns about it. And then the
past becomes a fulcrum rather than a burden.

Yet, importance often defers to availability. After Gutenberg invented
movable type, some scholars predicted that everything ever written in
manuscript would soon be published. Today, some prophesy that everything ever published will be digitized. Saving labor or not, the book, computer, television, fax, and xerography have made it more difficult to sustain authoritarian and totalitarian regimes. But less gross forms of

coercion thrive in a civilization unanchored to signs of the past. The *Titanic* has been found, photographed, and partly plundered, all courtesy of varied semiotic systems more powerful than any available to the ship's engineers and captain. One can now see it on video, recorded by a deep-sea submarine, much as Hardy describes in "The Convergence of the Twain," a poem about the meeting of ship and iceberg. "In a solitude of the sea / Deep from human vanity, / And the Pride of Life that planned her, stilly couches she." But now, on a television screen at home, the *Titanic* no longer rests deep from human vanity. Its whistle has been hauled up, the chance to sound it again won in a lottery before a cheering crowd in Chicago. A mammoth financial success, the recent movie turned the tragedy into a tale of romance and class envy in which a great jewel is thrown into the sea as an act of devotion. Marketing people rushed to advertise paste imitations on the airwaves. The movie's director blurted, "I'm king of the world!" *Titanic* the musical appeared and, incredibly, *Titanic* the children's cartoon. Rather than reflect on the hubris that doomed the liner and its passengers, there seemed a race to outstrip it.

Robert Proctor warns, "We live in a culture which, at both an individual and collective level, has at best only a tenuous relationship to the past." It is a relationship "characterized by nostalgia, which becomes ever more superficial as it is mined as a source for new commodities of mass consumption." Proctor quotes J. H. Plumb, the historian, who, in *The Death of the Past,* offers the origin of this mass amnesia: "Industrial society . . . does not need the past. Its intellectual and emotional orientation is towards change rather than conservation. . . . The new methods, new processes, new forms of living of scientific and industrial society have no sanction in the past and no roots in it" (Proctor, 136–37). But when the past is lost, all sense of how societies once directed and valued knowledge, a crucial guide to directing and valuing future knowledge, disappears.

• • •

Knowing the past won't reveal the future but it may help us prepare to shape it. Complexly coded natural semiotic systems of amino acids—genes—have now been mapped, systems not invented to represent nature but ones nature herself evolved to generate life. Genes contain four basic "semiotic" units, but those four amino acids combine at such length and so intricately that as means they determine the natural form of all organisms and species. Beginning with a monk growing peas barely more than a century ago, research mobilized words, numbers, images, computers, chemical formulas, books, x-ray diffraction, chemical notation—the whole range and panoply of sign systems—to understand this one system. Manipulating these natural signs can change life. It can change nature. This, to borrow a phrase from Emerson, is a new "method of nature," and the acceleration leading to it is astonishing: the beginnings of articulate speech are lost in the mists of time; a veil is thrown over the precise point at which humans first wrote or signed with their hands; petroglyphs are tens of thousands of years old. From the early lopsided pyramids to the great one of Cheops, the builders achieved an upgrade only every few centuries; and Stonehenge, thousands of years later, is no more sophisticated. Even relatively recent math is crude: Who would relish long division in Rome? Who could do quadratic equations in the Renaissance? And yet, in the last two generations, atomic structures come into focus, computation power increases a trillion-fold, and the reproduction of words runs so rapidly that the data equivalent of everything in the Library of Congress can be downloaded from a satellite in a few minutes. The genetic patterns of all sign makers and breakers, the natural symbolic codes of life, are decoded and rewritten in dozens of labs.

Whatever humankind can do, it has always done. There is nothing the species has been capable of that it has not developed, planned, pursued, refined, and executed. Even means with no possible benefit other than blank destruction are perfected. With its dangers and benefits, genetic engineering will be no different. In his remarkable fiction *Last and First Men* (1930), Olaf Stapeldon foresees a sweep of human development across tens of millennia: humans build and harness thinking machines, incorporate them directly into their own minds, set aside sections of the planet as wilderness for recreation, voyage to other planets and colonize them, live in groups arranged sexually and socially in ways foreseen. But what prevents the extinction and self-destruction of humankind is the ability of the species to reshape life itself. In his chapter "Man Remakes Himself," the First Men become Second Men, Second become Third, until finally there arise the Eighteenth and last men, eons in the future. Seventy years ago, critics judged Stapeldon to be a bit loony, a literary nut. Like many prophets with a vision, his work fell into obscurity.

Mastering and using signs and symbolic means is necessary for education but not sufficient. In *Paradise Lost,* Milton makes the best rhetorician, the best master of words, and the best poet the Devil, who prevails for a long time. So did the most captivating German orator of the early twentieth century. The fastest computer responds as faithfully to the finger of a terrorist as to that of a saint. Whoever sees advertising for cigarettes in Chad, Haiti, or Thailand knows the power of the hip jingle and sexually suggestive image, and the ruthless indifference of the people who deploy them.

Signs and symbols bestow the power to produce material things, to alter living organisms, to exercise values, to solve ethical problems. The university is no place for constant action, but it should not be passive. In the university, signs, symbols, language, notation, and images are perfected in the service of knowledge. The university is, or should be, where the hardest questions about the uses, ends, and values of knowledge and its semiotic systems arise. The chief place for the development and—to use Coleridge's word—the *interpenetration* of knowledges is the university. In the evolution of human institutions, the university is an adaptation to exponentially expanding, intersecting circles of knowledge. Specialization will continue, but at the boundaries of knowledge fusion will rule. This will alter the academic shape and organization of institutions. The false security that narrowness provides exerts a strong pull to be countered. As James Freedman notes, "Within law schools, no less than within undergraduate colleges, the insistent student demand is for specialized, narrow, practical preparation, not breadth of inquiry and general knowledge. Yet the world for which lawyers are being prepared will require, more than ever before, both more specialization and more breadth of knowledge" (1996, 86).

Distance learning attempts to transmute education by digitizing, storing, reformatting, and transmitting. The campus, physical classrooms and buildings, physical books and, above all, physical teachers and fellow students give way to monitor and keyboard. This is a powerful form of abstraction. Yet it is also a dream in which physical humanity, craving the sight and sound and contact of other people, and actual places of habitation become relative inconveniences. Distance learning works well for some subjects, but it will not substitute for education as a whole. It will re-create certain courses; it can never re-create a college or university. Moreover, the financial rewards originally sought in this venture now seem elusive. There are many casualties (Hafner). Most of all, amid the pros and cons of distance learning, it's worth keeping in mind that, like so much else, it represents a means for education, not an end.

In discussing Newman's *Idea of a University,* Jaroslav Pelikan notes that the first topic in Aristotle's *Nicomachean Ethics* is devoted to means and ends. As a corollary, says Pelikan, if knowledge is defined as the "chief good and end in itself . . . the moral consequences can be frightening. . . . The principle of knowledge [as] its own end, then, must be integrated with a larger and more comprehensive set of first principles" (43). It remains a world bursting with sin and sorrow, a world now bristling with missiles, anthrax, warheads, AIDS, pollution, and nuclear briefcase bombs. The new American Scholar—whether lawyer, economist, artist, corporate director, scientist, or public servant—can offer justice, medicine, insight, peace, hope, and help for pain, but only by recognizing the profound social and ethical interdependence of specialties in knowledge and the blending of their respective symbolic modes. To arrive at new syntheses demanded by specialized knowledge, to develop fresh governance of research and conduct, and to renew vitality for the arts, it is imperative to recognize the interdependence of all symbolic modes and to confront the fact that, as each develops, it touches and merges with others. Ethical considerations are never absent. All this is precisely why the word *university* was chosen for the place, the institution, where these activities are, as an entelechy, pursued together. *Universitas* means not only one whole. It also means "society."

7

PACKAGING ETHICS

A good judge in each particular field is one who has been trained in it, but a good judge in general is one who has received an all-round schooling.

—ARISTOTLE, *NICOMACHEAN ETHICS*, FOURTH CENTURY B.C.E.

All this knowledge, all our knowledge, has been built up communally: there would be no astrophysics, there would be no history, there would not even be language, if man were a solitary animal. . . . It follows that we must be able to rely on other people; we must be able to trust their word. That is, it follows that there is a principle which binds society together, because without it the individual would be helpless to tell the true from the false. This principle is truthfulness. If we accept truth as an individual criterion, then we have also to make it the cement to hold society together.

—JACOB BRONOWSKI, *SCIENCE AND HUMAN VALUES*, 1965

A movement to revitalize the teaching of ethics grew more visible and influential in the final decades of the twentieth century, and it continues to grow. It is designed to address knotty questions of means and ends, to prevent signs and symbols from eclipsing values, and to offset an ethos that regards money as an end rather than a means (see chap. 6). If not yet in the public eye, it has captured the attention of decision makers. American Express donates large sums to support the discussion and teaching of ethics in higher education. Princeton University is home to a center devoted to human values. Harvard runs a well-funded, esteemed program "Ethics and the Professions." Substantial contributions to business schools—especially Harvard's and Stanford's—help to make ethics part of the curriculum in management. Volumes on organized ethics in government, medicine, law, and business now cram bookstore shelves.

In short, an ethics boom has happened. It started chiefly with medical ethics and spread, in three decades, to most professional fields. In 1980, 58 percent of all codes of professional ethics had been developed in only the previous four years. In 1981, 241 such codes were on file; in

1989, a jump to 338; by 1997, a doubling to 764. Yet, as Michael Davis notes in *Ethics and the University* (1999), "The ethics boom is not a 'morals boom' . . . nor is it a boom in the study of . . . general standards of conduct. . . . The ethics boom is primarily a boom in 'professional ethics' and other forms of 'applied ethics'" (8, 20).

This enthusiasm and financial support for improved ethical awareness among the professional and academic elite must correspond to something in the broader society, but a correlation with national economic and social behavior (with the possible exception of its increasing complexity) is hard to pinpoint. By happenstance, the New Ethics came into its own just as a great financial scandal was coming to a head. Wickedly combining the ruthlessness of deregulated capitalism and the improvident generosity of socialism, the savings and loan fiasco damaged the economy by privatizing the profits of a factitious boom and transferring the losses of the ensuing bust to taxpayers. The unraveling debacle spun off 1,600 serious criminal referrals, to the discomfiture of the understaffed Justice Department, which could follow only a quarter of them. More than 1,000 were simply dropped. Evidence implicated officers of insolvent financial institutions by the score, "independent" accountants, lawyers, realtors, business schools, senators, and much of the revolving-door traffic between government regulators and private enterprise. A conservative estimate totals the mess at a $250 billion charge on the public treasury—$1,000 for every citizen. The average working taxpayer will contribute $2,000, plus interest. As a crowning insult, the less well-to-do, some of whom lost their life savings in the scams, are paying through their taxes a disproportionate share. A few criminals went to prison, some were slapped on the wrist, but most suspects went scot-free; many laughed their way to the local full-service bank in luxury cars, or in yachts to offshore vaults. After the scandal became public knowledge, some business schools injected ethics courses into their curricula, and the professions wondered aloud if they were policing themselves effectively.

The rage for ethics, at least in the business world, died down in the mid- and later 1990s. Why? The best short explanation comes not from any sideline moralist but from the dean of the University of Pennsylvania's Wharton School of Business, Patrick T. Harker: "We all got carried away in the gold rush." Then fresh corporate scandals—Enron, Arthur Andersen, MCI WorldCom, Tyco, Global Crossing, K-Mart, Sprint, U.S. Technologies, and Adelphia among them—prompted a new round of ethics courses to promote "values, corporate responsibility, and integrity." Closing the barn door too late might be an unfair appraisal of these initiatives, but as one business journal notes, "If the market picks up and the headlines feature fewer scandals, the newfound religion could fade." It had once before, so why not again? Thousands of managers run their companies in a responsible, lawful manner. Yet, it is hard to escape the fact that many more individuals—employees, investors, taxpayers— have been hurt, disenchanted, and robbed by the actions of a group large enough to inflict widespread loss (Merritt, 64, 66).

Reacting to the scandals, many business schools (among them Loyola, Duquesne, Penn, Bentley, Stanford, Harvard, Princeton, and Maryland) offer courses in ethics, but many schools still either do not offer ethics or do not require it. Martha Nussbaum of the University of Chicago sees weaknesses as well as strengths in the specialized approach taken by those programs that do address the question. Programs "in business and engineering pay lip service to the importance of ethical issues, including some attention to ethics in their regular courses; but they are not the focus of such courses and do not get covered fully; meanwhile, the existence of some ethical discussion in those courses reinforces the students' sense that they do not need philosophy" (299). Ethics is now ghettoized. It is a separate field. Paradoxically, educators would have been wiser to treat the term *ethics* neutrally—more like *health* or *nutrition.* This would avoid the misconception that ethical decisions are a lifestyle option, like choosing leather or fabric upholstery. One can have good ethics, bad ethics, shallow ethics, situational ethics, or inconsistent ethics, but one cannot live in society and have no ethics at all. It is gratifying to see the emergence of the New Ethics, and it is important. Yet, the nature of this educational and professional movement deserves scrutiny.

The Ethical Barometer

Objective assessment of the moral state of any society is absurdly difficult. Reactions based on characterizations of contemporary society— outrage, or outrage at the death of outrage—can contain (and often disguise) political, religious, or ideological agendas. It may be more fruitful to study the prevailing moral myths or self-perceptions that society constructs for itself. There at least a society, through its institutions and media, describes its own ethical integrity, or lack of it. History may validate or discredit such self-perceptions, but whether these characterizations, these self-portraits, are in fact accurate is but one facet of their importance. Whether true or false, such self-images exert powerful influences, at times self-fulfilling.

One recurrent theme of national self-perception is that social and educational institutions, religious and political life, and the professions in general are suffering a crisis in ethics, a confusion of values, even a moral vacuum. Harold Shapiro, former president of Princeton, notes, "From many quarters in contemporary society, one senses an increased concern over the lack of principled and responsible behavior in both public and private life, particularly with respect to our communal obligations, the web of mutual obligations and understandings that should bind us together as a community" (94). Robert Putnam has demonstrated that institutions of sociability, churches, civic clubs, adult sports leagues, and volunteer organizations, have declined since the 1950s. Noticing that Americans bowl but no longer bowl as much in leagues, Putnam entitles his study *Bowling Alone.* In his fiction, Walker Percy put his finger on the trend. Putnam to some extent blames TV, yet if identifying culprits repaired disintegrating communities and restored debased ethics, solutions would be easier. They are made more complicated by a now-reflexive cynicism.

Since 1980 the gap between rich and poor has widened. If all forms of taxation are considered (income, Social Security, Medicare, sales), the rich pay a far lower percentage of their incomes in tax than the hard-pressed middle class. A kinder, gentler nation still seems distant. During the last twenty years, to use Mario Cuomo's phrase from a National Press Club appearance, society has witnessed "the denial of compassion made respectable." In proportion to wealth, many surveys indicate that philanthropy is down.

The one activity that for decades claimed to represent elevated ideals of effort, striving, and commitment to a pursuit seen as its own end—the Olympics—succumbed to the corrosive influence of "gifts" and "scholarships." These were bribes. When cities saw, after the Los Angeles games of 1984, that they could turn aspirations into hard cash, they vied fiercely for the "honor" of the games. A volunteer investigating committee headed by former senator George Mitchell found that it was precisely this interurban competition that proved too tempting. It corrupted the International Olympic Committee, and it corrupted the citizens and businesses of cities hoping to host the games. An amateur, idealistic, and selfless spirit had become, in the ruling body of the Olympics and its host venues, professional, materialistic, and riddled with self-interest. To make matters worse, many months after the Utah Winter Games were finally cleaned up, in May 2002, Sandra Baldwin, president of the U.S. Olympic Committee, resigned, acknowledging that she had lied about her academic credentials. In early 2003, amid charges of conflict of interest, the new head of the U.S. Olympic Committee also resigned.

Yet, to insist that an unprecedented state of moral torpor now exists is appealing neither intellectually nor historically. Robert Frost, writing to a student at Amherst College, complained,

> You will often hear it said that the age of the world we live in is particularly bad. I am impatient of such talk. We have no way of knowing that this age is one of the worst in the world's history. [Matthew] Arnold claimed the honor for the age before this. Wordsworth claimed it for the last but one. And so on back through literature. I say they claimed the honor for their ages. They claimed it rather for themselves. It is immodest of a man to think of himself as going down before the worst forces ever mobilized by God.

Observations about a decline in authority, a decline in religion, or more concretely, about the lack of historical consciousness exhibited in many policies, can be useful. But it is more objective to remark how society has now come *to view itself,* rightly or wrongly, though for evident reasons, as having given way to a state of moral confusion, a corruption of values, an erosion of ethical life. How any society perceives itself becomes a substantial part of the reality of that society. Such a perception motivates its actions, not always in the direction of reform. A spreading disbelief in the viability of ideals invites defeatism and cynicism.

The response in creative literature, despite efforts of inspired satirists like Mailer, Vonnegut, Heller, and Wolfe, can't keep up with breaking scandals. Whether depravity has increased or simply the demand to know about it and the ability of twenty-four-hour news to answer that demand, scandals are so many and crowd on each other so quickly that the imagination falters; bizarre reality upstages inventiveness. In the postmodern era, satire finds itself in the predicament that Alexander Pope complained of in 1738:

> Vice with such Giant-strides comes on amain
> Invention strives to be before in vain;
> Feign what I will, and paint it e'er so strong,
> Some rising genius sins up to my song.

The investigative reporter, the author of the exposé, has largely taken the role of satirist. In the "information age," the availability of news channels and Web sites necessitates a greater demand for material to fill time and space, to which speculative reporting often replies in the only way it can, by outrunning the facts. The audience receives many stories based on conjecture, followed by more stories on whether the media should be running that kind of story. Reality, thus enhanced, outruns the satirist's fertile imagination and comments perversely on itself; in fiction, writers employ black humor, irony, the absurd, surrealism, and self-parody as the primary means of commentary, survival, and defense, the means to preserve moral integrity. It is no coincidence that these modes of literary expression have flourished since World War I.

An Academic Movement

The New Ethics is a pervasive response to a perceived moral problem. It is essentially unlike all previous ethical movements, and it is a phenomenon not restricted to this country. The New Ethics does not rest on a return to traditional values, whatever that may mean, nor on a return to family or church, though all those calls go out simultaneously as different responses to the same perceived "slide" and "confusion" in a shared moral life. The New Ethics is not epitomized by slogans. It is predominantly, almost exclusively, secular. It is thoroughly rational, at times intellectual and philosophical. It concerns itself with particular facts and problems; it is empirical rather than spiritual, professional rather than general, and for the most part, it is ahistorical. Its practitioners are primarily academics or intellectuals. The New Ethics is without overt political goals. It is not devoted to one stand on single issues such as abortion or nuclear arms, but addresses policy concerns in diverse areas of public life, particularly law, medicine, and business. In fact, programs in ethics flourish most vigorously in those professions where salaries are highest, both inside and outside the academy. It is a defining premise of the New Ethics that professional life presents cases or dilemmas that require specialized ethical discussion. It follows that to be a well-intentioned, well-educated individual is insufficient to confront such professional issues. One must be a specialist.

The New Ethics is an academic response to social dislocations real and perceived. It is seen—not just on campuses but in the world of public affairs—as an important way for the academy to reassert its relevance and usefulness. It opens a door for academics and administrators to escape the ivory tower and to enter what Milton calls the dust and heat of the combative arena. James Gustafson notes that the New Ethics deliberately moves away from more-abstract ethical speculation common earlier and, without jettisoning theory, engages ethical problems and case studies. In his view, the discipline of ethics—though he is careful to note that this should not be confused with actual ethical behavior—has been revitalized. The strongest wing of the New Ethics is in professional schools. Many fields—law, medical care, public policy, and business—now train a new professional species: the ethicist. Yet, ethicists often disagree with each other over basic tenets of their discipline. They are not authorities in the way someone is an authority on nuclear magnetic resonance or French prosody. Ethicists often testify as experts, for a fee, on opposing sides of legal cases. As Gustafson states, "Maybe the claims of expertise for ethicists will be diminished when people realize they are for hire." Some professions have spawned watchdogs and moral monitors, such as the Union of Concerned Scientists. But the battle over ethics has found common ground: educational institutions. William Bennett has complained that most courses in values offer simply "lifeboat stuff," in other words, worthy moral issues but ones so rare that they have little to do with cultural or communal values practiced daily. Derek Bok counters that moral education is a multiform process that involves many disciplines and courses, and that it encourages students to think ethically rather than to soak up an established creed. Here, again, the temptation to polarize the debate overwhelms common sense. There are, in fact, few teachers who advocate indoctrination in any moral code. Yet, reading the wisdom literature of the world is not incompatible with what is usually called, in discussions of ethics and liberal education, "critical thinking." Does it overstrain the imagination to picture the two not only coexisting but also, when taught and read imaginatively, strengthening one another? To these considerations Harold Shapiro rightly adds, "Complex moral reasoning is not a substitute for moral behavior" (96).

More fundamentally, to start ethical education in college or later, in the professional schools, is already too late. While training professionals "can help them understand that through their profession they can contribute to the larger aims of society, that professional ethics are not some last-minute add-on, but the very core of the meaning of professionalism" (Bellah 1999, 20), that core must be nurtured earlier. As Nussbaum remarks, separate courses in ethics provide the salve of examining the topic without integrating the resulting ideas into action. Even "action" compartmentalizes too much. Until students understand that human existence is ethical in nature, inescapably and always—that ethics is not entombed in a text or confined to good deeds—they are unlikely to see its interest or purpose as a subject. Athanasios Moulakis aptly notes: "To awaken and cultivate values is not to provide the learner with additional tools, not to add another facet to *what* he is—a neurologist, a scuba diver, a poor cook—but to bring about a change of *who* he is. Values are personal, or they are nothing" (111). Alasdair MacIntyre states this sense of values and of personal relationships from another angle. "We need then to be educated into the relevant kind of relationship with those others who participate with us in particular practices. And to be so educated we have to entrust ourselves to others who will act both as instructors and exemplars." To emphasize that these personal relationships differ fundamentally from taking a course, discussing case studies, or writing a paper, MacIntyre remarks of these exemplars: "Note that they won't so instruct us by professing to teach us something whose name is 'ethics'" (8). Practical moral instruction is either integrated into all teaching, including the teaching of professions, or it becomes window dressing. Once compartmentalized, it has lost.

Ethics in the root sense is what members of a culture do as a custom. Ethics has come to mean more than that, but custom and habit remain crucial to the concept. In part, ethics is the behavior honored by tradition. A cynic might say that the Greeks, who developed the word and the concept, owned slaves and demeaned women. But if, instead of castigating customary vices, one considers admirable customary behavior, then a more satisfying and challenging notion of what ethics can mean emerges. For instance, the Greeks—and not only the Greeks—accounted it a sin to turn away a stranger; custom obliged hospitality. Excellent historical and anthropological explanations account for this belief. And yet, to honor such a custom is, in part, to honor what makes *human* a laudatory word. Sometimes it is inconvenient or expensive to offer hospitality. It isn't entirely rational, it's not a rational choice, really, but it's hard not to admire it anyway—perhaps *because* it is not entirely rational. The Greeks did it because that's what you do (they thought) when a stranger appears at your door and does not threaten you. Not to do so is to behave like Polyphemus the Cyclops, the emblem of brutal selfishness.

If ethics were only a matter of rational choice, if rational choice theory could explain all ethical choices, and if one person's motives were identical to another's—or one group's or country's coincided with another's—then ethical issues would evaporate. We would be in the country of Swift's Houyhnhnms. Often, academic study of compartmentalized ethics encourages this confidence in rational choice. Robert Bellah remarks of this attitude, "Our modern quasi-Kantian university has decided to commit itself to cognitive inquiry and to push ethical inquiry to the margins as a subfield in philosophy or something the professional schools can worry about" (2000, 20). There, especially if the dimensions of history, religion, and ethnicity are neutralized in theory, ethical inquiry becomes a subspecies of cognitive inquiry. The trouble is, rational choice theory has never explained all human action, and whenever actions that it cannot account for are mixed with those it can, then none of them can be satisfactorily explained. A renowned economist and certainly a rational one, Joseph Schumpeter, warned, "Capitalist rationality does not do away with sub- or super-rational impulses. It merely makes them get out of hand by removing the restraint of sacred or semi-sacred tradition" (1950, 144; see also 1991, 324–25). Human conduct has always failed to provide evidence supporting only rational choice theories of ethics. Behavior has never reliably obeyed such theories. Motives, means, and ends are too complex to follow a clear decision tree.

The experience of sitting on fellowship committees or having frank conversations with students is sufficient to show how hard it is for students with aspirations not expressable in phrases like "lucrative career" or "professional success." Some of their peers have been running campus political campaigns for student government that would make spin doctors and old pols pause—ballot stuffing, reckless charges of racism, and forged e-mail messages (McGinn 2000a). It's hard to agree with those who think this "toughens" student candidates and prepares them for politics later. Doing something worthwhile without hurting someone else—whether playing the piano, experimenting in a lab, reading Borges, or working at a homeless shelter—is often difficult and frustrating. The young usually welcome the reminder that these activities are worth doing. To be told or shown instead that, in the eyes of society and their peers, selfless actions should be regarded primarily as tools for self-promotion and line items on a résumé is, to say the least, confusing. In time, for all but the strongest, it is dispiriting.

Success

Any education in ethics, new or old, confronts the unquestioned assumptions of a culture. Almost every citizen knows without thinking (in both senses) what his or her society regards as wrong and what it treats as necessary to self-respect. The wrongs of society have a Mosaic character—for example, it's wrong to steal. What society gives its approbation to, however, can grow strangely close to what it ostensibly decries. For many students seeking education, one goal, material success, is swallowing other goals and turning itself into an unquestioned good rather than a problematic objective. It is what William James called the American Bitch Goddess Success, the idea of winning, sometimes at any cost, the necessity of team playing if that is what winning requires, even to the suppression of individual moral qualms.

In the last thirty-five years this has been colored by the fact that—as Lewis Lapham points out in *Money and Class in America*—the universal yardstick of success has become, more than ever, money. It's become a civil religion, not just because a capitalistic economy exists without (thankfully) a state religion, but because in this pluralistic society the universally recognized measure of distinction is money. Alexis de Tocqueville hoped that Americans might offset greed by self-interest properly understood, finding equipoise between personal and collective advantage. But Tocqueville also worried that greed could undermine American civil society; the persuasion that I have too little or my neighbor has too much will in the end breed public vices. Ironically, much of higher education prepares students and encourages faculty to worship James's Bitch Goddess. Success begins with admission to the right day-care center, then advancement to the right schools and colleges with their high costs, which must be justified and repaid with interest, then acceptance into top graduate schools, with even higher costs, which require high-salary jobs to repay. The deleterious effects on higher education of this devotion to getting ahead can be read in symptoms like pervasive grade inflation. The foundation of this behavior is the conviction that if all the steps in this *cursus honorum* are duly trod, "success" or "security" will follow. In many advising sessions, these words now replace "citizenship" and "learning." The multimillionaire David Geffen, speaking on the TV show *20/20*, remarked on a fact that goes to the core of education in ethics and education in general: "Happy is harder than money. Anybody who thinks money will make you happy, hasn't got money."

In and of itself, wanting to get into good schools is admirable. However, the competition often seems for the advertisement value of the institutional name rather than for what might be learned in following the life of the mind. The effects on society considered as a whole cannot be healthy. In the absence of a universal draft or mandatory national service, most young people never encounter a true cross-section of civil society at work on tasks requiring discipline and cooperation. If college is as close to that as they are likely to experience—and it can be a rough approximation, better than most institutions afford—then the demand to succeed individually, and hence the ineluctable requirement to compete against others, placing everyone either behind or ahead of someone else, paradoxically undercuts the possibility of building a *national* community. The more that such values of competition and status take hold, the more pervasive their effect and its generational compounding. It's as if, one by one, every activity worth doing turned into high-stakes musical chairs.

All this has a subtle and underestimated effect on educational institutions that want actively to teach, if they dare, that success and security, money and professions, are not the locomotive of the train, with ethics coupled on like a caboose. Responsible ethics and moral action are themselves the engine that should be pulling everything else. There is an added irony when students see media attention focused on the funding and grants received by the New Ethics, particularly from successful financial corporations simultaneously doing business with the educational institution housing the ethical program.

Education in ethics faces another obstacle in the conflict-averse rhetoric of the polite community, the community unable to hammer out its values through open debate, disagreement, dissent, and consensus. The key words and phrases of this rhetoric are familiar: egalitarian, nonjudgmental, supportive, understanding, nonconfrontational, antielitist, and, in some contexts, politically correct. In most instances the rhetoric of tolerant, polite community has done considerable good. It can correct past prejudice and confront current bigotry. Yet, this rhetoric has a negative side. Actions that are courageous or extraordinary are often lonely and friendless, done with a conviction that it is better to act in a way other than that favored by peers and associates who have created the ethos of "right" values. An education in tolerance, if rigid and formulaic, can hinder principled decisions, all of which *are* judgmental in that they imply, and often express, judgment about the actions of others. In some of its conclusions, a conscientious ethics is certain to be controversial; it may regard all individuals with equity, but ethical judgments are by definition not egalitarian. At times they are fiercely hierarchical, not with regard to race, class, and gender—at least they should not be so—but with regard to right and wrong. An ethical action or judgment can be accusatory; often it is painful, confrontational. Whatever else it may be, it is, in the end, independent. Yet, as David Bromwich warns, in the atmosphere of much higher education, "The idea of personal thought, of making one's own experiment in life, often the very belief in intellectual liberty, is scorned. The watchword instead is 'community,' and this is likely to carry a meaning that is overtly paternalistic, or maternalist. I am to be judged not by what I say, think, feel, or believe, but by where I come from and by what and how much I am willing to do in a group whose moral soundness has already been judged acceptable" (1991, 36). It is, in other words, a belief in innocence by association.

Speech codes restrict student and faculty freedoms more than does the Constitution—ironic, since it is precisely universities and colleges that traditionally protect and foster free inquiry and free speech. The point is not to castigate the political left or right (both guilty, at various times, of clamping down on free speech), but to fight those instances where higher education decides what is socially acceptable in speech and then enforces it. This is not freedom. Its intentions are good, but a certain road is paved with those. Such codes dictate a prohibition not only against words and phrases but against ideas. They require that the community *already* agree on the meaning of the speech outlawed. Whether the child of this or that agenda, speech codes are a mistake (see Kors and Silverglate, 67–96).

While group thinking poses a clear danger, the tolerant spirit of most universities may make the academic world more of a battleground for debate than it now is, debate not just about ethical issues in society but about the actions of educational institutions themselves. Barring financial collapse and extinction, the most volatile, media-grabbing issues faced within a university regard its own governance as a moral and ethical matter: divestment, government contracts, conflicts of commitment, sexual harassment, campus recruitment, employment conditions, minority hiring and representation, tenure decisions, freedom of speech, and the disciplining of those who, in establishing their own moral stance, infringe the rights of others. As universities and colleges pursue education in ethics that can be applied to other problems and professions, the academic world simultaneously faces, as it has been facing, the fact that its most bitter disputes will focus on internal ethical issues. These cannot and should not paralyze the university or college, which has multiple responsibilities and duties, all to be carried on without interruption.

The general problem reveals itself in conflicts of interest where certain goals are set above others, or are set on an equal footing, when they should not be. The problem exists when no one at the institution has the will, courage, or power to insist that the more important interest must take precedence (e.g., literacy over excellence in athletics, excellence in athletics over video arcades). These conflicts may involve large sums of money. It is disconcerting to hear an official of a major university state, as reported by the *Harvard Crimson* on December 7, 1999, that one of the chief criteria for accepting a gift is not some internal moral sense—"Does this feel right to us?"—but instead a worry over public embarrassment: "Frequently, one of the things that is considered is, can we defend this if it's on the front page of The Crimson or the [Boston] Globe or the New York Times?" Presumably, the defense should invoke an internal ethical code, but so much concern over a public defense makes the internal rightness of the decision look like a secondary consideration.

Donald Kennedy, former president of Stanford, states, "Nothing is inherently wrong with conflicts of interest; they are frequently unavoidable in contemporary life. Universities are no less plagued by them than most other institutions, and most conflicts, when acknowledged, do not present difficulties for the institution or its faculty members" (1997, 249). Yet that seems too sanguine. It is hard to endorse the implication that something must be "inherently wrong" to warrant alarm. For example, the financial connection of drug companies to medical research has become, to use Frank Norris's metaphorical term about the old railroad monopolies, an octopus. So pervasive and lucrative are the money ties of drug companies to researchers and medical schools that on May 18, 2000, the nation's leading medical publication, the *New England Journal of Medicine,* took the unprecedented step of publishing an editorial entitled bluntly, "Is Academic Medicine for Sale?" The *Journal* noted, in its policy statement, that it requires authors of its published articles to reveal their financial ties to companies that might have an interest in their research, but those ties are in some cases so lengthy and intricate that space prevents printing them in the *Journal.* They appear on its Web site instead. In the editorial, Dr. Marcia Angell warns that the guidelines regulating financial ties between medical faculty and industry "are generally quite relaxed and are likely to become even more so."

Not just individual faculty, but whole institutions increasingly depend on industry. The transfer of research into products is one justification; another is the need for medical institutions to balance their books. Both justifications have merit, particularly the first. But, cautions Angell, clinical research rarely qualifies as technology *transfer.* It is rather the testing of technology. And "there is no conceivable social benefit in researchers' having equity interest in companies whose products they are studying." Companies lavish gifts, meals, trips, speaking fees, and various material blandishments on young physicians and medical personnel. If not enough to constitute bribes, these qualify as influence peddling. When disc jockeys accepted it to play certain records, it was called payola (from pay + [Victr]ola). Maybe doctors should think of the medical equivalent as payscriptions. Studies show conclusively that "researchers with ties to drug companies are indeed more likely to report results that are favorable to the products of those companies than researchers without such ties." Only when an eighteen-year-old died in a clinical trial of gene therapy conducted by the University of Pennsylvania—in an institute whose director did not, according to the FDA, "properly report the deaths of experimental animals or serious side effects suffered by volunteers"—did a university panel declare that financial relationships between researchers and private companies "may be ill advised" (Nelson and Weiss; Lueck). In her editorial, Dr. Angell concludes, "The incentives of the marketplace should not become woven into the fabric of academic medicine." Instead of blurring guidelines in this area, schools like Harvard should encourage others to adopt the more strict standard Harvard once prided itself on but now seems disposed to drop. Moreover, certain financial ties should be prohibited altogether, including equity interest and many of the writing and speaking arrangements. Money spent for those "gifts," conferences, meals, honoraria, and grants is provided, of course, by the rising price of drugs and devices. Taxpayers, elderly patients, and parents of uninsured children, among others, pay the tab. Or the tab becomes so high they go without.

In August 2000 a government-sponsored conference held at Bethesda, Maryland, concluded that integrity in research has measurably declined because of economic motives. Three years later, on August 21, 2003, Dr. Angell, along with numerous other prominent scientists, signed a letter to the prestigious journal *Science,* as well as to journals of the Nature Publishing Group. The letter protested that in five recent cases journals were still failing to disclose significant conflicts between authors' economic interests and their scientific research (Petersen 2003a).

Equally disturbing is the power of corporations to silence or discredit academics, or to pressure their home institutions to fire them. Nancy Olivieri experienced this at the University of Toronto. She came to question the safety of a drug manufactured by a potentially large donor to the university, Apotex. The company tried to prevent her from warning patients of side effects she considered life threatening. It cited the no-publishing stipulation it had insisted on including in her contract. Olivieri decided that people's lives were more important and published her findings. According to some reports, the president of the University of Toronto, Robert Prichard, fearing loss of the Apotex gift, mustered a publicity campaign against his own faculty member. At any rate, the university fired her from the post of director of its hospital blood disorders clinic. Only after international experts from Oxford and Harvard protested was she reinstated. Had she been an adjunct professor, who would have joined the fight? For adjuncts, academic freedom is a chimera. Olivieri said of Apotex what is true of the relationship between most companies and universities: "This company needs the university far more than the university needs it" ("A Drug Company's Efforts"; *CHE,* Dec. 10, 1999, A18–19). While medical ethicists are the most visible professional ethicists, they are far more likely to be engaged with the doctor-patient relationship than with the academic-corporate one.

Sheldon Krimsky, author of *Science in the Private Interest* (2003), contends that the temptation to profit is corrupting the motives for scientific research, disserving the public, and making objective research more rare. He documents the burgeoning ties between companies and academic science, arguing "that the trend has accelerated in the last 25 years" when "'a gold rush mentality began. . . . [N]egative attitudes toward commercialization disappeared over a fairly short period of time'" (Petersen 2003b).

The New Ethics—or any attempt at moral education—faces another difficulty. It will be hard to see progress in a short span of time; hard, even, to see progress over the long haul. In scientific fields, knowledge accumulates, theories are refined, and progress is marked. Some hard-won knowledge becomes obsolete or is modified. In other fields such as business, economics, and government, one expects that, over time, techniques and understanding will improve. Yet, for centuries, the wisdom of moral writers has indicated that it is a success—a word used advisedly—to maintain humankind in a middle state, to prevent slippage into injustice, savagery, even genocide. Most answers to human moral ills are not radical and curative but temporary and palliative. Abstract theory and specialization promise concrete action in some areas (new laws on suicide of the terminally ill, for example), but the New Ethics will be hard-pressed to hold up a body of accumulated knowledge that produces actual, demonstrable, positive effects. And as soon as the New Ethics addresses issues raised by new technologies, newer advances reformulate the questions.

The increasing specialization in ethics, its complexities and case studies in professional contexts, along with its perpetually changing object of study, make one question the viability of ethics as a separate, demarcated field of study with fixed principles and practices. Aristotle in the *Nicomachean Ethics* wisely and wryly prefaces his work this way: "Our discussion will be adequate if it achieves clarity within the limits of the subject matter. For precision cannot be expected in the treatment of all subjects alike, any more than it can be expected in all manufactured articles." Yet ethics now divides into ever more specialized, practical compartments. As one example, a research fellow in professional ethics at a major university devoted more than a year's study to the ethical implications of what it means to be called "professional" in the first place. Such specialization, even if inevitable, harbors dangers. It creates vocabularies impervious to the scrutiny of those not in the discipline. It suggests that ethics can, without difficulty, go on being divided into subdisciplines without detriment, that it progresses because of a mimicry of hard science, and that it requires professional specialists rather than educated citizens to understand and practice it.

Broader Concerns

While it is not, as noted, possible to participate in society and have no ethics, it is possible to live with blurred ethical vision so that only gross imperatives—it is bad to steal—are important. Fine ethical distinctions first fall into disuse, then are finessed, and finally begin to vanish. The ethical formulas of the culture eventually reduce to a checklist.

Donald Kennedy knows the meaning of loyalty but nonetheless, musing on the increasingly common practice of parlaying a fine university appointment into an even finer one, thinks its meaning has become newly problematic. He offers that there are now many kinds of loyalty. There are, but not long ago testing their variety openly for oneself went by the name of disloyalty. To select sides, institutions, or choices as they further one's own interests and advancement is certainly being loyal to something, often to one's self. To be loyal to one's discipline rather than to an institution may seem fine, but it is hard to avoid the sense that in some cases it means being disloyal to the institution. The problem here is that "disloyalty" is such a vice that one cannot bear to be identified with it. Professionally, it ranks up there with murder. It just sounds so bad. It suggests that you may be disloyal to the next place, too. Therefore, almost anything will be said or done to deflect any such charge and to turn the action that prompted that charge into a virtue itself, into "another kind" of loyalty. Obviously, there are valid reasons for people to move and change venues, yet selfish and ungrateful reasons prompt such action, too. It avoids ethical judgment to lump both kinds of reasons together under the banner of "a widening set of loyalties" (Kennedy 2002).

Education in ethics needs, at a fundamental level, to aim not just at specialization and the professions but at the ethical education of the whole individual. Conscience cannot be manufactured at the postgraduate level. It cannot be manufactured at all, but only nurtured at every level. So, James Freedman, former president of Dartmouth, states, "The morality of a professor's example is perhaps the most powerful force in the teaching of values" (1996, 57). Ethics is part of *any* field—one of Aristotle's "master sciences." Hence, it comes under philosophy, the method or integrative knowledge of all disciplines, the way to value knowledge in order to relate and apply it to conduct. Here, subjects such as ethics, aesthetics, rhetoric, linguistics, politics, and science conjoin and are regarded in the light of judgment that weighs conflicting goods and trade-offs, as well as evils, and then acts. As Robert Maynard Hutchins, drawing on Aristotle's *Ethics,* noted, "The end is the first principle of practical action." Many colleges and universities have mottoes conveying ideals or ends associated with this philosophical outlook. Those ideals and ends, such as truth, light, the good, the beautiful, justice, and knowledge for its own sake were esteemed, even revered, for a long time. The mottoes are usually in Latin or Hebrew or Greek. Symbolically and in actuality, many are replaced now with advertising slogans (for example, Hofstra's "We teach success" or Stanford's "A start-up since 1891"), or with mission statements, the latter at times unidealistic, prolix, and unreadable, even though in English.

The New Ethics might strengthen itself if it allied itself with the humanities. Or, rather, the humanities might rise to the occasion and include themselves in it. Before ethics gained a high profile on the academic landscape, some foresaw an age of Aquarius for ethics, with business schools housing guardians of commercial ethics, and corporations hiring experts on moral philosophy for sums that would make a Sophist blush. But ethics is too complicated, too rooted in custom, history, religion, politics, and difficult reading, as well as experience, to be boned up on and taught as a seminar sideline to the market economy, the board or the operating room. One cannot impart ethical understanding of any society without a decent foundation in literature, art, poetry, drama, philosophical traditions, and religions, the narratives that depict trauma and suffering, faith and betrayal, sin and atonement. Representing deep-seated practices often as strong as rational choices (though not ruling out rational choice), they are the repository and bedrock expression of ethical ideals and conflicts. They provide a broader understanding by which all case studies—legal, medical, and commercial—might be examined. Jefferson was not being flippant when, in 1771, he wrote to Robert Skipwith, "A lively and lasting sense of filial duty is more effectually impressed on the mind of a son or daughter by reading *King Lear,* than by all the dry volumes of ethics, and divinity, that ever were written." The abstract analyses and rare case studies of programs in ethics court superficiality if they are developed in a vacuum excluding the long traditions and record of cultural ethics that they cannot possibly stop and reserve the time to study in depth.

When Isaiah Berlin accepted the first Senator Giovanni Agnelli International Prize in ethics, he cited his reading of Tolstoy, Vico, and Herder as formative. Eminent American writers, among them Robert Penn Warren and Archibald MacLeish, have testified to the complex interpenetration of politics, history, government, and literature. Late in life,

MacLeish lamented that specialization had become so great that anyone attempting to fuse those fields, as he had done, would immediately be suspect.

However, the teaching of literature has largely abandoned its role as the examination of a complex set of ethical documents demanding agony over the choices, dilemmas, and ideals they present. The humanities have specialized, too. The teaching of literature in the last fifty years has witnessed a series of brilliant forays, for example, the New Criticism, structuralism, deconstruction, fashionable skepticism in interpretation, and the New Historicism. Yet, few of their practitioners ever evinced a deep involvement with ethical questions. (Feminists often did.) More recently, a "return" to ethics has been declared in literary studies, but to judge from its practice, this movement frequently confines itself to theoretical analyses or professional commodification. One critic, J. Hillis Miller, has written that literature is not a source of admirable cultural values. He regards that view as a warm, attractive, but false illusion. In other words, reading literature as an instrument for examining right and wrong, or for the formation of character and action, is often seen as delusive, insufficient, escapist. The "ethics of reading" ends up being about reading only, not ethics in the usual sense, not even ethics and reading.

Yet, even before Plutarch, humane letters not only contributed to ethical life and writing but represented its main support. Many authors during twenty-five millennia have thought it was worth trying. Literature written by great expressive spirits rarely inculcates didactic lessons, certainly not in tidy snippets like fortune cookies. Literary case studies are among the most complex. Because of its richness, its recognition of the fluidities and difficulty of ethical life, literature, in exploring the conditions of life and society, is apt to trouble our preconceptions. As John Dryden said, literature need not teach specific lessons; in fact, it is better if it does not, but poetry must *be* ethical. Tendentious writing and overly sophisticated literary theory age poorly: it is breadth of ethical and human interest that gives life to literature and keeps it alive. Even Oscar Wilde, condemning moral lessons as an "unpardonable mannerism of style" and protesting the blind conformity urged on by society, insisted nevertheless that the moral life contributes to the artist's subject matter.

While many teachers of literature elect to dismiss direct consideration of ethics, teaching the humanities can invigorate and give needed context to ethical education, not as the inculcation of "truths" or cultural standards, but as the representation, testing, and forge of values, the odyssey of personal experience in public venues. Countless poets and writers—Athol Fugard in South Africa, Alexander Solzhenitsyn in the

Gulag, Primo Levi in his concentration camp, Anne Frank in her confinement, Frederick Douglass in the United States, and Václav Havel in Czechoslovakia in the 1960s—all believed that literature is nothing if it is not ethical. The link between literature and liberty is freedom of the press writ large. The uses of literature are the uses of freedom, and the great tendency of vital literature has been to gain for its readers personal and imaginative freedom: the ability to ask and the drive to answer what Levin in *Anna Karenina* calls "Enigmas," the questions "Why?" and "What is to be done?"

Like the uses of all knowledge, the uses of literature exist in potential. Reading literature *guarantees* nothing. Its knowledge acts as an instrumentality. Like a scalpel or laser, it can heal or lance a cavity swollen with prejudice. It can also destroy, kill, or justify killing. Many SS officers were well educated. Many in authority at the camps loved fine music—often played by the prisoners—and avidly discussed the best plays. Willem Mengelberg, for fifty years the presiding genius of Amsterdam's Concertgebouw orchestra and one of the twentieth century's great conductors, spent the end of his life in disgrace, having supported the Third Reich throughout World War II. Slave owners could exhibit exquisite taste. Many knew their scriptures backward and forward; they just got the two directions mixed up.

Literature is open to everyone who can read; its uses parallel the uses of free will, a sobering as well as liberating prospect. This connection helps explain why some teachers of literature retreat into reliance on prescriptive methodologies or single-issue ideologies: those avoid raising the most troublesome enigmas that defy pat responses. It is hard to claim status as a teacher, an authority, if one cannot answer hard questions with certainty. Good writers know better. They explore those questions and are often the first to ask them. If they present ready answers, their own writing may teach the reader to distrust those very answers. Literature does not usually carry clear, concise ethical messages. If it does, we tire of it; as Keats said, we do not like poetry that has a design on us. But, in turn, any reader creates and is responsible for the ethical uses of literature, or lack of them. If readers do not develop their own taste or credo, then they become enslaved to the taste and belief of others. Not to decide is to have the decision made by others—by parents, teachers, colleagues, politicians, or someone willing to bully. Literature—with all its imperfections, subject to the pressures of history and the social conditions under which it's written and which it describes and represents—literature (both fiction and nonfiction) is still, of all human achievements, a secret nursery of change and reform.

Curricular aids to engagement can be of use, but only if well planned and well directed. Long before the New Ethics, there was recognition that the insularity of college life could breed detachment or apathy. In the 1850s Horace Mann pioneered the work-study program at Antioch College to combat those tendencies. The idea, though subject to abuse, has life in it yet. Mann's idea was to supplement education, not substitute for it, as is sometimes done now (e.g., academic credits for "life experience"). With careful oversight, though, community involvement programs and programs for public service offer real benefits. One contemporary success story is the Intercommunity Experience Program at Southern Methodist University. This program integrates reading and classroom work with community service, introducing SMU undergraduates to the realities of inner-city Dallas while providing tutoring and other assistance to the community.

The opposite of freedom and the free use of literature and art is individual fear. Fear, the progeny or sibling of ignorance, leads to cultural solipsism, to intolerance, and, finally, to hate. Hate, in turn, deepened and cultivated by habit, creates discrimination, tyranny, and genocide. If not actively fought, fear and hate are favored to win because they offer an easier path, one clearly blazed and attracting the more cowardly side of our natures. "The only thing necessary for the triumph of evil is that good men do nothing." This is attributed to Edmund Burke. Although the words cannot be found in his published work, he would own the sentiment.

The humanities offer not one social vision or theories of several, but actual instances of many, each one realized through individual character and feeling. Literature offers not one voice, but a debate of many dramatic ones, often as an exploration of ambiguity, and it offers at least one of the highest results of education. It aids in making difficult decisions by depicting those decisions, yet it refuses to impose answers. Literature rarely convinces by fear or authority—final choices and interpretations are left to the reader, challenged to make mature choices and interpretations independently.

Ethics should embrace the study of religion in Schleiermacher's general sense. This is not the inculcation or spread of doctrine, but the necessity of understanding and studying spiritual life as a worldwide anthropological phenomenon, everywhere indispensable to ethics and morality, even if, at times, as a bankrupt system to be repudiated or reformed. Only slowly have programs in ethics and courses in moral reasoning admitted that something other than secular, rational analysis shapes social ethics. In an interdependent world, religious life as part of ethics is as important as political ideology or rational theory. However many religions are practiced in a country, they all become connected to the nation's government and laws—even by the tension of constitutional separation—and they are never absent from customs and values.

As much good as it has done, the New Ethics will be even more effective if interest and involvement in ethics are encouraged early in the educational process and if ethics is treated as informing every field that touches on or depicts judgment and action. At the undergraduate and also at the professional level of education, scientists, doctors, lawyers, accountants, and managers will strengthen their ethical programs if they ally with humanists, but the humanists, in the proverbial expression, will need to step up to the plate. With thousands of years of collective experience, there is no doubt they can. The question is whether they will.

8

LEADING THE SELF INTO THE WORLD

Each one of us is always in peril of not being the unique and
untransferable self which he is. The majority of men perpetually betray
this self which is waiting to be; and to tell the whole truth our personal
individuality is a personage which is never completely realized, a
stimulating Utopia, a secret legend, which each of us guards at the
bottom of his heart.

> —ORTEGA Y GASSET, "THE SELF AND THE OTHER," 1939
> (TRANSLATED BY WILLARD R. TRASK)

The most authoritative, trusted study on the subject of student expectations and motives, a yearly poll of college-bound high school graduates
conducted by the Higher Education Research Institute at UCLA, reveals
that in thirty years, from the late 1960s to the late 1990s, a total flip-flop
occurred. Of all freshmen entering college, the number who expect
higher education to enhance future job security and assure high-wage
employment increased during those three decades from about 20 percent
to 80 percent. At the same time, those who expect to develop values, form
a broader social vision, experiment with varied forms of knowledge, and
formulate a philosophy of living slid from 80 percent to 20 percent. In
1998 three-quarters of all freshmen cited most frequently, and by a significant margin, as a "very important reason" they decided to go to college (a) to make more money (75 percent), and (b) to get a better job (77
percent). In 2002 these percentages remained almost the same. In 1998
fewer than half saw improved reading skills or becoming more cultured
as strong motivations at all. In 2002 the one final objective considered
"essential" or "very important" and identified by male freshmen more
than any other (75.3 percent) was "being very well-off financially," which
outranked raising a family. For female freshmen, raising a family barely
edged out being very well off financially as their top choice. For men and
women, the six lowest objectives considered important were "influenc-
ing the political structure," helping "clean up the environment," "making a theoretical contribution to science," "becoming accomplished in

one of the performing arts," "creating artistic work," and, last and least, "writing original works" (*American Freshman; CHE* Almanac 2003). As early as 1980, Arthur Levine, writing for the Carnegie Council series and entitling his study *When Dreams and Heroes Died: A Portrait of Today's College Student,* noted several distinct trends set in motion in the late 1970s. Grade inflation (see chap. 5) and careerism rose. Altruism and basic skills fell.

The idea of pursuing self-enrichment and material gain through higher education increased markedly in the late twentieth century, yet it had been common in the late nineteenth as well. At that earlier time, "No other theme so permeates the accounts we have of students' motives" (Veysey, 270–71). But historical precedent is a weak justification here. The motives described went hand in hand with a larger set of attitudes: study is good only for credit or for a credential, social and financial ambition should dictate intellectual life, and conformity to the crowd should not be sullied by too much hard work. Under this set of principles, many students kept their work, and especially their reading outside the classroom (see chap. 5), to a minimum. Thankfully, by 1930 such attitudes had diminished (Veysey, 272), and by 1968 they seemed fully in check. Now, in the last thirty years, the idea of self-enrichment and material gain has once again come to dominate students' motives.

How are the social and ethical goods of higher education (see chap. 2) to develop as individual students learn and mature? In a democratic society frankly multicultural, how can young people develop unique personal identities, yet also acquire a sense of shared concerns and some common cultural heritage? How can education foster values and social visions that go beyond the desire to be "very well off financially?" It may be plausible, even persuasive, to regard the situation this way: The individual psyche creates its identity by discovering what narratives, stories, and myths circulate in the ambient culture and then, by participating in language, the human activity par excellence, the self shapes its own personal narrative and private myths, which mesh but are not identical with the larger cultural ones in which it is involved. The individual grows with the aid and knowledge of ordered and meaningful language—narratives of various kinds. The self can be appealingly self-reliant yet not solipsistic. This understanding informs many bodies of knowledge dealing with human conduct and social institutions, among them history, anthropology, literature, ethnography, the study of religion, psychology, and political science. The active psyche creates itself in relation to already existing patterns and stories of personal development, in relation to fables and the quasi-magical tales of traditional myth. In addition, the individual psyche creates itself by absorbing and then criticizing the more abstract myths and cultural narratives that exert authority, so much authority that they regularly go unexamined. These animating narratives include, for example, the myth of the American frontier, the story of universal equality and equal justice under law, the promise of a new deal and a new frontier, and the progress of material culture. The more elastic the myth, the more grounded in history, the more powerful its different interpretations can be. "The American Dream," "the Underground Railroad," and "Horatio Alger" are instances. The psyche creates its singular inner life only as it simultaneously discovers these and other narratives embedded in a culture that permits self-creation in the first place. Understanding both individual psychology and collective culture hinges on seeing these two activities as symbiotic and acting in lively interdependence.

Giambattista Vico, the eighteenth-century Neapolitan scholar and teacher whose remarkable work *The New Science* was given wider circulation in the early 1800s by the French historian Jules Michelet, took special interest in the education of the mind in relation to language and civil society. Vico became one of the first social anthropologists. Thinkers as diverse as Coleridge, Goethe, and Isaiah Berlin admired him. Northrop Frye remarked on his power. James Joyce declared that reading Vico struck him more forcefully than reading Freud. The modern psychologist Jerome Bruner, a professor variously at Berkeley, Oxford, Harvard, and Jerusalem, has written on culture and personal development. The shared visions of Vico and Bruner offer an educational approach that delves to the core of individual psychology and cultural identity. Imaginative spirits—humanists, scientists, and social scientists—have known and practiced, but rarely analyzed, this approach. Together, the work of Vico and Bruner offers a perspective that examines fundamental aims and ends of education addressed to personal development and social well-being.

• • •

Bruner begins his *Acts of Meaning* (1990) by observing, "I have written it at a time when psychology, the science of mind as William James once called it, has become fragmented as never before." His characterization sounds familiar to anyone involved with the humanities. The British psychologist Liam Hudson echoes it and remarks that "the self-consciously scientific tradition in psychology emerges as a venue dominated by shabby scholarship and creative scandalmongering; objectivity becomes a slogan . . . the wilful promotion of one view of reality at the expense of all others is the norm. . . . Obviously, it is pointless to pretend that psychology is even a protoscience" (Kernan, 273). Bruner notes, "The wider intellectual community comes increasingly to ignore our journals" (xi). Researchers produce postage stamp-sized studies that cite others of similar scope. For all that, Bruner finds it hopeful that basic questions on "the nature of the mind and its processes, questions about how we construct our meanings and our realities, questions about the shaping of mind by history and culture" (xi) continue to be raised. Returning to basic questions takes courage, because who but a hack possesses ready-made, basic answers? Yet, without answers one seems unsophisticated in an intellectual milieu that, above all else, prizes sophistication.

In one ploy, an old but newly tricked-out brand of skepticism holds that any basic answer is no better than any other, that there exist no questions more essential than any others, that cultural conditioning means all. For all its purported shock value, this Pyrrhonian skepticism is simplistic, but embracing it looks like principled commitment, without the perils of committing to anything. It relieves one from the responsibility of ethical decision. (Of course, backing no ethical choices is a choice, too—a negative, lazy one.) This is actually a form of rigid cultural behaviorism, an abrogation of a search for meaning. For Bruner, the failure to see meaning and value as central betrays the flaw in psychology's cognitive revolution. The same concern might be applied to all the humanities. Beliefs are culturally conditioned and contingent, and—as Bruner implies in discussing Richard Rorty—truth is not one eternal, immutable essence nor a list of exact correspondences with "reality." But to suggest that relative or contingent areas of knowledge preclude decisions about what makes life meaningful or valued, or that individuals cannot defend what grounds they take to justify life's myriad, interconnected acts, acts charged with affect, emotion, cognition, and value—such as teaching, voting, raising children, loving our partners, spending money, and choosing careers—such a suggestion does nothing less than eliminate free will, what Coleridge calls our true and absolute self.

Bruner contends that the study of psychology divorced from the influence of culture is impoverished. As John Locke pointed out in his *Essay Concerning Human Understanding,* published a generation before Vico's major work and three centuries before Bruner's, culture exists through ready-made semiotic systems infused with custom, habit, and interpretation and shared, even if shared through debate, by a community. Language is at the core of cultural psychology because, as Locke noted, it is the most pervasive of semiotic systems, a fact recognized by Vico and by modern anthropologists such as Claude Lévi-Strauss: "Qui dit langage dit société." Whoever speaks about language speaks about society. As Bart Giamatti, former president of Yale, put it in another context, "Education is 'an intensely practical act of self-fashioning,' but one that proceeds in large measure through the discovery of other selves" (Axtell, 84).

For Bruner, what a "culturally oriented psychology . . . takes as central . . . is that the relationship between action and saying (or experiencing) is, *in the ordinary conduct of life,* interpretable. . . . This is what makes interpretation and meaning central to a cultural psychology—or to any psychology or mental science, for that matter" (19). Investigating meaning and interpretation thus links cultural psychology with literary and hermeneutic studies, with such figures as I. A. Richards, William Empson, Wilhelm Dilthey, Paul Ricoeur, and Hans-Georg Gadamer. Bruner mentions Ricoeur and Dilthey. Psychology and philosophy overlap in the individual interpretation of meaning and value. Bruner urges psychology to stop its attempts to be meaning-free—and, one could add, value-free. The mind and the culture to which the mind contributes—and can change—never are.

Bruner's stance may be familiar to readers of Northrop Frye or any systematic discussion of storytelling, narrative, or myth as these relate to culture, not just to literary taxonomy. Under the term "folk psychology"—unfortunately hinting at the primitive when he clearly intends "folk" to stand for what is commonly or customarily part of a culture—Bruner argues that the patterns of language that seam the bedrock of culture are at the basis of individual psychology. Those structures of language, in the most fundamental way, help *constitute* that psychology as well as supply the vehicle for its expression. If structures of language and narratives, what Frye calls the "verbal universe," cannot be quantified or predicted, if they become matters for interpretation and cultural history, this should not place them out of the realm of psychology but at its center. William James's *Principles of Psychology* presents a welter of storytelling, anecdote, and quotation; different stylistic voices and cultural signals populate it.

This essential connection with folk psychology expressed through language is, says Bruner, "where psychology *starts* and wherein it is inseparable from anthropology and the other cultural sciences" (32, emphasis added). This foundation in language makes psychology also inseparable from literature conceived as the study of language related to experience and values. This was once considered within the compass of rhetoric, and Aristotle insisted that rhetoric should not be divorced from logic or ethics. Humane rhetoric is intended by its great practitioners—Vico, Wollstonecraft, Lincoln, and Churchill are good examples—to embrace what Bruner has in mind. At its best, rhetoric relates language and persuasion to the moral imperative to act on behalf of the good. As Shelley points out, early in his *Defense of Poetry,* it is Bacon, one of Vico's heroes, who believes that "similitudes or relations," expressed in metaphorical language, give power to "the faculty which perceives them as the storehouse of axioms common to all knowledge." Not coincidentally, Bruner says that if folk psychology or "folk social science" is an unattractive term, we may call it "common sense." Related to the older *sensus communis,* this is what Adam Smith, Kant, and rhetoricians and philosophers of the late 1700s call it too, careful to distinguish this connotation from common and simplistic ones. Bruner here parallels Vico. For instance, folk psychology or "common sense" is philologically and practically related to the Greek *topikos,* an intellectual or cultural "commonplace," which Vico takes up in his philosophy of rhetorical topics, contrasting it to critical and analytical philosophies.

De Te Fabula

Moreover, as Bruner notes, "At their core, all folk psychologies contain a surprisingly complex notion of an agentive Self" (41). The narratives of folk psychologies are uniquely efficient in the way they organize, present, pass on, and retain the relation between the self and that larger culture of "common sense" with which it coexists, but which it can also reconfigure. Such stories may begin with "mama" or "dada," that is, naming the immediate creators. Later, as narratives grow larger and more complex they become, as Frye notes, quest narratives or searches. Their language depicts actions of meaning. Coleridge identifies a younger contemporary of Kant, Johann Gottlieb Fichte, as providing the real impetus to transcendental philosophy (that quest romance of the self), because Fichte insists not on "being" alone but on "acting," and acting not only physically but intellectually—psychologically. So, Goethe has this line in *Faust:* "Am Anfang war die Tat." In the beginning was the act. The deeper senses of Logos or the Word involve acting, creating, and evolving as well as language.

In this regard, every searching self is an active agent who quests and who is thus potentially a hero, an idea found in Frye and Vico, especially in Vico's *De mente heroica.* The variety of cultures expresses a variety of heroic types, Joseph Campbell's "hero with a thousand faces." One reason the figure of the hero in the modern world has become problematic is that individuals and readers recognize themselves as potential heroes, hence potential failures as well. The antihero is latent in all of us. In another sense, Logos, or the Word, takes on this active sense of quest, too, and the Bible, one of the world's prototypical narratives, begins simultaneously with Logos and an act of the ultimate "agentive Self." Frye begins his study of the Bible, *The Great Code,* by avowing his indebtedness to Vico. Frye says that reading the Bible is never done: the reader reaches the end only to return to the beginning, a never-ending story. As Wallace Stevens says in another context, the reader merges with the book. The popular movies *The Neverending Story* I and II are romance versions of this heroism, this merging with a book, where even the book's print disappears and reappears according to the young reader's reception of the story itself. This film innovation illustrates, anecdotally but vitally, the bond between the creative, individual self and the structures of language constituting culture.

Bruner takes up the rhetorical term *fabula* for the story that helps the self establish its relation to culture, and this recalls the ancient admonition of every romance narrative: *de te fabula,* this story is about you. This helps to fulfill one of the first injunctions of Western philosophy, "Know thyself." The initiate must participate in and learn the narratives of culture, diverse and pluralistic, and then create his or her own narratives out of them, sometimes by protesting against them. Every individual's story tends to ratify but also deviates from the related stories that the culture already provides. Bruner says, "The function of the story is to find an intentional state that mitigates or at least makes comprehensible a deviation from a canonical cultural pattern" (49–50). That deviation then joins canonical patterns so that traditions and cultures grow, but in growing they change or even merge. When retold, embellished, and especially when denied, myths take new forms. Any personal quest is in search of something new or lost, something not present, therefore imagined. "This method of negotiating and re-negotiating meanings by the mediation of narrative interpretation is, it seems to me, one of the crowning achievements of human development in the ontogenetic, cultural, and phylogenetic sense of that expression" (67).

Harold Shapiro, former president of Princeton, characterizes "much of the controversy over university education" in the last century as "the ongoing struggle between an intellectual vision that is secular and that focuses on the development of both the independent individual and new knowledge and an alternative intellectual vision that is less secular, emphasizes common cultural commitments, and focuses on traditional values" (64). But it is insufficient to see the controversy over university education in dualistic terms; such a dichotomy, however convenient to participants in a debate, is damaging in the end because it implies that one side or the other might or should win. A victory for either side is an overall defeat. The individual personality and its new personal, secular myths must grow along with the culture and its old communal ones. They educate and change each other. The process is not so much a controversy to be resolved as a continual conversation to be scrutinized and entered into fully, advisedly.

Claiming as much, Vico believes that the imaginative processes of personal development begin and flourish when we are young, receiving education through cultural myths and narrative language, before we enter into routine forms of rational analysis and specialization. As Donald Verene explains, Vico "holds that studies should be introduced to cultivate first the powers of memory and imagination in the young and that too early an emphasis on the mastery of philosophical criticism and logic will make the mind sterile. The sense of wisdom and eloquence found in the Ancients should not be easily thrown over for the rapid assimilation of the techniques of modern invention and science. The arguments and ingenuities of the Moderns should be mastered, but only by mature minds that have been educated in the art of topics" (Vico 1990, iii). This interrelation of cultural and personal growth anticipates Bruner's depiction of folk psychology as the topics of common experience embedded in cultural narratives. Like Vico, Bruner wants to know how "the young human being achieves (or realizes) the power of narrative" (68), a power of realization Vico calls imagination. Without awakening and constantly exercising this power (see chap. 9), education leaves the student with little recourse but to seek the lowest common denominator of means (money), rather than to pursue ends that are imaginatively conceived.

Vico contends that imagination acts most strongly in childhood and youth. But the imagination natural to children—and to nascent societies—should never atrophy. Care must be taken not to lose it in the procedures and proliferation of knowledge that characterize higher learning and the professions. Civilizations hobble themselves when they over-refine, looking only for rarefied, theoretical abstraction on the one hand, or immediate material utility on the other. Abstraction and concrete utility, seemingly poles apart, both depend on the refinement of analysis and efficient methodologies. Vico cautions that before descending into the inevitable theories and techniques of specialties, the student should educate the imagination firmly and fundamentally, turning all faculties at the outset to capacious subjects. He states, "Young people at an age when memory is tenacious, imagination vivid, and invention quick . . . may profitably occupy themselves with languages and plane geometry. . . . But if they pass on while yet in this immature stage to the highly subtle studies of metaphysical criticism . . . they become overfine for life in their way of thinking and are rendered incapable of any great work" (159). He is warning against what Bacon, in *The Advancement of Learning,* identified as a vanity of learning.

The child collects a mass of images from stories and from sense experience directly. Soon, imagination acts to recombine, reorder, and fuse images. "In children memory is most vigorous," remarks Vico, "and imagination is . . . vivid" (211). Then, with words—in stories and other kinds of discourse—the growing youth creates original narratives. The best realization of imaginative growth in the young mind as itself an actual subject of poetry is perhaps Wordsworth's *Prelude.* It is Wordsworth's poetry that pulls John Stuart Mill out of his early depression. According to Mill, reading Wordsworth released a new joy connecting his interior life with the hopes he held for social reform. Mill experienced an ecstatic reconnection with a childhood freedom of thought denied to him, and from which he had been diverted, by a regime of constricted study, rote memory, and incessant drill. Invention or creative imagination, is, as Vico affirms in his *Study Methods of Our Time,* "the faculty of youth," its hallmark. Yet its capacity and inclination to transform stories and experience into new images and evocative language can be retained in maturity as central to an adult's engaged intellect knowing the world and its relations.

As David Hume concluded (and Samuel Johnson, too, although he never liked to agree with Hume), imagination thus forms individual mental character and the psychology of the self long before it alters or contributes significantly to specialized knowledge. Once the imagination establishes first directions and opens the psyche to more ways of perceiving and understanding, it can proceed not only to form new knowledge but also to form and collect knowledge in relation to human character: to history, types of economy, forms of social organization, or human impact on the environment. Modern culture can hardly recapture, in any authentic way, the imaginative force of "primitive" societies, which perhaps explains why their art is prized so highly. Yet, that does not mean that the virtues of those "first natures" and "first customs" should not be emulated (*New Science,* 916–21). At an early age it is vital to address the imagination in ways fanciful and marvelous, yet also immediate and real. Hence, in all cultures, children's teaching texts have for millennia included fictional fables, animal stories, fairy tales, quests, and ballads, yet also factual biographies and histories, stories of ancestors, the tribe, or the nation. In these myths and narratives, either fantastic or to some degree historical, we locate personal identities, character, and the essentials of ethical decision, family life, law, and social reality. For "the first fables," says Vico, "must have contained civil truths, and must therefore have been the histories of the first peoples." And "the first science to be learned should be mythology or the interpretation of fables." This foreshadows Bruner's sense of *fabula.* Vico stresses that the arts stem from the first poetic activity of imagination, analogous to the imaginative activity of every child (198, 51, 217).

Imaginative Language and Communal Ends

Paying heed to the situational appropriateness and cultural shadings of language, to the acquisition of vocabulary and the grasp of structures and rules called syntax and grammar—this all aids the imaginative construction of meaning and value. Every person in part mimics others but ends by uttering a personal style, a self. In referring to this crucial process, poets and writers use a deceptively simple phrase, "finding a voice." Every significant writer to re-create the world in defamiliarized, arresting language has constructed an identifiable style. For this reason, talented writers are parodied more than mediocre ones. It is possible to pick up a book blindly, read one paragraph, and then say, this sounds like Austen or James or Hemingway. A line or two may be enough to recognize Dickinson's voice, or Dickens's. The same is true for Shakespeare, except that he creates many selves and so writes many styles, a "myriad-minded" dramatic genius, as Coleridge calls him. (Shakespeare led a life of allegory, Keats remarks, and "his works are the comments on it.") Each such construction in language interprets both self and culture. Language is also *languages,* and Goethe's adage that learning a foreign language gives us a new world can be supplemented: *and* a second self. Each human language interprets the infinite complexity of the world anew. The categories with which an Italian or Chinese child begins to piece together a coherent set of perceptions are not identical to those a Masai or German child uses. Being "an author" is thus bound up not only with one's own self—as personality or autobiography—but also with the languages of culture and how such languages interpret the very act of being an author in the first place. Hence, one can ask with Michel Foucault the question he posed in 1969, what—and not only who—is an author? Interpretive approaches and cultural experiences—the answers—may differ. The differences may be personal, ethnic, or geographic. They may be extreme. Nevertheless, some shared commonality of language and of narrative holds individuals and society together if those individuals are to create culture.

The self develops out of imaginative, language-sensitive acts of meaning constructed first by children just getting a handle on words and stories. Eventually, the self reaches a stage when it interprets life in retrospect, through the rearview mirror. In these inventions, tellings, interpretations, and retellings, which take place on the individual and cultural levels, the young earn the hard-won realization that different kinds of knowledge and identities cannot isolate themselves in self-contained fields and categories: the essence of narrative interpretation is connection. Education, which leads out into the world, and which transforms that world, affirms that different types of knowledge are akin to a large set of narratives, myths, and interpretive procedures. In the *Poetics,* that most influential of critiques on art, language, and education, Aristotle signals the confidence his society invests in art by calling its effect *psychagogia,* the leading out into or the educating of the individual self in the larger world of action.

Precisely because of exponential growth in knowledge (and not despite it), the case Vico made in the early modern world is now more urgent and demands more vigilance. No matter how many methods are mastered—apprenticeship to even one requires great effort even as it is apt to rapidly grow obsolete—and no matter how many subjects are encountered, such activity does not inquire into the aims of education beyond learning a series of utilitarian means. Nor does it ask what connected purposes and relative values might be attached to differing bodies of knowledge.

In "The Academies and the Relation between Philosophy and Eloquence," Vico reiterates the importance of feeling and language, heart and tongue, if civil society is to conceive how different spheres of knowledge relate to each other. He defines wisdom as "mind and language . . . the perfecter of man in his properly being man." This stands as a gloss for Bruner's *Acts of Meaning,* whose first chapter is titled "The Proper Study of Man." That phrase comes from Pope: "The proper study of mankind is man." A contemporary of Vico, Pope conceives of imagination and rhetoric shaping education, civil polity, and ethical character. The full couplet harkens back to that basic tenet of philosophy invoked above: "Know then Thy-self, presume not God to scan; / The proper Study of Mankind is *Man.*" In the *Study Methods* (33–34), Vico identifies the chief sin of education in his day: insufficient vigilance in fostering those kinds of eloquence, those kinds of language and narrative, that (as Bruner also believes) secure the core of cultural life and the development of the self.

Vico's project, a humanizing of knowledge through the power of language, does not mean salvaging an arid roster of "traditional values" mistakenly associated with "humanism." Rather, he desires to render knowledge relevant to social institutions and personal decisions, to save knowledge from being inert, to help it serve welfare and justice, to make it operative for what Jefferson calls the "living generation." The faculty for this is the mature imagination, and the key instrument it uses is language—the medium by which knowledge is often first made, then made relevant to needs and desires, and by which it is placed before society in legislatures, boardrooms, universities, and courtrooms. As Vico tersely formulates the connection, he conjectures "that ideas and language accelerated at the same rate" (234). Facts or information alone may be represented by other symbolic systems, but the relevance of facts to values is expressed chiefly through the languages we speak and write. Language often constitutes and always expresses the social and human relevance of knowledge.

Vico's idea of imagination is not of one faculty distinctly analyzed but of a complex activity that assimilates, combines, and sympathizes. Imagination employs language and images to cross borders and to connect provinces of knowledge. Conceiving of imagination similarly, Bacon, one of Vico's "four authors," calls in *The Advancement of Learning* for "a science of the imagination" itself. How to organize different kinds of knowledge and how to order knowledge about the peculiarly human—what we know about the world and what we know about ourselves and our happiness—become inseparable tasks.

Vico formulates rhetoric as "wisdom speaking eloquently." He feels revulsion at deceptive language and the ingenuity of argument simply to persuade, merely tactical rhetoric severed from ethical foundations. Nor is rhetoric for Vico based on analytic procedures for categorizing figures of speech. To catalog is not its essential function. Rhetoric includes the study of methods, but its final goal is to elevate language in the service of human virtue, to learn language in order to exert power for what is good. This, at least, was its final goal for Quintilian, too, who introduced the idea of a canon of literary works long before arguments about the canon of the Bible. Imagination and the products of imagination find a central practicality in rhetoric, in language that speaks eloquently to habitual thoughts and feelings. The expression of wisdom in memorable language is paramount. Learned Hand, perhaps the greatest American judge never to sit on the Supreme Court, remarks of this wisdom:

> [I]t may now begin to be clearer why I am arguing that an education which includes the "humanities" is essential to political wisdom. By "humanities" I especially mean history; but close beside history . . . are letters, poetry, philosophy, the plastic arts, and music. Most of the issues that mankind sets out to settle, it never does settle. They are not solved

because . . . they are incapable of solution . . . being concerned with in-commensurables. . . . [T]he opposing parties seldom do agree . . . and the dispute fades . . . though perhaps it may be renewed as history. . . . It disappears because it is replaced by some compromise that, although not wholly acceptable to either side, offers a tolerable substitute for victory; and he who would find the substitute needs an endowment as rich as possible in experience, an experience which makes the heart generous and provides the mind with an understanding of the hearts of others. (214)

For educated adults, imaginative wisdom remains as important as technical expertise to govern and change the world. Well developed, this wisdom is the synoptic ability to imitate, create, embody, and express a set of narratives that depict different cultures at different times. Then these pictures and myths are brought together to form a mural or surview, a picture of the human condition conscious of its status in history and its possible future. (Vico calls this *storia ideale eterna*.) This surview gives a context for individual ethical and social decisions, decisions not possible to analyze in isolation, for they arise out of the dense and involved knot of that larger context. It is from that poetic or imaginative spirit that a student can "learn the adequacies of the imagination and the inadequacies of things as they are" (Bromwich 1995, 74). Exercising such an imaginative surview separates the statesman from the politician, the leader from the drill instructor, the teacher from the grader.

Vico apprehends imaginative wisdom in the way that argument, language, and metaphor—which is myth in miniature—condense and transmit social institutions, ideas, and ideologies. In his search to construct truths relevant to experience, he favors an art of topics rather than a rationalistic method that judges what is assumed to be existing as either true or false. An exclusive premium on "clear and distinct" ideas raises obstacles, for no metaphor or cultural myth is precise. Metaphor challenges the boundaries of known, literal definition in order to bring more knowledge within the ken of language, or some other semiotic system. This can include discussions of language and narratives related to law, psychoanalysis, or business. Bruner and Anthony G. Amsterdam have together written *Minding the Law,* a study that demonstrates how Supreme Court opinions themselves rely on various modes of storytelling, myths, and narratives all embedded in a larger culture. Legislators, lawyers, and judges write and interpret laws and rulings, which themselves result from previous cases, that is, from particular, multiple narratives of experience and conflict. The most desirable attribute of judges is wisdom; their wisdom, consonant with Vico's emphasis, comes through the eloquence of interpretation, their "decisions" or "opinions." Psychoanalysis draws on and contributes key elements to the larger process of stories, culture, case studies, and interpretations. At its best, it helps people see more deeply into their own psyches and into the psyches of others with whom they have close relationships. This helps to construct the permissible limits of action and to recognize the motives for actions that they have already taken. It often leads to a more fulfilling life. (Freud, Jung, and others drew on both ancient myths and modern stories.) Business case studies chart decisions caught in large, complex sets of conditions and contingencies. To discern and manage new combinations of these circumstances is best apprehended by learning to read and interpret what are basically narratives of previous management experience.

Narrative and storytelling also play key roles in science. Roald Hoffmann, 1981 Nobel laureate in chemistry, remarks that "storytelling seems to be ingrained in our psyche[s]. . . . Scientists are no exception." He observes, "In thinking about theories, storytelling has some distinct features," but that in published accounts of the final scientific theories, "much of the narrative" is left out because of a "desire to show us as more rational than we were" in arriving at them (3–4). When he emphasizes how powerful a part storytelling can play in scientific discovery, Hoffmann cites Jerome Bruner's book *Making Stories* (2002).

A New Rhetoric

Lévi-Strauss's axiom "Whoever speaks about language speaks about society" implies that mind, language, and society are mutually enabling. They are realized only in and through one another. The language that produces a nation or society need not be the language of writing and books; Vico says it can exist solely in speech and memory (*New Science,* 67). Such language embodies the principle Vico calls *verum factum,* truth that is made. In a passage that exemplifies *factum* as the process of being made through imagination and *verum* as social truth, Vico claims that Orpheus, "through the fables, in their first meaning, first founded and then confirmed the humanity of Greece" (81). Imaginative language helps to create the reality and virtue of civil society. Vico realizes that human beings, no matter how much they know, possess far less than perfect knowledge; imagination suggests new directions. Imagination, not knowledge, prompts the quest for more knowledge. Human fables, from religious services to engagements with the world on the Web, from Dostoyevsky's novels to catchy jingles hummed by children, depict society and culture, as well as individual quests and destinies. Imaginative narratives and narratives interpreted imaginatively are synthetic in their activity; they counteract the atomization and trivialization of knowledge. Vico's concept reflects a rhetorical tradition, now transformed as it confronts a modern world of self-consciousness, accelerating knowledge, technical advances, and new social pressures. In his attempt to see the relevance of knowledge expressed in eloquent language, in his premium on the polymath over the side-blinded specialist, he is, as Alain Pons remarks, "the last philosopher of the Renaissance." He is also one of the first of the modern world.

Vico calls for an alliance between philosophers and philologists, an interpenetration of the "knowledge of the true," which comes from reason, and of the "consciousness of the certain," created by words and choice. Here philology means not the graveyard of language but the active history of meaning and significance. It involves the history of peoples, institutions, values, social systems, and gods. Philology traces the history of words, not only as part of but as the begetter of the history of peoples and nations (138–40). Expressing this synthetic principle of language, ideas, and history, Vico claims, "The etymologies of the native [earlier] languages" relate "the histories of the institutions signified by the words, beginning with their original meanings and pursuing the natural progress of their metaphors according to the order of ideas, on which the history of languages must proceed" (354). Language is a primary vehicle for imagination. The study of one engages the other.

As a corollary, a purely utilitarian language produces a purely utilitarian people, devoid, as Emerson says, "of analogies," bereft of any sense of transcendence. If Vico's thought hovers between the conviction that "Man is the measure of all things" and the admonitory question "What is man that Thou art mindful of him?" then the principle of action he fears most, and to which his third age of men—the present age—is most susceptible, could be stated this way: "Things are the measure of the mind."

"Cultivate Knowledge as a Whole"

Vico uncovers the first acts of vivid imagination in the child's realm. How that imagination becomes educated, how it grows in the world, then how imagination itself leads others, determines its service to community and to humanity. As imagination marks youth, imaginative wisdom marks the development of adult virtue. This is one way to understand Wordsworth's lines "The Child is father of the Man; / And I could wish my days to be / Bound each to each by natural piety." In *De mente heroica* Vico exhorts students, "Cultivate knowledge as a whole." He means not only knowledge bound by academic definitions, or by an aesthetic divorced from experience, but all knowledge, *tekhne* and *topoi:* grasp their interconnections in human terms. The examples of achievement Vico offers—Columbus, Alexander, Galileo, Descartes, Grotius—display variety of endeavor, a respect for the differing modes of operation in feeling and cognition. It is true, Vico's list is dead, white, male, and European. But their race and gender did not make their lives easy or guarantee acceptance for their discoveries. Columbus was reviled; many thought him mad. He was sent back to Spain in chains and died almost forgotten, a joke and a disgrace. The church accosted Galileo for his scientific boldness; Grotius, the founder of international law, avoided incarceration for life only by a daring prison break.

In the vivid experience of youth, then in mature ethical conscience and wisdom speaking eloquently, Vico proposes a sequence of the educated imagination. He is concerned not only with how to educate the imagination but with how imagination in turn continues to educate the individual, a growth that asks for sacrifice, sympathy, and dedication. With his call to cultivate all knowledges, his range and curiosity, and his vision that the best form of knowledge is that which makes it relevant, through eloquent language, to human need, Vico provides a fresh perspective on what a liberal education in the arts and sciences can be.

The leading of the self out into the entirety of the world—education or *psychagogia*—matches Vico's scorn of solitude. He does not condemn the solitude of contemplation, the loneliness of a tragic figure, or the disaffected alienation of a virtuous individual slandered and persecuted. What revolts Vico is the solitude of self-interest, the cult of the self perfected in a refined, comfortable, or even luxurious society. Deadened to sympathy and the primacy of justice, mental ingenuity becomes selfish, and finally cannibalistic. This self-absorption or solipsism is identified in studies by Christopher Lasch and Robert Bellah. Blake remarked on it long ago in his poetry and considered it the worst form of hell. The solitude that Vico fears so much is the opposite of social connection. In Vico's "Age of Men," which now prevails, the culmination of barbarism is the ever-inward focus of the psyche and the closing spiral of the self. The self turns away from history, away from other societies, away from the history and the alien qualities contained within its own society, away from the formative ideal of knowledge as a whole, and finally away from the needs of fellow beings. Ultimately, like late Roman society in Edward Gibbon's depiction, the woven texture of society and government can no longer support the stupendous weight of a fabric whose individual threads have for too long been selfishly or blindly spun. Harry Huntt Ransom, who headed the University of Texas system, remarked that "a university opens paths for each of its members to pursue knowledge according to his or her need. That is an old precept, and still a sound one." He then qualifies this immediately: "But it has never been sufficient for complete education. Moving outward, self-knowledge gropes toward an understanding of others" (6).

No educational problems, especially systemic ones, find easy solutions. Yet the ideas of Vico and Bruner (and those of many others like them) point the way to a larger, capacious mode of education. They reorient the psychological and cultural basis of education itself. Their ideas hold promise to reconnect disciplines in the humanities and natural sciences. They provide a deeper sense of self and culture as interdependent. This reunion has the potential to reverse the accelerating fragmentation and specialization that expend their necessary energies but too often produce unrelated and unnarrated activities. Vico's and Bruner's visions create a larger understanding of acts of meaning achieved by the self, acts capable of expression in a social language, acts capable of passing on to the next generation a complex culture, yet a culture also criticized and improved by individual quests. In this larger understanding, things are not the measure of the mind, but rather ideas about things, and ideas about ideas themselves. The ends of education are endowed with more meaning, and they become richer in many ways.

9

SCIENCE, ART, AND DEMOCRACY: A PARTNERSHIP

Through the repeated alternation between flights of the imagination and the accretion of hard data, a mutual agreement on the workings of the world is written, in the form of natural law.

—EDWARD O. WILSON, "THE DRIVE TO DISCOVERY," 1984

The unvarnished truth is that the extraordinary compact between state governments and their flagship universities appears to be dead—or at least on life support. For more than a century, these two parties had a deal: In return for financial support from taxpayers, these universities would keep tuition low and provide broad access for undergraduates from all economic strata, train graduate and professional students, promote arts and culture, help solve local problems, and perform groundbreaking research. Unfortunately, the agreement between the states and their flagship universities has deteriorated for 25 years, leaving public research universities in a purgatory of insufficient resources—low tuition and flat appropriations.

—MARK YUDOF, FORMER PRESIDENT, UNIVERSITY OF MICHIGAN, 2002

Leaders of higher education invariably explain and defend the primary functions and essential purposes of college and university life as the discovery and transmission of knowledge. Yet, Albert Einstein, a definitive model of intellect, states flatly, "Imagination is more important than knowledge." His claim expresses more than the opinion of a great scientist. It summarizes the single most profound shift in the arts and the sciences since the Renaissance, arguably since the pre-Socratics. This reorientation toward imagination shows no sign of reversal. Future intellectual historians will regard it as one of the principal steps in the mental self-development of the species. Darwinian evolution itself does not proceed at a regular, slow pace. Rapid changes in species and multiple adaptations over a comparatively short time punctuate its course. The same is true of ways of thinking about and exploiting our own capacities.

The new emphasis on imagination is pervasive; it will be long lasting precisely because it does not formulate one specific method or procedure to ascertain knowledge. Instead, it reenvisions and redefines the power of discovery and insight, anchoring it in images, analogies, and metaphors, the progeny of imagination itself. The imagination has become a model, a metaphor itself for the ways the mind generates all methods, metaphors, and models. It deals with the unpredictable and the unsuspected, which have also risen in intellectual esteem. Many pivotal experiments in modern science are *Gedankenexperimente,* thought experiments, performed chiefly by an act of imagination—among them Galileo's on falling bodies and Einstein's concerning relativity. The turn to imagination in the last ten generations coincides with, and in large measure caused, the rise of modern science and the coming of the modern age in human and social inquiry, the attainment of an intellectual majority. Kant advocates this coming to maturity in answering the question, "What is Enlightenment?"—an inquiry quite different from the historical one, "What was the Enlightenment?"

The avowal "Imagination is more important that knowledge" voices no naive declaration of faith that the sciences and arts are identical under the skin. They aren't. It is unlikely that if academics and professionals only crawled out of their career fiefs, then the problem of C. P. Snow's "two cultures," scientific and humanistic, would vanish. The complex situation resists neat bisection. The sciences, as Northrop Frye notes, practice detachment and examine the natural world; the humanities practice concern and ask what kind of world we might or should create, as well as what kind of world we have created. In a prophetic observation, as pertinent now as it was prescient in 1966, Daniel Bell identified what "will be the most urgent cultural problem of the university." The university increasingly embraces technocracy, professionalism, specialization, and public service. At the same time, the university remains "devoted to *humanitas.*" However, the arts and humanities, "eroded by formal pieties" and "in danger of being swept away by the swift-running currents of the post-modern moods," can hardly keep themselves whole, let alone welcome and join the technocratic. Thus, the "confrontation between these two modes," one growing and the other uneasily shifting, emerges as an urgent cultural predicament and challenge (311). Far from having outgrown or solved the two-cultures syndrome, the academic world has too readily adjusted to its widening crevasses and fissures. Yet, in view of how many prominent scientists and artists place a premium on imagination, is it possible that a mutually comprehensible appreciation and cultivation of this power might aid in bridging those crevasses?

The creative imagination as a valued idea or quality of mind associated with positive achievement is, remarkably, a relatively new phenomenon. Until three hundred years ago, thinkers looked on imagination as suspect, delusory, and far inferior to reason. As scientific investigation, amid a series of dramatic advances, rose to its modern level of respect and influence, and as literary criticism and the philosophy of art became more psychologically attuned and considered the effect of art on the individual psyche, something else was happening, too. The power called imagination—as it denotes force of invention and insight—began, not coincidentally, to be much more highly prized. This period of intellectual ferment and discovery stretches over most of the seventeenth and eighteenth centuries and continues to inform the twenty-first. Wide-ranging thinkers such as Bacon, Descartes, Adam Smith, Joseph Priestley, Kant, Goethe, John Dewey, and Carl Sagan all talk about the imagination in reference to science, art, and ethics. They pursue both differences and affinities in the exercise of imagination affecting those realms. Their attitude has not grown obsolete. Wolfgang Pauli, a great theoretical physicist of the twentieth century, declares that, "contrary to the strict division of the activity of the human spirit into separate departments—a division prevailing since the nineteenth century—I consider the ambition of overcoming opposites, including also a synthesis embracing both rational understanding and the mystical experience of unity, to be the mythos, spoken or unspoken, of our present day and age" (Heisenberg, 38).

Unless society and its educational institutions can grasp basic imaginative processes in terms of both the sciences and the arts, society will fail to address the hardest problems facing its citizens. For those problems indicate that the manipulation of matter and the pursuit of human happiness are inseparable undertakings. Those problems crystallize the relation between technology and values. Among them are arms control, human effects on the environment, the understanding and treatment of mental illnesses, nuclear power, famine, human rights, disease control, ethical and technological issues in population growth, and the distribution of finite global resources.

Cultivating the Capacity for Creation

Robert Scott Root-Bernstein, former MacArthur Fellow at the Salk Institute for Biological Studies in San Diego, in his "Creative Process as a Unifying Theme of Human Cultures," asks, "If unity in culture is possible, how can it be accomplished?" The answer, he believes, "will fundamentally influence the future course of cultural evolution." He suggests that "the cultural split . . . must be examined" as one not "between scientists and everyone else, but between those who innovate or create and those who do not." A strong affinity exists between his thought and one ideal of the Enlightenment, which prized a larger imaginative unity in human achievement and transformation. Root-Bernstein quotes Paul Weiss, the biologist, who sees that "the time has come when we must face the decision of either implementing the desideratum of unity or else reverting to jungle warfare of mutual extinction among conflicting doctrines, each claiming a monopoly for its particular brand of diomomborod culture" (198, 203, 217). Similar inferences can be made from reading Arthur Koestler's *Act of Creation*. Koestler sees creativity as a *bisociative* act, one that interpenetrates at least two elements considered dissimilar or incompatible. This bisociative principle can be applied to the context of two kinds of imagination, two cultures. A larger model of creative process is needed to achieve any harmony and connection. Einstein insisted that scientific thinking was a refinement of everyday thinking, not a new species of mental operation.

Genius, said Samuel Johnson, is an ample power of mind turned accidentally in one direction. By this criterion he argued that Isaac Newton would have written a great epic poem had Newton first chosen that challenge. Johnson, moral philosopher and poet as well as journalist and single-handed creator of the first complete English dictionary—he also performed chemistry experiments and wrote a preface for a book describing how to determine longitude—is not making idle speculation. He had written reviews of Newton's proofs of God and, fearing his French accent poor, discussed in Latin Newton's achievements in mathematics with members of the Académie Française. They were impressed. Johnson's longest work, rarely read, comprises half a million words. In it he records numerous debates in the House of Commons. Many of these speeches later editors anthologized and attributed to the lawmakers rather than to their true author, who sold them to a magazine. Johnson's essay collections were what we nowadays would call best sellers. Jane Austen judged him her favorite prose writer. Right or wrong about the nature of genius, Johnson is entitled to pronounce on it.

Other views on how genius develops suggest it is specialized or that, once turned in a particular direction, it can succeed in following few others. Vico in his *New Science* (see chap. 8) argued that different kinds of imaginations create different systems: "It is impossible," he says, "for anyone at the same time to be a sublime poet and a sublime metaphysician." Is the case so settled? Coleridge, long before reading Vico, didn't seem to think so. In a remark apparently contradictory, he writes his friend William Sotheby, "A great Poet must be, implicitè if not explicitè, a profound Metaphysician." Many important thinkers engage the issue but fail to arrive at one conclusion. They offer no formula to follow, yet they all insist on the importance of imagination.

Snow, originator in 1959 of the "two cultures" label, might have been taking an evidential leaf out of a book written exactly two centuries previously, when intellectuals and writers freely compared the arts and sciences, a book by the novelist, poet, and journalist Oliver Goldsmith. In his *Inquiry into the Present State of Polite Learning in Europe* (1759), he comments that the "arts and sciences grew up together and mutually illustrated each other. But when once pedants became law givers, the sciences began to lack grace and the polite arts solidity; these [the sciences] grew crabbed and sour, those [the arts] meretricious and gaudy; the philosopher became disgustingly precise, and the poet ever straining after grace caught only finery." Since the late eighteenth century, increasing specialization in science and art, necessary for advancement in both, has nevertheless made the two areas of endeavor seem more remote and even antagonistic. The resulting refinement and detail in both areas are such that new syntheses prove elusive even though, as knowledge accumulates, such syntheses are more crucial for the civic good.

When thinking about creativity in science and the arts, why choose earlier thinkers—Kant, Descartes, Samuel Johnson, Adam Smith—to illustrate present concerns? It is just at this time, the period of the Enlightenment, that experimenters, critics, philosophers, and psychologists face a new, modern world of constant change, new science, and historical awareness of different cultures. They realize that knowledge and divisions of knowledge might continue to accumulate and accelerate past all previous habitual comprehension. This is when the word *accelerate* is first applied to the acquisition of knowledge. Teachers, students, philosophers, manufacturers, politicians, and theologians struggle to find the proper methods and foundations of certainty or probability for acquiring this seemingly infinite new knowledge, and they begin to ask how it might be applied. They inquire into the very nature of the imagination.

Previously, thinkers had judged it a neutral quality, even negative. Writing in the seventeenth century, Thomas Hobbes defined it as "decaying sense," the faculty of representing to the mind what is no longer present to the senses—a form of memory emancipated from time and space. Many early psychologists and moralists designated the imagination as "unregulated," that is, emancipated from the conscious control of reason and authority. Imagination, it was thought, permitted religious prophecy, a form of madness to a rationalist like Hobbes, and it could cause madness outright. An admired poet was traditionally praised more often for judgment, a good "scientist" for cataloging. The idea of imagination carried powerfully pejorative connotations. In Shakespeare's *Midsummer Night's Dream*, Theseus warns: "The lunatic, the lover, and the poet / Are of imagination all compact." Yet, by inquiring about it and testing it against new types of knowledge and new forms of artistic originality, these thinkers *create* a new concept of imagination. For, not being a natural phenomenon like a rock or a star, but a human one, it can change and is constructed and reconstructed by the very way we debate, talk, and speculate about it. Hippolyta, Theseus's consort, counters his view and asserts that imagination brings about something strange, yet of "great constancy." Through the 1700s and early 1800s, thinkers elevate it to utmost importance, where it remains.

How, exactly, does the change occur? For one thing, reason itself undergoes a process of redefinition beginning in the seventeenth century. It comes to be viewed increasingly as rationalistic, a power largely iterative and deductive, a logical ladder rising in the manner of Spinoza's *Ethics* or Newton's *Principia*. Associated with observation and proofs, with comparison and "ratio," this concept of reason disallows the older belief that reason could be intuitive as well as discursive. As the concept of reason is reshaped and narrowed, it leaves room for the concept of imagination to grow.

There isn't space here to do more than touch on high points of the evolution of the idea of imagination, for example, the burst of new investigations in psychology and perception. Edmund Burke exemplifies this. Early in his career he writes a treatise on aesthetics relying heavily on the idea of imagination. His *Philosophical Inquiry* attained popularity in the Old and New Worlds. Kant handles the imagination as a particularly rich, problematic concept. It plays a key role not only in his critique of aesthetic and teleological judgment but also in his critique of pure reason. So powerful and suggestive is the idea that, once Kant pursues it, it almost overmasters the master. He relies on it at crucial points in his thinking but never arrives at an adequate definition. At one point he seems to throw up his hands and says that the imagination "is a mysterious power hidden in the depths of the soul." This very un-Kantian description virtually admits failure in every attempt to pin down an idea that is absolutely indispensable to his achievement. A generation later, Emerson, influenced by Kant's thought through the medium of Coleridge's writing, develops a new philosophical attitude. According to George Santayana, Emerson is the first thinker to predicate his philosophy on the superiority of imagination, not reason. Joseph Priestley, discoverer of oxygen and later a political émigré to the United States, writes a series of lectures on rhetoric as well as one on jurisprudence. He also abridges an influential early study of psychology, David Hartley's theory of Associationism, which draws on Aristotle and Locke and which is still familiar through the terms "free association" and "association of ideas." In all these books, Priestley emphasizes the power of imagination.

So does Adam Smith. Sixteen years in advance of *The Wealth of Nations,* he publishes in 1759 *The Theory of Moral Sentiments,* an influential book without which his economic theory cannot be properly understood. In it he posits that moral principles in society are based on "fellow feeling" or sympathy. Smith sees imagination, here the ability to feel as someone else would, as the essence of ethical action and social stability—and hence equally as vital to consider as any theory of rational choice if one seeks the basis of an economically prosperous and just society. Nonrational or even "irrational" as it may seem, the exercise of imagination for Smith affects economic life. Economists today still ponder various extrarational effects. John Kenneth Galbraith wrote an amusing novel about them. Smith's broader lesson is that an economist who works only with theories of economic self-interest and the law of supply and demand and who bypasses the effects of imagination is left with something insufficient.

All his life Goethe felt proud of his original theory of colors. It remained competent and perceptive enough that Edwin Land, founder of Polaroid, used some of Goethe's observations and principles, specifically on black and red, in devising methods to develop, literally, his first films. And it was a child's imagination, not knowledge, that first stimulated Land's famous invention. He began research on "the Land camera" at the prompting of his three-year-old daughter. After he took photographs, she asked why she had to wait so long to see them. Goethe conceived of imagination working in art and poetry but also in scientific research, and he speaks of an imagination that anticipates "the measure of the real and what is known, [and then] proceeds to probable things."

Land's daughter and Goethe strike a common chord. Imagination thrives in the strange soil of wonder, doubt, and uncertainty. It prompts action and investigation. So Plato describes the beginning of philosophy as wonder, and Matthew Arnold locates both the urge to write poetry and the motive of valid social criticism in one quality, curiosity. And to what does Einstein attribute scientific thinking?—to doubt and curiosity combined, adding the question, "What, precisely, is 'thinking?'" The danger, as George Grant noted a generation ago—and the danger has increased—

"is that in science the motive of wonder becomes ever more subsidiary to the motive of power, and that those scientists still dominated by wonder have a more difficult time resisting the forces of power" (22). Humanists are not immune to those same forces. In *The Dons,* Noel Annan, a man of long and detailed academic observation, notes, "Success . . . can easily corrupt scholars" (29).

Hegel inherits and studies the evolving systems of Friedrich Schelling and Johann Fichte. All write passionately about imagination. So does the naturalist Alexander von Humboldt, who died in 1859 at ninety, author of the monumental *Kosmos,* a forty-volume work describing the physical universe. More places on earth are named after Humboldt than after anyone else. He didn't conquer or claim them for any country. He discovered, explored, mapped, and explained them—for example, the Humboldt Current. From Humboldt's great treatise the astronomer Carl Sagan borrowed the title and something of the overarching concept for his television series *Cosmos.* And Sagan's fictional starship was not the *Enterprise.* He called it *Imagination.*

By the late Enlightenment, then, thinkers, poets, philosophers, and scientists alike regard the imagination as the chief source of creativity and discovery. It is seen to synthesize human experience in aesthetics, ethics, science, and even religion. The poet William Blake is not eccentric for his time when he speaks of a "divine-human imagination." For him, this represents the sanctity and potential of every life. The imagination connects the material and spiritual worlds. With it, the eye can see the apocalyptic in the mundane. It is a source of dialectic in philosophy and art, and a source of new theories in natural science. Nikolai Lobachevsky's non-Euclidean geometry, a monument of creative mathematical imagination, dates from this same period. Samuel Taylor Coleridge, poet, theologian, and friend of scientists such as Sir Humphrey Davy, calls imagination "that synthetic and magical power," a theme taken up more recently by Silvano Arieti in *Creativity: The Magic Synthesis.*

Kant and Adam Smith both praise a now-obscure Scotsman, Alexander Gerard, as the foremost writer on the nature of genius. Gerard's *Essay on Genius* (1774), widely read for more than a century and still worth reading, devotes an entire section to the difference between scientific and artistic imaginations. While seeing similarities in them, he doesn't think they are identical. Soon, however, romance novels, archetypal and popular in appeal, begin to interchange, as they still do, the figure of the gifted "mad" scientist and the character of the original, possessed artist. Both transform the world. The most enduring versions remain popular—Mary Shelley's *Frankenstein,* Hawthorne's "Rappaccini's Daughter," Jules

Verne's *Twenty Thousand Leagues under the Sea,* H. G. Wells's *The Is-land of Dr. Moreau.* There are countless more, and in many stories the scientist is a medical doctor with artistic or creative impulses, often per-verted ones. Even the evil scientists in James Bond fictions, Dr. No, for instance, are megalomaniacs exercising refined aesthetic pursuits in music, painting, gardening, and wine. Nonfictional science, too, provides its own aesthetic experience. As James Freedman points out, the diaries and autobiographies of scientists "make clear, again and again, that in-spiration was a prominent, if mysterious, source of their creativity. Ideas flash into the minds of scientists as unaccountably as lyrical phrases form in the minds of poets." Newton decodes the riddle of the universe "by the leap of his curiosity and the magic of his imagination" as much as "by any formal powers of concentration" (1996, 80). Michael Dixon, who teaches English at the University of Toronto, originally studied math and science. He holds degrees in philosophy and science as well as English, and before teaching literature he worked for IBM. "I have always thought," he says, "that my English students should be as clear-thinking as physics students, and I suspect that the methods of thinking, the or-ganization of thought and self-correcting processes, are very similar" (Tei-tel, 15). In the early nineteenth century, Karl Gauss, mathematician and astronomer, experimenter in magnetism and electricity, felt that learning languages kept his mind flexible, and he read widely in several. At sixty he took up Russian and mastered it in two years. The way in which the mind works in general, manipulating signs and symbols, deducing, using inductive reasoning, cross-checking, performing midcourse corrections, invoking metaphors, or creating placeholders, these and many other op-erations function across many fields.

Yet, as Alexander Gerard avowed, while occupying common ground, the overall operations of science and art are not the same: the same things are not produced, the goals are not identical, and as Max Black notes, their "aims and methods" diverge. Any glib equation of scientific and artistic imaginations fails. They are siblings, not twins, or if twins they are fraternal, not identical. However, if it is delusory to look for identity, there remain analogy and metaphoric similarity—of the essence of imag-ination itself—a sense of process and of new relations. Beyond any elu-sive neurophysiological explanation of "the" creative process, the prin-ciple of the imagination connects discovery of the natural world with invention in the artistic one. In *Atoms of Silence,* a book about cosmic evolution, Hubert Reeves compares the cemetery near his home in Mon-treal to the Orion nebula. "On one side were vigorous flowers and trees, thrusting their roots out from the moist banks of the graves; on the other, the polished wood coffins that men eased down into the dark holes. It was at once the beginning and the end, life and death—the ephemeral and the eternal immediately intertwined. . . . I rediscover my cemetery of the Côte des Neiges in the constellation Orion." This insight reaffirms that no single exercise of the imagination, scientific or artistic, is sufficient to society as a whole. Each influences and overlaps others. A larger paradigm of imagination seeks organic growth, process, and interconnection. It recognizes the drive not merely to learn by method but to uncover new method, to transform.

To cultivate such a power requires accepting significant risks, not the least of which is the virtual guarantee that flat failure, or at least failure to be recognized, will result often enough. If success arrives, it can encounter opposition in discovery and delay in recognition. This resistance frequently extends beyond the lifetime of the scientist or writer. At the beginning, the end results of innovative research are, by definition, never obvious. As a consequence, promoting the exercise of imagination in education—genuinely promoting it and not just talking about it—involves risk and partial failure. Students and faculty who learn to follow the prompting of imagination can encounter an initial, and sometimes a prolonged, lapse of productivity, which is not easily distinguished from no work at all. Imagination is a skill hard to test. It takes time to recognize. Its creations are not ordinary and frequently do not display immediate utility, whether in theoretical mathematics, theoretical physics, or literary theory. To invest in the imagination requires long-term views, a sense for and a faith in long-term returns, a faith harder to create than quantitative assessments, and a willingness to be repaid in a currency different from immediate fame and the coin of the realm.

Many writers on higher education—Freedman, Giamatti, Nussbaum, Axtell, and Pelikan—affirm the importance of imagination in that enterprise. (Pelikan adds that discipline must go hand in hand with imagination, which cannot be unregulated.) Yet, these voices are in danger of being buried in the avalanche of programmatic writing on higher education, or suffocated in its administration. In social and educational environments that worship specific measures of competition, "success" that is immediate and quantitative almost always looks better. Society often demands fast results, fast food, and fast profits. But imagination works unpredictably. It can be excruciatingly slow. Optimism about the prevalence or even the appeal of imagination in what Robert Reich calls the "second Gilded Age" is unwarranted. The valuing of imagination is endangered. Impatience for results exerts pressure that favors results *of a certain kind.* Even if work slow to develop becomes high in quality and beneficial in use, that work will develop only if given the chance. And it will be given the chance only if the imagination needed to produce it is supported and encouraged during inevitable frustrations and failures, not just at the hour of success.

• • •

In the university, the system dividing knowledge into departments, divisions, procedures, and methods, ingrained through decades of practice, must constantly be addressed not only within each field but also through the whole of the university. As the philosopher Stephen Toulmin remarks, "By its very nature, the problem of human understanding—the problem of recognizing the basis of human authority—cannot be encompassed within any single technique or discipline for the very boundaries between different academic disciplines are themselves a consequence of the current divisions of intellectual authority, and the justice of those divisions is itself one of the chief questions to be faced afresh" (7).

As a warning or admonition, certain Enlightenment thinkers tried to keep in mind that when faced with problems of universal scope, even strong intellects can cling to rigid procedures or latch onto buzzwords, what two centuries ago was called "cant." Carried to large, almost intractable issues—arms control, the grab for land amid a growing population, and the abyss yawning between the haves and have-nots—carried to such issues, imagination takes on a new dimension. No single paradigm of scientific or artistic creativity can solve such problems. Yet, imagination is, after all, a form of power, a creator of new modes of creation with the ability to transform old ones, too. It can move emotionally, persuade, symbolize and concentrate energy, affect the economy, and give understanding and technical means to work out desires and ambitions. Because imagination is power, or at least potential power, what William Blake calls "Energy," it is among the most hopeful of human capacities, whatever the field. Harder to gauge and more elusive than either productivity or knowledge, it is also more important.

What values and goals will powerful applications of knowledge serve? Can imagination help to establish those goals, what Northrop Frye calls "primary concerns," and Aristotle "chief goods"? Among these are welfare, health, education, and the defense of civil liberties and justice. In the sciences and arts, one primary concern is to preserve the freedom and the desire to uncover more than it is necessary to know, to discover more than a practical problem dictates for its solution. Concerns and goods such as comfort and wealth are vital, too. However, they derive their added value and reveal their relative importance only in the light of imaginatively conceived primary concerns and chief goods, without which the other goods never rise above self-preservation, amusement, or luxury.

The Power of Metaphor

How does the imagination overleap the bounds of the obvious and make headway into new areas of knowledge, boldly connecting fields seemingly separated by a rigid wall? In science, as in art and religion, when faced with the unknown, human beings turn to the use of metaphors. In his *Preface to Logic,* Morris Cohen remarks that metaphors express "the vague and confused but primal perception of identity which subsequent processes of discrimination transform into the clear assertion of an identity," or the more exact discovery of a new relation. Hypotheses to be tested—electricity as a "fluid," the atom as a miniature "solar system," the "stream of consciousness" in psychology—become fruitful and lead to further discovery. "In trying to visualize the unknown, the imagination must clothe it with attributes analogous to the known" (83–85). Einstein used locomotives and trains to visualize the theory of relativity. Edward Purcell, like Einstein a recipient of the Nobel Prize in Physics, and whose love of poetry tended to Robert Frost, remarked that at a high plane of thinking, in science and art, the common ground is an ability to think metaphorically. Dudley Herschbach, a chemist and another Nobel laureate, reaffirms that one "aspect emphasized by a language metaphor is the kinship of neophyte students with research scientists. Nature speaks to us in many tongues. They are all alien" (4). To translate and interpret these alien languages, metaphorical thinking makes substitutions, equivalencies, leaps, and transformations. Its activity is part of the answer to Einstein's difficult question, "What, *precisely,* is 'thinking'?" And, paradoxically, this suggests that when first encountered, the best creative thought, while never haphazard or utterly random, is often not precise, clear, or distinct. Every act of imagination that succeeds will alter the very standards of judgment that govern its subject. Einstein's question is emphatically not field specific. The subject at hand may be truth, beauty, or goodness, and it may be considered in practical or idealistic terms. Yet each subject, as Wayne Booth notes, is "relevant to study in every division within the university; the humanities, for example, have no corner on beauty or imagination or art, and the sciences have no corner on speculative truth" (1987, 27).

Ultimately, "every division" impinges on every other one. The possibilities and connections are as infinite as the prospect of all possible knowledge itself. For example, for centuries it puzzled scholars and readers why many ancient texts, in many different languages, all gave an account of a great flood. Could something so outrageously spectacular possibly be true? Now, after seemingly specialized work drawn from archaeology, religion, literature, geology, satellite mapping, ecology, and several other fields, it is clear that there was a sudden, great flood in the region of the Black Sea. This would never have come to light without the convergence of those different "separate" disciplines. Bruce Wilshire, a professor at Rutgers, puts the general case this way: "The limits of the imagination are unimaginable. . . . Ever new images and metaphors . . . loom as possibilities, as sheer *thats,* not-yet-knowns. So perceptions of actual things and connections in the world, to be made possible by these currently unimaginable images and metaphors, are themselves unimaginable" (206).

The twentieth-century philosopher Max Black was trained as a mathematician and published his first book on mathematics. He has also written highly regarded studies on the nature and imaginative uses of metaphor. He insists, "There will always be competent technicians who . . . can be trusted to build the highways" for mechanized and logical vehicles. "But clearing intellectual jungles is also a respectable occupation. Perhaps every science must start with metaphor and end with algebra; and perhaps without the metaphor there would never have been any algebra." As Edward O. Wilson indicates in the epigraph that opens this chapter, imagination works hand in glove with empirical observation. Black notes that an imaginative model or archetype "can yield to the demands of experience. . . . The imagination must not be confused with a strait jacket." He makes the case that "all intellectual pursuits, however different their aims and methods, rely firmly upon such exercises of the imagination" as the construction of metaphors and models. These have the power to cross-pollinate; "a sociologist's pattern of thought may also be the key to understanding a novel. . . . When the understanding of scientific models and archetypes comes to be regarded as a reputable part of scientific culture, the gap between the sciences and the humanities will have been partly filled. For exercise of the imagination, with all its promise and dangers, provides a common ground." He concludes that "science, like the humanities, like literature, is an affair of the imagination" (242–43). C. S. Peirce, a brilliant logician, philosopher, practicing astronomer, and physicist, as well as a historian of science, affirmed this in 1896. He anticipated Einstein's pronouncement about the importance of that key faculty. "It is not too much to say," noted Peirce, "that after the passion to learn there is no quality so indispensable to the successful prosecution of science as imagination" (43). Peirce was writing more than a century ago. However, his insight is recently reaffirmed by the biologist and geneticist Richard Lewontin, who states at the opening of his book *The Triple Helix* (2000), "It is not possible to do the work of science without using a language that is filled with metaphors."

The Arts and Sciences *as* Culture: Knowledge from the University Creates Society

Built in by past imaginative accomplishments in all fields, metaphors that were once as startling as "quantum leap" or even "poetic justice" become common. But unless that same principle of metaphor can fashion new, bolder connections between different areas, between what is scientific, social, and humanistic, then education will build a house divided. While specialized scholarship may be removed from the everyday preoccupations of society, what society itself treasures and keeps, its secular ark, is in the sum total of all the arts and sciences, which balance social, economic, and ethical goods. The word used to signify this conception is *culture,* which first entered English with this meaning, according to the *Oxford English Dictionary,* in 1805, when Wordsworth uses it in his autobiographical work *The Prelude,* a poem with the explicit theme of the imagination. Wordsworth had, a few years earlier, divided knowledge into that pursued by the poet and that discovered by the scientist, but he saw no contradiction or antagonism between them. Both, he said, afford pleasure. Earlier, for Hume, Bacon, Hobbes, and for anyone interested in education, "the arts and sciences" stood for culture itself. And as Stanley Aronowitz concludes in 2000, "The fundamental mission of higher education should be to play a leading role . . . in the development of general culture." Colleges and universities alone have "the intellectual and physical resources" to perform this service (172).

Such a vision explains why Northrop Frye can state, "What real society is, is indicated by the structure of the arts and sciences in a university. This is the permanent body of what humanity has done and is still doing, and the explanations of why the world around us changes so suddenly and so drastically are to be found only there" (64). In other words, the force of change—to which the university is constantly said to need to react—actually *originates* in the arts and sciences, which, to a large extent, are discovered and related to one another in the university in the first place. At bottom, then, every citizen holds a stake in what Edmund Burke describes as "a partnership in all science; a partnership in all art":

Society is, indeed, a contract. Subordinate contracts for objects of mere occasional interest may be dissolved at pleasure; but the state ought not to be considered as nothing better than a partnership agreement in a trade of pepper and coffee, calico or tobacco . . . to be taken up for a little temporary interest, and to be dissolved by the fancy of the parties. It is to be looked on with other reverence; because it is not a partnership in things subservient only to the gross animal existence of a temporary and perishable nature. It is a partnership in all science, a partnership in all art, a partnership in every virtue and in all perfection. As the ends of such a partnership cannot be obtained in many generations, it becomes a partnership not only between those who are living, but between those who are living, those who are dead, and those who are to be born. (*Reflections on the Revolution in France*)

Colleges and universities sustain and uphold this partnership. They are at its center. They generate it. Higher education in the United States, despite its problems, is arguably the best in the world for many reasons: diversity, research faculty, graduate training, the mix of private and public, intellectual competitiveness, extensive library and laboratory facilities. Yet, the *one* feature that American higher education enjoys that no other country exhibits to nearly the same degree or extent is a tradition, at the undergraduate and the graduate levels, of learning and working in an atmosphere of liberal education. Here the ultimate vitality of the sciences and arts is pursued and prized. Only a few other institutions in the world can claim this tradition of the combined liberal arts and sciences. (It was first established in Europe, but then declined; only now is it being revived again at institutions such as the European College of Liberal Arts, associated with the Humboldt University in Berlin.) A paramount reason for the high quality of American higher education is its continuing tradition of the liberal arts and sciences. If this tradition erodes as it did in Europe, the erosion will damage the one quality most clearly responsible for the unique strengths of American higher education. This tradition produces leaders and managers, as well as professional academics, artists, and scientists.

Many professors and administrators have at one time or another played a Machiavellian game of poker. But cooperation often wins more for everyone than competition, especially competition of the zero-sum variety. "Building bridges"—what lesser minds dismiss Kant as doing when he relies on the idea of the imagination—means opening traffic not only between different faculties of the individual mind but also between different faculties of higher education engaged in varied forms of knowledge. It means respect for different, even opposing claims to relevance in society because, in a real sense, all these claims taken together *are* society. If the university is not to become a house divided, or a house for sale, a reduction in the professional suspicions and prejudices that crowd the arena where varied forms of the arts and the sciences find a common home seems paramount. The hope to reduce intellectual provincialism and the hope for higher education to remain independent are not just realistic, they are matters of survival and progress, and imagination can achieve them.

"An Object of Primary Importance": Imperatives for Democracy

Any good tradition survives by more than sheer inertia. As it is honored, it must be reinvented and made present. "Liberal education" in the arts and sciences is an idea given that name two thousand years ago, but one whose enduring value has been secured only through historical evolution and adaptation. Such persistence through the vicissitudes of war, politics, and religious strife implies how central—and centrally debated—this idea is in Western civilization. In closely related forms it emerges from the thought of Confucius and Mencius, and from other philosophical and ethical systems in cultures around the world. The tradition of broad general education through the first year or two of college, and an overall emphasis on the liberal arts and sciences, still predominates in many selective institutions, without which American higher education would not ever be judged superior to that found in other nations.

It is possible to cultivate the liberal arts and sciences in many institutions, not just in highly selective ones. It has been done successfully, and it is especially important to do so, in a participatory, deliberative democracy. A staunch advocate of practical higher education, extension studies, agricultural improvements, and technological transfer in the land-grant universities, George R. McDowell, affirms that extension programs in areas such as history and child psychology add to the involvement of the university with society. Such programs meet "the need to have the society understand, engage, and affirm more than the technological part of knowledge and the university. Indeed, it may be that the fullest appreciation of the university in society will come through extension and outreach in the humanities, the arts, and the social and behavioral sciences, rather than in the physical and biological sciences." As a result, McDowell is disturbed at the emerging likelihood that "fields of study embraced by the university will simply be ignored because they appear to have no or limited commercial value" (176, 175).

From the start, a paradoxically idealistic strain informed the great practical universities. Developments in agricultural science, engineering, forestry, pharmacy, and eventually law characterized state and land-grant universities. However, the distinguished historian Allan Nevins asserts, "The most important idea in the genesis of the land-grant colleges and state universities was that of democracy." It was the "ideal of an open, mobile society." One of the reasons why the University of California is so strong today is that in the last quarter of the nineteenth century a move to curtail instruction in "physics, mathematics, English literature, and French" in favor of courses purely in agriculture and industry was defeated. The land-grant colleges and state universities soon produced civil and mechanical engineers, and later electrical and chemical engineers, but they also discovered that "the more extreme champions of practical education" actually undermined the strength of useful applications that they themselves advocated. In fact, Justin S. Morrill, father of the Morrill Act establishing the land-grant institutions, expressly stipulated that those universities "be not merely technical but also liberal" (Nevins, 16, 17, 60–61, 75).

Liberal education—the pursuit of knowledge and the inquiry into how it should be used as well as how it can be used— requires stability but must encourage change. These undertakings, based largely on past experience, exert real effects on the present and future. In his First Inaugural Address, Lincoln spoke of the "mystic chords of memory" that from generation to generation bind a people together and help to ensure their individual freedom. At every level and in every field, education shares in and strengthens those chords of memory; they extend forward through "every living heart" to an uncertain future in which citizens have so much hope. This idea explains why Harry Huntt Ransom, president and later chancellor of the University of Texas system, stated that "all that a university is now or can become relates to a simple concept, man's fate" (6). Yet, no homogeneous or "pure" form of higher education exists. Instead, the endeavor represents an evolving process. In Burke's phrase, this process "preserves *in order* to reform." Faced with pervasive changes in social and cultural conditions, it responds by encouraging and resisting them selectively, criticizing and cherishing alike what is new and old. The headstone of Willa Cather quotes her novel *My Ántonia:* "That is happiness; to be dissolved into something complete and great." Human life finally means little unless devoted to something larger than the self. That "something complete and great" requires the creative power and participation of each generation.

The republic itself, a public *res* or "thing"—the Romans in their wisdom used the most capacious term in their language—becomes the responsibility of each of its members; freedoms incur responsibilities, a set of duties related to the public good and general welfare. To pursue knowledge reveals how the local, national, and global connect, how one area of endeavor or professional training merges with others, whether in law, international relations, human rights, history, genetics, economic development, literature, or the environment. The structure of every college or university reflects the fact that while schools, divisions, and departments exist to pursue, analyze, specialize, and augment specific realms of knowledge, the larger issues facing complex institutions, society, and government ultimately draw on multiple, converging forms of knowledge. One body, one body politic, one university: each draws life from all its vital organs.

Unless dealt with imaginatively and with greater ends in view, the pressures facing colleges and universities will produce results whose effect on the republic is frankly antidemocratic. Because, to a very large degree, knowledge is power, anything that turns knowledge purely into a commodity to be bought and sold threatens democracy. Improving "productivity," a term now used within the university almost as often as outside it (Johnstone), is desirable, but it is worth recalling Northrop Frye's warning that "the natural drive of the producing society is not democratic but oligarchic or managerial: it increases inequalities of privilege instead of reducing them, and in itself is no longer capable of leading us to the vision of the just state" (73).

One fact that confirms this warning comes from financial aid and admissions data. The rate of increase in college admissions for students coming from the bottom economic quarter of American families is "no better . . . than for groups of higher-income quartiles, and the overall percentage of college attendees among the lowest quartile is stalled at around 50 percent compared to 85 percent of attendees coming from the highest quartile" (Losco and Fife, 67–68). In his 2001 study "Assessing the U.S. Financial Aid System: What We Know, What We Need to Know," Thomas J. Kane reports pessimistically that from 1980/82 to 1992, college entry rates increased for middle- and higher-income families, but not for lower-income ones. During a time of national prosperity, policies and practices failed to reduce an already significant gap. Moreover, "differences in college-going by family income remain wide and, according to some recent evidence, appear to be widening" (33). William C. Symonds points out that "only 3% of students" at top or "selective" schools come "from families in the bottom socioeconomic quartile and just 10% from families in the bottom half. Meanwhile . . . 74% of the students hail from families in the top quartile—defined by family income, parental education, and other factors such as neighborhood affluence" (66). The title of Symonds's article is, appropriately, "College Admissions: The Real Barrier Is Class." This is demonstrably the case, yet it receives less attention that other factors, such as race—though, to be sure, race is often one element in the class barrier. A society that decreases its social and upward mobility by, in effect, using its system of higher education as a filter to perpetuate economic privilege is not serving either economic or social goods very well for many of its citizens. Rather, it is perpetuating advantages for some and making them difficult for others to obtain.

The Center for Higher Education in San Jose reports that a family in the lowest economic quartile in 1980 needed to spend 13 percent of its median annual income for tuition at a public college. In 2000 it was 25 percent. In 2004 it is even higher. Is it possible that the competitive money ethic of higher education bears some responsibility for making that education itself less affordable for those young people without much money to begin with? If so, this constitutes a terrible irony for a country where education should help even the odds. The meritocratic outlook fostered and expanded in the middle of the twentieth century (through the GI bill, scholarship aid, and various forms of social outreach) has stalled and is in danger of reversal. One practice has to some degree always existed but recently has been ramped up. "To attract prospective donors, colleges are," aside from favoring children of some alumni, "also bending admissions standards to make space for children from rich or influential families that lack longstanding ties to the institution. Through referrals and word-of-mouth, schools identify applicants from well-to-do families. Then, as soon as these students enroll, universities start soliciting gifts from their parents" (Golden 2003; Leonhardt). In addition, it is increasingly common at many institutions to attract top students by offering scholarship aid to them even though they and their families clearly do not need it. This raises overall costs and threatens democratic education. It means that the institution pays for some students who could already pay. And because attending a selective college does, on the average, affect lifetime earnings, this practice perpetuates and exacerbates income differentials. It contributes to the education plutocracy.

To build a larger national spirit is, as Jefferson claimed, a task performed by every living generation. Al Smith phrased this idea another way: the only cure for the ills of democracy is more democracy. Institutions of higher education can take greater part in this task. Even when statutorily private, they exist for the common good; they educate citizens as well as prepare job applicants. One of their functions is similar to the workings of the ancient virtue of hospitality. We give to a stranger something valuable and sustaining, not in hope of immediate return, but in acknowledgment of the tacit bond that sees hospitality as a custom circulating slowly yet inevitably, binding us together so that one day we too might receive it, at the hands of another stranger. So it is with many effects of higher education. A democratic society requires that education not become an engine whose chief effect, even if unintended, is to maintain or exacerbate economic hierarchies. The more that higher education and economically useful knowledge find themselves closely coupled, the greater this danger is. To repeat a point noted in chapter 6, Tocqueville warned a century and a half ago that the prime danger inherent in American democracy is this: absent other establishments of status or measures of distinction, soon material possessions—money—will universally mark all forms of worth; and then what will become important is not the common good but the race to accumulate wealth.

In 1783 Washington remarked on the unprecedented *diversity* (the word is his) found in the new republic that he had personally sacrificed so much to create, and for which he had called on so many others to do the same. Thirteen years later in his Farewell Address, he warned the nation against entangling itself in foreign alliances—that is the part always quoted. But he opens his address with another, more important, admonition: against letting the very diversity of the republic turn into a rock on which it might split. Sectarian, geographical, and party concerns, "discriminations . . . local interests . . . jealousies and . . . misrepresentations . . . tend to render alien" one group from another, he says. Such separations still exist, growing in tension, yet they must accommodate themselves justly in one union. Washington concludes with several imperatives. Chief among them for our purposes is this: "Promote, then, as an object of primary importance, institutions for the general diffusion of knowledge. In proportion as the structure of a government gives force to public opinion, it is essential that public opinion should be enlightened." Washington assumes that the national form of representative democracy gives to public opinion the greatest possible force; therefore, he urges that public opinion "be enlightened" to the greatest possible extent.

Shortly after the Civil War, many educators begin to link democracy with higher education. The connection can mean, as it meant for Washington, a wide diffusion of knowledge aimed at improving civic welfare. It can also mean higher education as an agency of individual success, as long as this is not carried out at the expense of communal good. Inside colleges and universities, it can mean a general equality of fields, a point advocated elsewhere in this book. And it can mean, too, the possibility of admission and hiring not tied to financial or social status (Veysey, 62–68). All these meanings are laudable, and they are not mutually exclusive. Through the ROTC program, colleges have also provided educated officers for military service. (That program received early support from Joshua Lawrence Chamberlain, who began his career as a professor of rhetoric, modern languages, and religion at Bowdoin College. At Gettysburg he commanded Union troops on Little Round Top, and after the Civil War served as governor of Maine and later president of Bowdoin.) The hope that higher education will strengthen democracy and the reverse as well, that democracy will improve higher education, has proved well placed, but to fulfill that hope each generation must renew its dedication and labor.

The myth that higher education needs and has but one benefit and that such a benefit is solely individual or institutional economic advancement is the nucleus of our current situation. Unless and until that myth is dispelled, and until it is understood that economic advancement is but one of several other interdependent benefits conferred by higher education, American colleges and universities will labor in peril. And so will university systems in many other countries, including Canada, the United Kingdom, Russia, and China (see "How to Influence People"). Whether imported or produced locally, the same attitude is now taking its toll around the globe. For a while yet, the shift of values may seem unremarkable, even natural. Just about anything is convertible to material gain, after all, including the ideals of a society. "The reverse of disinterested, in American culture, turns out to be not 'engaged, passionate, socially committed,' but rather 'functional, corporate, scientifically cashable'" (Bromwich 1992, 233). After the transaction is complete, all is transformed. One can, in fact, put justice up for sale, but after that it isn't justice. One can sell love, but then it's called by another name. With education the situation is no different. Institutions can experiment with compromising their ideals or ignore them for a time, but once those ideals are well forgotten, or sold, then they are gone.

The ideals and practices of democratic free speech and the conventions of open, scholarly debate and discourse are mutually dependent and mutually reinforcing. This means a continually expanded, revised, and improved awareness of what degrades or promotes the general welfare. And this awareness should not impose conformity of thought; it should protect freedom of expression. It is a huge task. We can't ask more of higher education—and we can't accept less.

10

THE HIGHER UTILITY

The distinction between pure and applied science would, one feels, have puzzled Kelvin and Rankine. Where, they might have asked, does it leave Sadi Carnot's Réflexions sur la puissance motrice du feu? *Is it a work of "pure" science or is it merely a manual for horny-handed engine builders that might, possibly, by accident as it were, have significant consequences for science? One has only to pose the question to realise how inappropriate it is, for science and technology have never been separate; they merge and in many places overlap. This has always been the case and it is even truer now than in the past.*

    —D. S. L. CARDWELL, *TURNING POINTS IN WESTERN TECHNOLOGY,* 1972

. . . the academes,
That show, contain, and nourish all the world.

    —SHAKESPEARE, *LOVE'S LABOR'S LOST,* 1596

At the end, as at the beginning, this book addresses the issue of utility, the arbiter to which society refers many questions of value and even of values. But simple tests rarely explain complex issues. An exclusive and strict standard of utility produces distortions. For once evaluation is restricted to the primitive dichotomy of "useful" or "useless," this legitimates other simplistic dichotomies that citizens might also defer to with little thought or question. "Science" and "technology" are seen, falsely, as separate. "Pure" or "basic" research is regarded, erroneously, as the opposite of "applied." The reality behind these pairs of terms—each of which stands for a set of complex activities—is hard to grasp. It is clear that when all the weight is put on one side, the symbiosis between the two starts to break down and both become endangered. Shortchanging one eventually devalues the other.

    The pair "theory" and "application" is one instance. These terms should be understood in their meaningful and necessary sense as describing an interdependent relationship. To be worthwhile, a theory must be susceptible of being tested by applying relevant empirical data. Whether those data come from physics experiments, the U.S. Census, or Shakespeare's sonnets will depend on the nature of the theory. Neither term—theory or application—can gain precedence over its partner. To prefer one to the other is nonsensical, as meaningful as declaring bones more important than muscles, or nouns superior to verbs. For example, "By the close of the nineteenth century, both the mathematicians engrossed in 'pure' theory devoid of fresh physical inspiration, and the engineers absorbed in accumulating experimental data without adequate rationalisation by deductive theory, seemed each to have reached blind alleys of their own" (Singh, 48).

Nonetheless, society can establish an invidious primacy by taking "application" and "applied" in a special, limited sense. Properly speaking, without some means of application a theory is empty, because a theory that cannot be validated or invalidated has no explanatory value. But in loose contemporary usage, theories and theorizing that do not lead very soon to demonstrable, practical benefits—"applications"—are often despised. In such an ordering of priorities, a theory like that of marginal utility is valuable because it can affect economic behavior, but a theory like Grimm's law is insignificant because it affects only linguistic understanding. Avogadro's law is important because it aids aviation technology, but Hubble's law becomes an interesting luxury because the expansion of the universe has no relevance for material improvement in any comprehensible time frame.

The reductive criterion of utility alone for evaluating intellectual activity is not a recent development. While its force has been growing considerably in the last thirty-five years, it has been a part of the American scene, and of American higher education, since the middle of the eighteenth century. Richard Cox plausibly traces the utilitarian dichotomy, with its emphasis on the "useful," to the manner in which many advances in knowledge were interpreted in the seventeenth and eighteenth centuries:

> The ancients spoke of the vehicle of human knowledge as psyche or soul; they conceived of the highest activity of the soul as *theoria*—active wondering and gazing at the cosmos and its various parts; and they concluded that the true object of *theoria* is simply knowledge for the sake of knowledge . . . knowledge that nature is an end in itself, complete and perfect. In contrast, the moderns [1600–1800] increasingly spoke of the vehicle of human knowledge as the mind; they conceived of the highest activity of the mind as the discovery of methods by which the mind may penetrate

Nature's secrets by developing a dialectic between theory and experiment; and they concluded that the true object of the dialectic is acquisition of human power over natural processes. Knowledge is for the sake of human power. (Cox, xi)

Ideally, knowledge for its own sake and knowledge for the sake of power and economic usefulness cohabit and reinforce one another. A lively cross-pollination then exists between the practical on the one hand and the imaginative and exploratory on the other. However, once the idea of "useful" gets the upper hand, and once "usefulness" is translated into any common currency of exchange, including money, then the balance between the two is destroyed. Once the special, complex utility of higher education is reduced only to determinate goals and specific problems, and especially once those goals become easily symbolized by their monetary value, then the false dichotomies of "practical" versus "speculative," "applied" versus "theoretical," and "useful" versus "useless" achieve a ghastly and deleterious reality. Historically, needs that are broadly economic and needs that are chiefly inquisitive or driven by curiosity have built on one another in ever-shifting ways, especially since science and technology formed their mutually supportive alliance as early as the sixteenth and seventeenth centuries. In learning and research, a reciprocal and productive relationship springs up between learning for its own sake and learning for utility. American universities have developed this dynamic relationship with particular success. Today, in biotechnology, for example, it is extremely hard to separate out the technical from the scientific, the scientific fact from its use. A discovery of previously unknown natural phenomena can inextricably involve an application of those phenomena. But, in part because of this very close coupling in the most heavily funded of all research areas in the nation, it is becoming easier and easier to regard the "useful" as the golden yardstick of all measures in every field. The present danger is that society will accept the "useful" and the wealth creation or power it promises to individuals, and the profit it offers to universities, as the one sufficient and satisfactory objective for higher education. And then everything that detracts from such an objective will be judged as mere intellectual games and puzzles.

To put it another way, it is no demerit (quite the contrary) in the land-grant schools that they run large and active extension programs, which include consulting to farms and businesses. That is, it is no demerit until the extension faculty metamorphose into paid operatives of commerce and industry severed from their special commitment to disinterested scholarly standards and to the larger endeavor of knowledge formation that binds scholars to institutions, and to one another, in the enterprise we call education. It is no demerit (quite the opposite) in the elite research universities that they actively pursue programs in engineering and biotechnology, which include consulting to multinational corporations and drug companies. That is, it is no demerit until the university faculty metamorphose into hired hands of specific company objectives or into officers of their own companies spending more time managing their own businesses than educating students or colleagues. It is important for college freshmen to hope that what they learn will help them live better, more rewarding, and more productive lives, but it is sad and ultimately socially destructive to regard "better," "more rewarding," and "more productive" as synonyms for one thing and one thing only: "higher paid."

The rise of "utility" in its various forms occupies a strong chapter in the history of higher education (Nevins, 2–22; Veysey, 57–73). In the decade following the Civil War, "almost every visible change in the pattern of American higher education lay in the direction of concessions to the utilitarian type of demand for reform." The change permeated both state and private universities. In addition, vocational training soon shaped the undergraduate curriculum at many colleges (Veysey, 60, 66). Reconstruction after the war, westward expansion, new technical knowledge that could be applied to the labors of reconstruction and expansion, and a long-standing conviction that higher education should serve not only culture but also industry and agriculture, these all prompted the new ideal of utility. Yet, it is important to recall that from its inception another ideal always tempered the stress on utility. This was the sense of public or civic service, where utility was not to be confined to the individual, the company, the profession, or the profit expected, but to a greater social good, to "a sweeping social sense." Vocational ambition thus "also meant the service of the society by way of one's calling" (Veysey, 72, 66). Even as David Starr Jordan of Stanford proclaimed in 1903 that the entire university movement "is toward reality and practicality," ten years earlier, George Elliott Howard of Stanford had advocated "that spiritual utilitarianism whose creed is social perfection." Exclamations such as Howard's may seem innocent or too lofty now, but they did produce a tonic effect. They kept alive "the realm of educational ideals" and encouraged not only "training for success within the existing order" but also new arrangements and further reforms (Veysey, 61, 72, 73).

As first presented in chapter 2, the question is not which ideal or pursuit is "right" or "better"—that is the wrong question to ask—but how to balance those ideals and pursuits so that they reinforce and, as it were, keep one another honest. The issue of "utility" is well more than a century old, but the conditions and forces shaping it have changed. In 1865 or 1905 the drive for "utility" was relatively new. As it grew, it often devolved, remarks Laurence Veysey, "into a merely deft pragmatism" (89).

The Paradoxical Origin of Unexpected Progress

The college and the university, with their tendency to conservatism born of the ruminative and disputatious character of higher learning, would seem exactly the institutions needed to maintain and promote the delicate, vital linkage between knowledge for its own sake and knowledge for the sake of economical usefulness. Their position as major repositories and disseminators of culture obliges them to respond. They are doubly obligated: paradoxically, the current situation is, to a great extent, a creature of their own making. Science, medicine, and technology would not exist in their current states had higher education not fostered and supported them in the first place. Even if a sense of responsibility fails to produce action, the real chance that the economic interests invested in the technologies that colleges and universities have helped to create will consume their parent institutions (or force them into subaltern status) ought to stimulate the efforts of those institutions. Yet, higher education has been slow to respond. Events threaten to overwhelm it, and many opportunists who would use it for their own self-interest are eager to sell it a bill of goods.

The response cannot be isolation and disdain but, at the other extreme, the response cannot be enthrallment, hawking higher education to the highest bidder. "A key challenge for the next century is maintaining a balance" among the missions of "teaching, research, public service, and contributions to the U.S. and global economies" (Mowery and Nelson et al., 118). However, "maintaining a balance" suggests that the missions are in some way regarded as equal already. For some, that may be true, but the fact is that the monetary and utilitarian incentives now have the very clear advantages of both institutional momentum and public perception. In other words, the response cannot be simply a pragmatic compromise brokered between the missions; it must include a strong streak of idealism. It should champion the essential purposes of higher education as advancing the life of the mind and the long-term good of society, not just certain segments of it, in a way that no other institutions or organizations can, a way that has been, is, and will remain invaluable to society. This is the higher utility.

The monastic origins of the university contribute to academia's tardiness in addressing this dilemma. After all, the semi-isolation of academic institutions had not, historically, presented a liability. Over the years, the unworldliness of scholarly communities, their relative detachment from practical affairs, had been mainly an advantage. They survived intact eight hundred years of social and political evolutions and revolutions. This unworldliness proved a good defense against external hostility, but poor preparation for the worldly success that the academic acceptance and fostering of the experimental sciences brought with it. Not long after these disciplines became thoroughly identified with academia in the nineteenth century, advanced research began its unprecedented association with useful (or usable) discoveries. Researchers who earlier would have been independent scientists like Leeuwenhoek, Lavoisier, or Cavendish began in the nineteenth century to rely on the support and protection of universities. Colleges and universities provided human, organizational, and pecuniary resources, including students to assist in research, all of which enhanced scientific productivity and the production of knowledge. Practical consequences for industrial innovation, medicine, business, and the military followed. In such conditions, even those hostile to the academic world were hard put to deny that higher education made material, economic, medical, and "security" contributions to society. The admirable, almost spiritual, habit of investing in thought for the sake of thought itself began to weaken in the face of a self-explanatory rationale for continued support of higher education. Colleges and universities had shown themselves immediately useful, so much so that before long much of the general population believed that their only purpose was just that.

In the early stages of academia's interactions with commerce and industry, it may have seemed improbable that the whole system of higher education could ever fall under the spell of accountancy, productivity, quantitative measures, and profit. In many ways the early twentieth century was an idealistic time, and it accorded respect to unapplied learning and knowledge. With a *richesse oblige* that now seems endangered, a major corporation at that time might choose to support research in the interest of something as vague as "science." In 1909 the great chemist Irving Langmuir took what he thought would be a summer stint at General Electric's laboratory in Schenectady, New York. GE soon appreciated his ability and offered him a permanent position on their research staff. At first Langmuir hesitated. "Would it be fair, he asked [the head of the laboratory, Willis R.] Whitney, to spend the money of an industrial organization like the General Electric Company for purely scientific work which might never lead to any practical application?" Whitney believed most new and significant practical applications could be traced to scientific curiosity. "It is not necessary for your work to lead anywhere," stated Whitney. Langmuir made up his mind—he would remain in Schenectady (Jaffe, 239–40). Interested first in solving a theoretical problem, the nature of atomic hydrogen, Langmuir nevertheless made discoveries that eventually—but not immediately—led to the modern incandescent lightbulb, saving Americans countless billions of dollars on energy and lighting costs. Although there remain exceptions, a question like Langmuir's and an answer like Whitney's are less likely to be voiced today.

Today in universities, "curiosity-driven" research is, comparatively, increasingly less well funded. For some, it even carries a negative connotation. The National Science Foundation, according to many scientists, has increased its emphasis on the usefulness of the projects it funds. After a massive study, two investigators concluded of academic research in the 1980s and 1990s in Australia, the United Kingdom, the United States, and, to some extent, Canada: "The freedom of professors to pursue curiosity-driven research was curtailed by withdrawal of more or less automatic funding to support this activity and by the increased targeting of R&D funds for commercial research. . . . Policies for academic R&D, the lifeblood of graduate education, became science and technology policies, more concerned with technoscience innovation and building links with the private sector than with basic or fundamental research." The eventual effect on academic research is clear. "As corporations reduce their investment in their own industrial R&D laboratories or disband their industrial laboratories altogether—as was the case with Bell Laboratories—and move their R&D dollars into short-term efforts in their business divisions, they are likely to turn to universities for more of the R&D once performed in industrial laboratories" (Slaughter and Leslie, 211, 223).

David C. Montgomery holds a named chair in physics at Dartmouth. He reports that at some institutions the "discussions of faculty hiring and promotion frequently do not delve into the details of a candidate's research or scholarship, but rather cut immediately to the person's success at the chase after external money. . . . It would be redundant to develop in any more detail how willingly (or how quietly) the American university is surrendering its insistence on the primacy of values unrelated to the marketability of a 'product,' whether that be a research paper or a graduate. And this transformation has happened quickly—in less than one long academic lifetime." This surrender would not be so problematic if it did not affect the quality of the science being done and the stock that one can put in its results. The real fear is that "we have inherited a legacy of credibility that may not last much longer if we proceed in the directions we are going" (Montgomery). Once that credibility is gone, recovering it will be the work not of one but of many generations.

The old-style university, relatively unproductive of direct material benefits, was sustained by faith, faith in the intrinsic value of education, learning, and scholarship. The new-model, practical, and efficient university not only took shape among a host of brand-new institutions but also came into being on the very campuses occupied by its older incarnation. The idea that a university could take a leading position in the march of material progress was seductively modern and hard-headed. Soon, the ability to take on such a role could be seen as the *only* qualification required for an institution to be identified as a leading one. Universities could now justify their existence, it seemed, without resorting to anything so nebulous as faith; they could offer society a tangible and immediate return on investment, not a long-term, indirect, unpredictable (but historically generous) one. The immediate return would prove a great point in fund-raising, too—so great that it began to convince higher education itself that this immediate return was the primary, even the sole reason for its own existence. Eventually, "knowledge that is in practical terms 'useless' but in cultural terms significant" gets "shortchanged" (Aronowitz, 173).

In a world that seemed to belong to the doers rather than the dreamers, Charles W. Eliot, a man of integrity and intellect, the long-serving president of Harvard, could sketch the character of the dawning era with assurance. In "The Tendency to the Concrete and the Practical in Modern Education," he described the new wave: "We all agree that the present generation is characterized by two strong desires. One is the desire for sound knowledge, not knowledge of the myth, the fable, or the dream, but knowledge of the fact, the truth; and the second is the intense desire to be of service to mankind" (15). In the atmosphere of his time, even Eliot was prepared to believe that for higher education the two strongest motives were to apprehend "facts" that were clearly factual and "truth" that was plainly true, and then to help solve society's problems. Good will would take care of the rest. So sweeping a vote of confidence for the utilitarian outlook would have been incautious at any period, but Eliot's timing proved unlucky. He delivered the speech in 1913, on the eve of the most advanced and bloodiest war the world had ever seen.

But even if he was capable at times of advocating a constrained view of the aims of education, Eliot was a broad-minded intellectual with a firsthand understanding of how higher education worked and what multiple objectives it could pursue. Educational reform was important to him, and he took an active role in shaping the university, especially the curriculum. He proved an effective reformer, and he reenvisioned the university's relation to society in important ways, in large part because he had been a practicing teacher.

Today, to be visionary, or even intellectually curious, is viewed as suspect at times, not only outside the campus but on it as well. "'Why is that man reading books?' asked a distinguished faculty member when he saw Harold Shapiro, then president of Princeton, reading in the university bookstore. 'Why isn't he out raising money for us?'" (Kernan 1999, 269). Would that such an attitude—at Princeton, of all places!—generated surprise. But in the current climate, it is not anomalous. Nor is it unusual nowadays to hear a prominent state university advertise itself on public radio as turning out graduates with "entrepreneurial spirit," advertised above or totally in lieu of intellectual spirit, the spirit of curiosity, or of science. After a while an institution begins to believe its own advertising and rejects other claims on a mission that has grown single-minded. And it was not surprising to hear Bill Clinton, then president of the United States and himself the beneficiary of a first-rate education, willfully disregard high-school drop-out rates and widespread adult illiteracy by holding out the false promise of college education for everyone, right on the horizon. Clinton's vision was proposed on behalf of a trivialized and misrepresented version of higher education—that is, on behalf of college study as one thing only: job training. Neil Postman presented this critique: Clinton's "solution is to provide the young with more practical vocational skills [in college]. . . . Of course, this is exactly the wrong solution, since the making of adaptable, curious, open, questioning people has nothing to do with vocational training and everything to do with humanistic and scientific studies." Far from looking ahead, the president and his colleagues "have difficulty discarding outmoded assumptions, including their belief that if something is not working—for example, training people [in college] for jobs—then what is needed is more of it" (1995, 32).

As noted in chapter 4, a pervasive myth directly links higher education with employment and economic productivity. Alison Wolf, writing for the *Financial Times,* states the myth succinctly. "To stay competitive, we need to be top in numbers of graduates, to have more of our young people gaining qualifications than our rivals, and to make education more responsive to skill shortages in the economy." Yet, when one searches for data to support this apparently self-evident and widely accepted position, the data support no such conclusion. After citing studies from many countries, including Hong Kong, Egypt, Korea, Switzerland (the lowest university attendance and graduation rate in the Organization for Economic Cooperation and Development), and Zimbabwe (one of the top rates of literacy and higher education in Africa but an economy in shambles), Wolf concludes, "This theory, however, is wrong. Wrong, in that education doesn't simply deliver up economic growth in the way our politicians and businessmen believe, and wrong because this very expensive belief is distorting education." While one study (see Krueger and Lindahl) contests Wolf's debunking, the larger point is that the link between economic growth and higher education is now held pervasively. For many "politicians and businessmen" it thus becomes the only reason to promote or care about that education.

If colleges and universities increasingly face the danger of demotion to credentializing services and ancillary laboratories for government and industry, they are in large part victims of their own past success. Having done so much to bring into being the technological and information age, they can find themselves subordinated to that achievement, tempted or compelled to serve its ends before their own. Set against the information age economy, colleges and universities of the traditional mold cannot help looking elderly and obsolescent. As the third millennium succeeds the second, not many leaders are apt to consider their world much beholden to a type of institution conceived of in the Middle Ages. It is easy to dismiss the slow-paced, inefficient, and traditional characteristics of higher education as holdovers from a time when advanced thought (and everything else) ran slowly. From this point of view, the remnants of idealism in higher education look like a dispensable part of its archaic charm. It is a rude adjustment to go, in a few decades, from receiving praise as a disinterested participant in learning and thought to receiving scorn for the same. Protected in many ways from the rough and tumble and the perpetual compromise of practical affairs, institutions of higher learning were unprepared for their value to society to be sharply and openly challenged.

The Perils of Silence

The legal system, however, offers an instructive comparison. The traditionalism necessitated by respect for procedure and precedent gives the law an archaic character and a slow pace equal to anything in academia. The institutions of law in the United States are plastered over with the cobwebs of medieval England and ancient Rome, peppered with old French, late Latin, and, in some places, the Napoleonic Code. American law is still mindful of the barons' revolt against King John (cited in President Clinton's impeachment proceedings) as if it were last week's news, not contemporaneous with the Crusades and Kublai Khan. The machinery of the law moves as slowly as any Elizabethan oxcart. For tedious inefficiency, it is hard to match a jury trial or a congressional deliberation on an appropriations bill. And then the results aren't always pleasing. In any legislative session, some money will be cut from vital services to squander it on boondoggles. Inevitably, as a consequence of due process, in some court actions the innocent are punished and in others the guilty party walks free.

Society complains and periodically demands reform, but it puts up with the presence of these imperfections as the unavoidable deficiencies of democracy and the rule of law. The maddening slowness of courts and legislatures, the hemming and hawing and backing and filling, the insistence on minuscule details—these evils, though deplored individually, are accepted, in principle, as necessary. Even the unfairness of many trial verdicts is, in a deep if reluctant way, endured as an unfortunate concomitant of due process. As Mark Twain remarked of the weather, everyone complains about the rule of law, but nobody does anything about it. To eliminate its exasperating characteristics, one could trade it in for something else entirely, but chaos and confusion would ensue.

Such an attitude suggests respect, grudging but sincere. For, unlike the weather, there are alternatives to democracy and the rule of law; but our respect for the law grows out of a cultural memory of those alternatives, of the much higher price that dictators and monarchs have exacted in return for efficiency and swift justice. This awareness is not biologically inherited; it is taught and learned, at first perhaps in high school civics classes, but thereafter by the makers and agents of the law itself. The majesty of the law is rarely sufficient to obliterate the everyday associations attached to politics and the courts: calculation, compromise, hypocrisy, and tedium, even greed. Democratic institutions and legal due process function only if they are accepted, and they are accepted only when they are believed to be necessary. Not every important thing is delightful. Power lines, asphalt, and ambulance sirens are rarely fetching. The law is not always more attractive than these physical necessities, and it is far more complicated to justify and explain. For this reason, legislators and lawyers have made it their business to remind impatient critics of the alternatives already rejected, and to explain that there are reasons why everyone suffers with the limitations of legal and legislative institutions.

By comparison, higher education has had it too easy. Its dignity, its authority, its mystery, and even its antiquity once exerted great charm. A brief experience of its collegiality can bind people to it with a lifetime's loyalty rarely accorded government service or corporations ready to downsize. The faults of colleges and universities, though real, are small by comparison with those of any legislature. After all, higher education does not have the responsibility to govern anything but itself. It is not the negative features of higher education that are at issue, but the positive ones: How important is it? Is it a necessity, a luxury, or worse, an ornamental parasite? For a long time, these were hardly questions at all, let alone serious ones. The eminent position of higher education seemed assured. Lulled into complacency by centuries of acceptance and admiration, colleges and universities were as unprepared for a serious assault as the Ottoman garrison at Aqaba when the troops of Lawrence and Faisal appeared out of the desert.

Higher education long abstained from self-advocacy and self-justification largely because it could, but also out of patrician abhorrence. The consequences have proven dire. Few people would advocate streamlining the judicial system by eliminating jury trials or reforming government by forgoing elections. Society does not believe—because it has been taught otherwise—that more criminal convictions or fewer pork-barrel appropriations would compensate for the loss of freedom. But many people (and most politicians) now advocate a more practical, workplace-oriented and industry-oriented system of higher education. Voters are a little chary of taking civil liberties entirely for granted, as if they grew unassisted out of the soil of civic affairs. Yet, many citizens have few reservations about treating fiber optic cable, microchips, the Internet, the National Weather Service, and the polio vaccine as the simple and direct products of results-driven research. None of them was. Enough ignorance of the history of higher thought abounds to foster the belief that the present state of sophistication is the simple consequence of people imagining better mousetraps, then building them.

The irony in this situation is that colleges and universities have garnered great benefits not because they simply adopted or conformed to the values and standards of industry and profit. Rather, colleges and universities created these benefits out of a dedication to inquiry, education, science, and disputation inherited from the Middle Ages, the Renaissance, and the Enlightenment. The persistence of these institutions in the inefficient, chancy, arduous pursuit of the true as well as the useful has, paradoxically, opened up even greater possibilities for efficiency, productivity, and utility. It seems more efficient to do research with one assigned goal in view, knowing in advance what one is looking for; it also severely limits the scope of inquiry. Spacecraft now transmit signals at the speed of light while orbiting Jupiter, and computers communicate across local area networks but not, however, because someone imagined those things and then achieved them. Rather, for example, J. J. Thomson wished to know why a magnet could bend a beam of light and had the time and the facilities of Cambridge University to help him find out. Or, for another instance, Wilhelm Ostwald could use the resources and prestige of his professorship at the University of Leipzig to help the young Svante Arrhenius test the validity of his shockingly novel theory of ionization. For yet another example, James Clerk Maxwell of Aberdeen, King's College (University of London), and Cambridge University wanted to know about the stability of Saturn's rings and later about the nature of electromagnetism. He had no design to invent spacecraft or the wireless, both of which, however, would have been impossible without his advances. A relative backwater in mathematics known as Knot Theory now all of a sudden seems able to help reveal how DNA strands order themselves. Three centuries earlier a similar moment of convergence transformed architecture and building. For generations the science of statics had developed independent of its practical applications. This development "was largely the work of physicists and mathematicians. It is only at a comparatively late stage, during the eighteenth century, that the attempt was made to apply the scientific knowledge gained . . . to the design of structures and to the solution of practical building problems." This signified "the birth of modern structural engineering; it revolutionized the entire art of building" (Straub, xvii). This revolution owed its force to theoretical knowledge that had developed for two centuries before being applied in a utilitarian manner. This happens repeatedly. "Fundamental research," notes mathematician Daniel Goroff, "has fantastic payoffs in ways no one could have expected" ("The Science Economy," 4).

To be certain, it is hard and at times inappropriate to separate pure from applied research, and the progress of the two often go hand in hand. But the point remains that a growing commercial or monetary emphasis on the results of research will soon limit the nature of all research. Karl Compton, former president of MIT, went so far as to say that "pure scientific research, carried on simply with the objective of discovering new truth, is the best long-term investment which can be made." Compton even had a rule for this. He believed that "if there is one practical problem which I want to solve, and just one scientific fact which I know, the chances that this scientific fact will solve that practical problem are very small." However, two facts give "a much better chance," and "ten facts" mean there are "probably a hundred times as many chances to solve my practical problem as if I know only one fact." His resulting rule is that "the rate of development of engineering is proportional to the square of the amount of our scientific knowledge" (60, 61). The situation is no different outside the laboratory and material sciences. It would be convenient and efficient to study language, social structure, ethics, law, and government without an account of epistemological controversies, cultural diversity, religious and political history, literature, or psychology. Such shortcuts fail, and only ignorance or heedless impatience counsels following them.

Colleges and universities have for centuries enriched society with the mental and moral ingredients for cultural adaptation, critique, and advancement—to no small extent through their role as preservers of culture. As one aspect of this gift, they have also made possible a host of scientific discoveries and technological innovations. Grown accustomed to this bounty, society may take its original investment for granted. It might ignore the origins of much scientific, intellectual, and technological capital, or conceive of higher education as a temporary holding company. Many people promote such opinions, or act as if they did. Implicitly, and increasingly often explicitly, political leaders and academic administrators treat education as subservient to "problem solving" rather than treating progress as indebted to education. Yet, far from being obsolescent cogs in the smooth workings of modernity, institutions of higher education are chief instigators of modern technological understanding and competence. They have encouraged these and much more, not mainly by serving industrial demands, commerce, political creeds, or medical corporations *directly,* but by perpetuating the beautiful but scarcely innate habits of disinterested inquiry, open debate, and independence from external intellectual or economic authority. As a case in point, Japan is now trying to "break out of the scientific ghetto of applied research, the long-favored emphasis on research with direct commercial applications" (French). By contrast, industry can gain much, even much more, from long-term investments. Andrew P. McMahon, the chair of molecular and cellular biology at Harvard, and Andrew W. Murray are among the recipients of a research gift from the pharmaceutical giant Merck. As reported by the *Harvard Crimson* (February 27, 2003), Murray believes that "the traditional contractual structure of academic industrial collaboration had a 'chilling' effect on the openness of scientific research and represented a 'poor return on investment for the industry.'" This gift assigns no specific project or problem, but the research it permits may be incredibly useful to Merck and many others.

• • •

To propose, in ignorance of what colleges and universities are actually good at, that society can enervate and abase the constitutive activities of higher education and yet continue, indefinitely, to obtain its derivative goods is a counsel of folly. A healthy system of higher education offers many collateral rewards: scientific discoveries, eventual and even unforeseen applications, thoughtful political leadership, intelligent public discourse, cultural vitality, and an educated workforce. But these will materialize only if the original spirit informing the institutions that produced them in the first place remains a spirit that is cherished. Again, we stress that in its capacity to generate an entelechy (see chap. 2), higher learning serves several goals in coordination, goals that are mutually reinforcing. The aims are at once personal and social, private and public, economic, ethical, and intellectual. To make any specific objective or set of objectives the defining aims of higher education is an exercise in common sense of the flat earth variety. It has been tried to a considerable extent in Great Britain, with what seem rather disastrous results (Annan; Gombrich; Wolf). Hot for quantitative measures of productivity and "excellence," much of British higher education has developed myopia so complete that few advocates of its new utility can see beyond the next hedgerow, or the next election. The newly appointed chancellor of Oxford, Chris Patten, a former diplomat, declared in 2003 "that the school must be run in a businesslike manner." His advocacy for increased access for families of lower incomes is welcome, but his stress on intellectual evaluation by "quantification" (his word) and on more training for job markets, whatever that means, misses both the historical and current strengths of the university he now heads ("New Chancellor"). Given its head, this attitude will before long reduce higher education to an obsequious dependent of the rest of society, not its independent servant. Eventually, higher education will produce mundane but no spectacular benefits, only the ones sought by external direction, not the surprising ones that come with the force of multiple blessings. If, on the other hand, there is courage to see the collateral rewards of higher education in their true colors—as the natural by-products of a healthy system focused on learning and thought—then those rewards will be obtained. They are and will be a dependable derivative benefit of higher education only so long as faith abides in higher education's *intrinsic* value. An easy insistence only on narrow, goals-oriented activity, however, will diminish higher education and choke off long-term benefits. If one argues to redirect the goals of higher education to the exclusion of a healthy symbiosis of the practical and theoretical, the applied and basic, then the expected collateral benefits will constrict and the educational system will degrade. Many things—higher education among them—are easier to preserve than to restore.

For an analogy, consider the national parks system, which provides recreational opportunities to tens of millions of people each year. Americans value the national parks primarily for recreational uses, which is understandable, since most visit them on vacation. But if, from now on, the parks were managed with recreation as the sole or even primary objective, the parks would cease to be preserves of natural country and habitat, and their recreational value would soon decline. Should that time arrive, there would be no going back. As Lech Wałesa said, it is easy to make fish soup out of an aquarium, but who can make an aquarium again out of fish soup?

Recreation in the parks is not in danger until the parks are. Recreation is a dependable derivative benefit of preserving the national parks in a natural condition. And in order for them to be maintained in that condition, tourist and recreational activities are necessarily regulated, even curtailed. Yet natural parks take up a great deal of space. As providers of relaxation and amusement, they are far less efficient and more expensive to maintain than artificial alternatives like theme and amusement parks, which make a profit. National parks should, of course, be managed as efficiently as possible, but their relative inefficiency compared to purpose-built, for-profit parks is no flaw, it is a condition of their very existence. Recreation and preservation are not mutually exclusive, but their interests are not identical, and when those interests clash in a serious way in a system like the national parks, it is preservation, ultimately, that must be preferred. Recreation can defer extensively to preservation without harm. But when preservation constantly yields to recreation, both, ironically, become subject to rapid decline.

This is the way it is with higher education and its relation to immediately practical objectives in society and the economy. There should be no firewall between the two, just as there should be no firewall between pure and applied research (there sometimes cannot be), but in each case the former cannot simply exist to serve the latter only and still preserve its intrinsic functions. Different institutions will contribute different parts to the overall equation, but the upward tension of a higher, long-term utility must be kept alive by those institutions that originally dedicated themselves to that ideal, the select liberal arts and sciences colleges and significant elements of the larger research universities. Moreover, higher education at present suffers a liability not generally shared by the national parks system. Very few people know in any detail what higher education is, how complex it is, why it takes the forms it does, and what functions it serves that no other institutions serve so well or so effectively.

Some critics are ready to portray the spoliation of higher education—the demotion of learning, the de-idealization, the importation of image-based values—as inevitable. They are wrong. The speed of light is inevitable, and the specific gravity of silver, and the passage of time. Voluntary human activities are not. In the words of the historian Hugh Trevor-Roper, "The irresistible is very often merely that which has not been resisted" (324). There are choices; there are things to do. It is up to us to do them. But let us begin by differentiating what is a choice from what is not. No evidence suggests that the fate of higher education is sealed. Those in it and those supporting it have many choices to make, and those choices will make a difference.

What Is to Be Done?

No reform of higher education will occur unless its leaders take the first step, which requires courage. As Aristotle observed, courage is the most important of all virtues, because without it none of the others can be exercised. This book has offered suggestions aimed at redirecting the contemporary college or university away from increasing atomization toward a more organic, cooperative, idealistic condition, yet one that will do no worse—in the long run, it will do better—in furthering technological advancement and economic well-being. (Twenty years ago, it was heresy to suggest that business practices that were ecologically responsible could reap both social benefits *and* more profits than environmentally dangerous practices; now it is commonly accepted.) Understood in a superficial way, concepts like "progress" (which cannot be blocked), "the market" (which must be deferred to), and the "information age" (to which lives must conform) are dangerous to the extent that they forestall thought and induce reflexive compliance. The philosopher Karl Popper writes,

> Neither nature nor history can tell us what we ought to do. Facts, whether those of nature or those of history, cannot make the decisions for us, they cannot determine the ends we are going to choose. It is we who introduce purpose and meaning into nature and into history. Men are not equal; but we can decide to fight for equal rights. Human institutions such as the state are not rational, but we can decide to fight to make them more rational. . . . It is up to us to decide what shall be our purpose in life, to determine our ends. (278)

Preserving and improving higher education is one such end, and a good one. Colleges and universities must be supported and promoted by those who esteem them for what they distinctively are and for what they uniquely can do, not for what they can be made to symbolize or for what they can be used to buy. They will be saved by solidarity, or not at all— by the solidarity of those who value them for their service to the ideals of learning, knowledge, thought.

Higher education cannot survive in any meaningful form—that is, as distinct from high school on the one hand and commerce on the other— unless its institutions inspire among their members, both transient and permanent, a rational loyalty to the institution and to the ideals it serves. "The responsible university has made its greatest contribution by sticking to its principles" (Ransom, 6). Students who value college only as an aid to doing well personally and who then go on to do well are perhaps a source of development money, but they drain the school's morale. Their loyalty is limited, almost contractual, and they will rarely advocate educational improvement or reform. A college that exhibits and expresses interest in learning and scholarship, however, has a good hope of reaching these students during their years there; a college that does not, has none. Furthermore, a college existing only to credential will alienate and disenchant a large segment of the student population eager for education but who will not, on their own, sift it out from heaps of classes. To scant labor-intensive teaching that gives freshmen and sophomores the rudiments to build on, or to exploit graduate students and adjuncts in order to devote more resources to fancier buildings, more administrative bureaucracy, or a few superstar faculty: these practices discourage all but the hardiest and most brilliant students and young scholars. And it has a follow-on effect of weakening upper-level classes. The graduates who emerge will be confused or enrolled among the cynics, because they will not have been exposed to the transformative, expansive experience of real education.

Aside from the manner and spirit of teaching, there is a specific topic of instruction that can be of great value in returning education to its mission. It has been all but ignored. Students at committed institutions do indeed experience education, if they wish to, but they often are obliged to do so willy-nilly, unadvised. A college or a university is a living, evolving thing. It has a relevant, individual history, in addition to sharing the history of higher education in general. As noted in chapter 2, it is anything but self-explanatory. What student (or teacher!) knows how American colleges resemble or differ from English universities, or Scottish, Chinese, or Continental ones? What student knows how and when college majors and specialized departments arose, or why? Who, on a campus full of Ph.D.'s and even Nobel laureates, has a clear idea of the history of the Ph.D.? American universities are, indeed, among the best in the world. But not to know why—and the reasons are historical—endangers that superiority.

The lack of this knowledge reinforces the impression held by many students that everything that happens on a college campus for any purpose other than career advancement or entertainment is empty ritual. They could and should be taught otherwise. If given pro forma or anti-quarian treatment, this teaching would only add to the problem it is supposed to remedy. Taught from a conviction and understanding of its active, continuing relevance to every scholar and student on campus, not only is it worth attempting, its worth may be inestimable.

Undeniably, a commercial, popular culture bombards the young with anti-intellectual slogans and innuendoes. It discourages reflection in countless ways. The resulting atmosphere is not conducive to sympathy with or understanding of higher education. Nonetheless, misconception of the purposes of higher education is not a student problem; it is a problem permitted to arise among students by faculty and administrators who do not comprehend higher education themselves, or who have abdicated their duty to transmit that comprehension. One cause of this dereliction is the widening divide between faculty and administration, a matter discussed in chapter 2. To a degree unconscionable—and with (sometimes) the exception of positions like provost or dean of faculty—many faculty members nationwide have washed their hands of the day-to-day dirty work of running the institution. They sit on endless departmental committees but have little to do with alumni, government, or difficult budgetary decisions. They have preferred, or have been forced, to turn educational decisions over to professional administrators who, no matter how conscientious, cannot reasonably be expected to understand the teaching and scholarly functions of a college or university in the way that a career teacher and scholar does. To repeat what is obvious but often forgotten: almost every budgetary decision is, in effect, an educational decision of some kind. If nonacademic professionals are running colleges as they would an insurance office or a generic NGO, is it really their fault? The unnatural segregation of faculty and administration sets up bad feeling and bad faith. It is a sad fact that many faculty members despise their administrators and are repaid in the same coin. Collegiality cannot stop at the department door—not at any healthy institution. When loyalty does not transcend mistrustful interest groups, self-interest can be counted on to replace dedication to learning as the common denominator. On a divided campus, self-interest is a purpose in common, but it is not a common purpose. Competing self-interest cannot replace the strong but collegial dialogue and disagreements that are components of good scholarship and sound management.

The ill-advised partitioning of faculty and administration helps to create a divided campus, but an even greater cause of fragmentation is disunity among the faculty. This is not to imply that faculties should be, or ever were, unified like a marching band. A level of mutual incomprehension may occur between fields like chemistry and classics, or art history and psychology; but the division into specialties and disciplines should not cause mistrust and animosity. As long as there is a general agreement on purposes, a college or university need not be—and perhaps, given the specialization of most research, cannot be—more than a confederation of departments. But when division becomes the order of the day, when discord attends lack of unity, then the pursuit of learning gives way to paralysis. Suspicion breeds suspicion.

Although the laboratory sciences, along with all other departments, bear some responsibility for the atomization of the modern college or university and the consequent diffusion of its energy, they are not chiefly at fault. Their declared area of study is, after all, physical phenomena. It is the social sciences and the humanities that claim for themselves the less orderly domain of human structures and intentions. The connecting purposes around which the multifarious parts of higher education coalesce, and the relation of colleges and universities to society, is surely their duty to explain. By virtue of their area of study and their history, the humanities above all inherit this responsibility. They are the traditional core of a highly traditional enterprise. They have the longest experience of what makes higher education distinct from other human endeavors; if teachers in the humanities cannot roughly agree on and to some extent embody a sense of higher education's general purposes, who can—or should? If other organizations, unlike and at times at odds with the distinctive mission of colleges and universities—government, the media, or commerce—succeed in parasitizing or absorbing higher education, the inaction of humanists will have played a decisive part.

The traditional independent college or university, whether public or private, needs the support of internal constituents and the backing of an external constituency. It needs faculty and administration who agree on some unique set of purposes that justifies the institution's existence, and who can, as a function of their teaching role, communicate that belief to students. (As explained in chap. 2, this set of purposes will vary from institution to institution, but must be well defined for each one.) Students are badly served if that belief, that dedication to learning and the pursuit of knowledge, is not implicit in the actions and expectations of faculty and administrators. After graduation, ex-students form the basic constituency of higher education. If they graduate without having been exposed to the ideals of higher education, in theory and in action, they can hardly be expected to extol and defend those ideals as alumni and parents.

Humanists have arrived at a fateful juncture and face questions they can no longer postpone. Is it worth it to them to agree that they should agree on anything in the way of a general ideal of education? Or, to put it differently, do they like what they have wrought? Many faculty members in the humanities have for decades—decades of their own retrenchment and decline—preached the doctrine of fragmentation in a variety of forms and have for their efforts reaped a harvest of fragments and fewer students. Small denominations reposition themselves with respect to one another without a discernible common purpose, but often with an appeal to objectivity as a common enemy. Absolute objectivity being unobtainable, and therefore absolutely impartial evaluation being equally unobtainable as well, all but a very restricted class of positions and assertions fall under automatic suspicion. The ambitious—or merely circumspect—humanist knows that affirming or pontificating on the elusiveness of objectivity is safe and doing it cleverly can provide professional advantages. Louis Menand argued in 1990—and things have not changed—that "what ought to be most distressing" in literary criticism "is the utter predictability of the great majority of the academic criticism that gets published" (38). The humanist knows that it is always safe and usually rewarding to take a position, though not necessarily an action, in support of the oppressed. Any other decision, affirmation, or evaluation often is either left unexpressed or else qualified within an inch of its life.

The vestiges of serious and sometimes effective protest movements can be seen in the limited menu of safe choices. To expose oppression and give voice to the voiceless recalls and depends on the memory of important past efforts. But the fight for civil liberties and tolerance has not for some time been centered on college campuses, and what at another time was advocacy for the downtrodden has, with few exceptions, settled into a status contest among the advocates. Constructive protest has dwindled or gone elsewhere, leaving behind a reflexive fear of hegemony and objectivity, of decisions and evaluations that are not programmatically (and therefore safely) political. Decision and evaluation—tainted by class, cultural, and generational biases, some of which in our lifetimes will not even have a name—remain the live third rail of the academic humanities. However, the ideal of pursuing knowledge carries with it the hegemonic possibility, even necessity, of some agreed-on standards for that pursuit, agreed on not by *dictat* but by conversation, debate, and compromise, and a shared sense of calling. Yet, this notion seems too dangerous or distasteful for many humanists to contemplate. Without noticing the irony, a few even decry it by claiming that their own judgment of the impossibility of shared standards should be precisely the standard everyone must share. Karl Popper, having been at the University of Vienna after World War I and therefore knowing how rapidly a great institution could deteriorate, puts the situation this way:

> [N]either logical argument nor experience can establish the rationalist attitude; for only those who are ready to consider argument or experience, and who have therefore adopted this attitude already, will be impressed by them. . . . [N]o rational argument will have a rational effect on a man who does not want to adopt a rational attitude. . . . [T]his means that whoever adopts the rationalist attitude does so because he has adopted, consciously or unconsciously, some proposal, or decision, or belief, or behavior; an adoption which may be called "irrational." Whether this adoption is tentative or leads to a settled habit, we may describe it as an irrational faith in reason. So rationalism is necessarily far from comprehensive or self-contained. . . . Since an "uncritical" rationalism is inconsistent, the problem cannot be the choice between knowledge and faith, but only between two kinds of faith. The new problem is: which is the right faith and which is the wrong faith? (230–31, 246)

Pinned in trenches by the friendly fire of humanist colleagues, and communicating with potential allies in other fields in a language often opaque, humanists are losing the struggle for a serious place in a serious academy, as well as for a serious place in society. Neither the prudential nor the aleatory approach to intellectual judgment will sustain higher learning in the humanities and social sciences much longer, above all because the ultimate effect of those approaches alienates the young. Obscure or sensational language and simulacra of intellectual daring may at first stimulate students by appealing to their forgivable desire for adult-sounding vocabulary and their age-appropriate wish to distress their elders. But when the thrill has passed, little curiosity remains to inspire another stage of intellectual development.

• • •

Rescuing the liberal arts and sciences from marginalization and rescuing the humanities from self-terrorized immobility will require a renewed faith in critical rationalism. This calls for an "emphasis upon argument and experience, with its device 'I may be wrong and you may be right, and by an effort we may get nearer the truth,' [an attitude] closely akin to the scientific method" (Popper, 238). Success in restoring that faith requires action and courage, and not, at first, the action and courage of graduate students and untenured faculty. The realities of the humanities job market are sufficient to deter any academic who is not guaranteed employment from attempting an open challenge to the status quo. The first stage of any challenge in this area belongs to scholars less vulnerable to criticism or retaliation. Tenured faculty discontented with the present state and wishing to see it modified will need to make those feelings public. If they have faith in reason and rational discourse, they will need to testify to that faith, in hiring committees and tenure decisions, in learned journals and classrooms. There are, of course, many campuses and departments where the prospect of publicizing such beliefs is not inviting, even to high-ranking professors; but continuing to conceal intellectual beliefs is worse. It gradually deprives one of professional integrity and satisfaction and leads nowhere at best, except perhaps to the bottle or an unhappy early retirement.

That said, speaking out on one's own can seem, and at times is, an exercise in futility, a mere gesture, quixotic and painful. Solidarity is all-important. Achieving it requires leadership. On some campuses, senior faculty can supply that leadership unaided, but an initiative by the administration offers the best hope of gaining support throughout the institution. Although lately many have been relegated—or relegated themselves—to the job of head fund-raiser or chief headhunter, college and university presidents are still the likeliest leaders. They have in the past, and can still now, set the intellectual tone for an institution. Their backing, even if at the start taking the form only of presidential addresses, could prove the deciding factor in mobilizing faculty reluctant to be lone martyrs but willing to make common cause with like-minded colleagues. Theodore Hesburgh describes this leadership: "The most important contribution a president can make to institutional advancement is to articulate his vision of the institution so persistently and persuasively that it becomes shared by all constituencies, internal and external, who adopt it as their own. Whatever else he is clear and enthusiastic about, the president must most of all elaborate his specific vision, re-think it as times change, perfect it as he learns from experience, and make his contribution to an evolving sense of institutional purpose" (1980).

In the search for faculty support, the sciences should not be ignored or permitted to sit out the fight. The world of scholarship is unified across disciplinary boundaries: humanists, social scientists, and scientists need to wake up to the fact that, in the battle to preserve the pursuit of knowledge and its ethical applications as the most defining activities of higher education, they are allies. The physical sciences deceive themselves if they think that the struggle for reason being played out in the humanities and social sciences does not concern them. The potential forces arrayed against science and technology cannot be underestimated. A weakening of the liberal arts and sciences to the point of debility—and that point is too near—would be a blow that cripples all of higher learning. It would more speedily deliver the laboratory sciences to the control of profit-driven or government-directed organizations. Less-"productive" sciences would join the social sciences and humanities in premature retirement. Ben Franklin's admonition to the signers of the Declaration of Independence remains apt advice today for academia as well: hang together or hang separately.

In "Five and a Half Utopias," Nobel physics laureate Steven Weinberg argues cogently about civilization, scientific research, and the free market: "Another thing that is manifestly not maximized by free markets is civilization. By 'civilization' I mean . . . the whole range of public and private goods that are there not merely to help keep us alive but to add quality to our lives. . . . The aspect of civilization that concerns me professionally is basic scientific research . . . research that cannot be justified by foreseeable economic benefits" (2000, 109). If only foreseeable economic benefits become what universities pursue militantly, then what we call civilization will suffer grievously.

Many citizens and scholars have sustained the multilayered, positive conception of higher education advocated in this book. Jefferson shared it. He founded the University of Virginia and ranked its founding as high as any of his other accomplishments. Washington shared it. Speaking eloquently of this conception in his Farewell Address, he regarded higher education as a bulwark against special and narrowly local interests. For him, it represented a common good. Robert E. Lee shared it. After the war, he served as president of Washington College (now Washington and Lee), and he made it one of the leading institutions of the nation. Frederick Douglass shared it. He considered education the first, indispensable step toward freedom. W. E. B. Du Bois shared it. He went from a small southern institution to the Ivy League to the University of Berlin, and then back to this country. His veneration of higher education informed his struggle for racial justice and his broad intellectual vision. Susan B. Anthony shared it. She advocated college training for women at a time when many thought it unthinkable. Elizabeth Cady Stanton shared it. A graduate of the Emma Willard School, she believed that advanced education and the development of civil rights are inseparable. Woodrow Wilson shared it. He arrived at the presidency from another presidency,

Princeton's, and, before that, positions at Johns Hopkins, the University of Virginia, Bryn Mawr, and Wesleyan. Andrew Carnegie shared it. He endowed 2,800 libraries, an institute for teaching, and a university. Andrew and Paul Mellon shared it. They strengthened Carnegie's university and established a philanthropic educational foundation. Dwight Eisenhower shared it. He too held a university presidency, that of Columbia, before election to the presidency. John Kennedy shared it. He believed in university life and, speaking in praise of Robert Frost, advocated a republic where the work of the artist can act as a check on the exercise of power.

All these men and women believed in the calling of higher education as a faith. And then, either as supporters or participants, they roused themselves to act. If no action is taken, then other institutions and other interests will outmaneuver, outtalk, outvote, and outspend what is great and good in American higher education, by degrees domesticating it as an indentured servant. Academic freedom and freedom at large support one another by a bond deeper than many casual observers surmise, and deeper even than most teachers credit. The independence of higher education is no less vital than individual freedoms, which in truth owe their first existence and no small part of their continued survival to the life of the mind, and to those who pursue and defend it.

ANNOTATED BIBLIOGRAPHY

CHE = *Chronicle of Higher Education*

Academe. Published by the American Association of University Professors. Starting with the July–August 1985 issue, the journal has useful tables based on reports of the National Association of State Universities and Land-Grant Colleges; since 1987 these have often appeared in the annual special issue devoted to the economic status of the profession.

Adams, John Quincy. 1810. *Lectures on Rhetoric and Oratory*. Cambridge, MA: Hilliard and Metcalf. Adams reflects on broader aims of liberal learning and on educating the professions of law, the clergy, and public service, all of which use rhetoric extensively.

American Freshman: National Norms, The. Los Angeles: Higher Education Research Institute, UCLA. Published annually, a standard study of student attitudes.

"American Higher Education: Toward an Uncertain Future." 1974–75. Special issue of *Daedalus* (Fall and Winter). See esp. pp. 1–38, essays by E. H. Gombrich, Northrop Frye, and Eric Weil on the humanities.

Amsterdam, Anthony G., and Jerome Bruner. 2000. *Minding the Law: How Courts Rely on Storytelling, and How Their Stories Change the Ways We Understand the Law—and Ourselves*. Cambridge, MA: Harvard Univ. Press. Examines the influence of cultural narratives and mythic structures on legal opinions, including those of the Supreme Court. This dovetails with discussions in chap. 8.

Angell, Marcia. 2000. "Is Academic Medicine for Sale?" *New England Journal of Medicine* 342 (May 18): 1516–18. Editorial sharply questioning the integrity of practices and results in academic research and clinical trials because of the financial and business interests involved.

Annan, Noel. 1999. *The Dons: Mentors, Eccentrics and Geniuses*. Chicago: Univ. of Chicago Press. A history of intellectual leaders of Oxbridge during the last two centuries. The last chapter, "Down with Dons," provides Annan's assessment of recent directions.

Appleyard, Joseph. 1982. "The Limited Prospects for Liberal Education." *Thought* 57, no. 225 (June): 234–56. Sane, perceptive; since proven correct in many of its judgments.

Arieti, Silvano. 1976. *Creativity: The Magic Synthesis.* New York: Basic Books.

Aronowitz, Stanley L. 2000. *The Knowledge Factory: Dismantling the Corporate University and Creating Higher Learning.* Boston: Beacon Press. This study takes a skeptical view of corporate developments characterizing the last three decades of higher education in the twentieth century (see discussion in chap. 1).

Ashby, Sir Eric. 1958. *Technology and the Academics: An Essay on Universities and the Scientific Revolution.* London: Macmillan. Thoughtful and historically grounded, this study examines connections between pure research and utility.

Association of American Universities. 1985. *Financing and Managing University Research Equipment.* Washington, DC: Association of American Universities, National Association of State Universities and Land-Grant Colleges, and Council on Government Relations.

Astin, Alexander W. 1992. *What Matters in College?* San Francisco: Jossey-Bass.

———. 1997. "Liberal Education and Democracy: The Case for Pragmatism." In *Education and Democracy: Re-imagining Liberal Learning in America,* ed. Robert Orrill, pp. 207–23. New York: College Entrance Examination Board.

Averill, Lloyd J. 1983. *Learning to Be Human: A Vision for the Liberal Arts.* Port Washington, NY: Associated Faculty Press. Acute criticisms and suggestions abound in this often-overlooked volume.

Avery, Christopher, Andrew Fairbanks, and Richard Zeckhauser. 2003. *The Early Admissions Game: Joining the Elite.* Cambridge, MA: Harvard Univ. Press. A thorough study based on empirical evidence concludes that the process can improve chances for acceptance but has gotten out of hand.

Axelrod, Paul Douglas. 1982. *Scholars and Dollars.* Toronto: Univ. of Toronto Press. Chap. 2, "Corporate Aid to Higher Education," is informative about business attitudes.

Axtell, James. 1998. *The Pleasures of Academe: A Celebration and Defense of Higher Education.* Lincoln: Univ. of Nebraska Press. Well intentioned and well informed but sees no real reason for alarm over higher education and accepts its current state somewhat uncritically.

Barber, Benjamin. 1989. "The Civic Mission of the University." *Kettering Review* (Fall): 67.

Barnes, Brooks. 2002. "Museums' New Mantra: Party On!" *Wall Street Journal,* July 19, sec. W.

Barnett, Ronald. 1990. *The Idea of Higher Education.* Ballmoor, Buckingham: Open Univ. Press. An important statement.

Barzun, Jacques. 1959. *The House of Intellect.* New York: Harper & Brothers. Especially pertinent are the essays "The Three Enemies of Intellect," "Education without Instruction," and "Philanthropic Businessmen and Bureaucrats."

————. 1968. *The American University.* New York: Harper & Row.

Bate, W. Jackson. 1986. Interview by John Paul Russo. In *Coleridge, Keats, and the Imagination,* ed. Robert J. Barth and John L. Mahoney, 201–18. Columbia: Univ. of Missouri Press.

Bell, Daniel. 1966. *The Reforming of General Education: The Columbia College Experience in Its National Setting.* New York: Columbia Univ. Press. Remains relevant almost four decades after its first publication.

Bellah, Robert. 1999. "Freedom, Coercion, and Authority." *Academe* (January–February): 17–21. Concern over higher education as merely an instrument for other, chiefly practical and economic, ends. The "market" is not identical with freedom, either academic or political.

————. 2000. "The True Scholar." *Academe* (January–February): 18–23. Morality and self-interest in higher education.

Ben-David, Joseph. 1983. "Research and Teaching in the Universities." In *The Western University on Trial,* ed. John W. Chapman. Berkeley and Los Angeles: Univ. of California Press.

Bondor, Thomas, and Carl E. Schorske, eds. 1997. *American Academic Culture in Transformation: Fifty Years, Four Disciplines.* Princeton: Princeton Univ. Press. Studies economics, English, political science, and philosophy; finds trends include the desire for theory, the use of "scientific" models, and the hope for direct utility in economics and political science.

Berg, Ivar. 1971. *Education and Jobs: The Great Training Robbery.* Boston: Beacon Press. A critique of American credentialism before the term was coined.

Berkman, Johanna. 2001. "Harvard's Hoard." *New York Times Magazine,* June 24, 36–41. Examines the nation's largest endowment and, by implication, the phenomena of endowment building and spending.

Berlin, Isaiah. 1988. "On the Pursuit of the Ideal." *New York Review of Books,* March 17, 11–18. Warns that entrenched ideologies often lose sight of their founding idealism.

Bérubé, Michael, and Cary Nelson, eds. 1995. *Higher Education under Fire: Politics, Economics, and the Crisis of the Humanities.* New York: Routledge. The introduction is articulate, very good on part-time graduate student labor and workloads in different disciplines. Authors defend the accomplishments of theory.

Birnbaum, Norman. 1973a. "The Carnegie Commission: The Politics of the Future." *Change* (November 1973): 28–37. Argues for higher education to produce a citizenry ready to critique as well as serve society.

————. 1973b. "Students, Professors, and Philosopher Kings." In *Content and Context,* ed. Carl Kaysen, 401–90. New York: McGraw-Hill.

Black, Max. 1962. *Models and Metaphors: Studies in Language and Philosophy.* Ithaca: Cornell Univ. Press. Black, an excellent thinker on the nature of metaphor, investigates processes of research and discovery in numerous fields through their shared use of metaphors and archetypes.

Blackburn, Robert T., and Mary Jo Clark. 1975. "An Assessment of Faculty Performance: Some Correlates between Administrator, Colleague, Student and
Self-Ratings." *Sociology of Education* 48 (Spring): 242–56. See esp. p. 244 on
the widespread assumption that teaching and research are positively related.

Bloom, Allan. 1987. *The Closing of the American Mind: How Higher Education
Has Failed Democracy and Impoverished the Souls of Today's Students.*
New York: Simon and Schuster. Indictment, by a professor at the University of Chicago, of liberal education in its failure to address basic questions
of the good, the true, and the just. Even if one disagrees, the book's intellectual argument cannot be dismissed as simply ideological or politically
motivated.

Bok, Derek. 1982. *Beyond the Ivory Tower: Social Responsibilities of the Modern University.* Cambridge, MA: Harvard Univ. Press.

———. 1990. *Universities and the Future of America.* Raleigh-Durham: Duke
Univ. Press. Bok, president of Harvard for almost twenty years, envisions
a university directly aiding society without becoming politicized or com-
promised by entanglements. He warns universities against setting up their
own for-profit companies, yet feels it appropriate for faculty to do so, or to
hire themselves out; how to track and stop conflicts of interest or of commitment depends, he admits, on how much the faculty care about the university. While admitting potential abuse and harm at every level, Bok remains confident that the system can be administered within acceptable
levels of risk.

———. 2003. *Universities in the Marketplace: The Commercialization of
Higher Education.* Princeton: Princeton Univ. Press. Bok reverses somewhat his rather sanguine assessment expressed in the 1980s and 1990s (see
discussion in chap. 1).

Bombardieri, Marcella. 2004. "What's Your Pleasure?" *Boston Globe,* March 11,
sec. B.

Boorstin, Daniel J. 1958. *The Americans.* New York: Vintage. Includes history
of higher education in the United States.

Booth, Wayne, ed. 1967. *The Knowledge Most Worth Having.* Chicago: Univ. of
Chicago Press. Booth leads off essays by ten distinguished hands. Not out-
dated in philosophical issues, often wise. Essays by Booth, Northrop Frye,
Richard McKeon, and Edward Levi are especially relevant.

———. 1987. *Idea of a University as Seen by a Rhetorician.* Chicago: Univ. of
Chicago Press. Unfortunately overshadowed by Bloom's book of the same
year, Booth offers a vision that began to wane a century ago but now, with
support from scholars such as Robert Scholes, might help revive a humanist undertaking tied not so much to particular subject matters as to
methods of approach and rhetorical skills with language.

Boutwell, W. K. 1973. "Formula Budgeting on the Down Side." *Strategies for*

Budgeting, New Directions for Higher Education 1, no. 2 (Summer): 41–50. Frank appraisal of reason for adjuncts: they're cheaper and can be fired.

Bowen, Howard R., and Jack H. Schuster. 1986. *American Professors: A National Resource Imperiled.* New York: Oxford Univ. Press. See esp. pp. 3–8, 113–62.

Boyer, Carol M., and Alfred Ahlfren. 1982. "'Visceral Priorities' in Liberal Education." *Journal of Higher Education* 53, no. 2 (March–April): 207–15.

Boyer, Ernest L. 1983. *High School.* New York: Harper & Row. See p. 99 for a table showing decline in high-school foreign-language enrollments since 1915.

Branch, Mark Alden. "Deciphering the Admissions Map." *Yale,* November 2000, 32–37. Reports on the bewildering, not always reassuring developments in college admissions practices and behaviors.

Breneman, David W. 2001. "Speaking Out, Giving Back." *Harvard Magazine,* January–February, 54.

Brinkman, Paul T. 1989. "Instructional Costs per Student Credit Hour: Differences by Level of Instruction." *Journal of Education Finance* 15 (Summer): 34–52. Also detects cross-subsidization. This article, by no means the hardest, gives some idea of the complexity of cost analyses.

Brod, Richard, and Bettina J. Huber. 1996. "The MLA Survey of Foreign Language Entrance and Degree Requirements, 1994–95." *ADFL Bulletin* 28 (Fall): 35–43. Both types of requirements are significantly less common than in 1965, but the trough was 1982–83. The situation is complex, the more so because stringency of requirements must be taken into account as well, and that is not the focus of this article. Our search of recent college catalogs revealed that among the most elite institutions, a year of foreign-language study often sufficed for the degree requirement—if there was any degree requirement at all.

———. 1997. "Foreign Language Enrollments in United States Institutions of Higher Education, Fall 1995." *ADFL Bulletin* 28 (Winter): 55–60. Foreign-language enrollments have lagged behind total enrollments for decades, settling into a steady low of just over 7.5 percent from 1977 on.

Brodhead, Richard H. 1994. "An Anatomy of Multiculturalism." *Yale,* April, 45–49. A critique both of multiculturalism, in its current form, and of those who are opposed to it in any form.

Bromwich, David. 1988. "The Cost of Professionalism in the Humanities." In *Learned Societies and the Evolution of the Disciplines,* 9–16. ACLS Occasional Paper no. 5. New York: American Council of Learned Societies.

———. 1991. "Higher Education and Group Thinking." *Raritan* 11, no. 1 (Summer): 32–42.

———. 1992. *Politics by Other Means: Higher Education and Group Thinking.* New Haven: Yale Univ. Press. Fears the inroads of new-style conformity in what should be a community fostering independent, individual thought and expression.

———. 1995. "A Note on the Romantic Self." *Raritan* 14, no. 4 (Spring): 66–74.

Bronner, Ethan. 1998. "Winds of Change Rustle University of Chicago." *New York Times,* December 28, sec. A.

Brooks, David. 2002. "Why the U.S. Will Always Be Rich." *New York Times Magazine,* June 9, 88–91, 124. The tone is given by the alternate title on the cover, "How Money Makes Americans Virtuous."

Brown, David K. 1995. *Degrees of Control: A Sociology of Educational Expansion and Occupational Credentialism.* New York: Teachers College Press. Interesting historical account of the growth of this phenomenon, dating it to the late 1880s and offering an explanation for the mainly irrational demand for bachelor's degrees that has sustained credentialism.

Bruner, Jerome. 1990. *Acts of Meaning.* Cambridge, Mass.: Harvard Univ. Press. The narrative imagination in the development of self in society.

Buckles, Stephen. 1978. "Identification of Causes of Increasing Costs in Higher Education." *Southern Economic Journal* 45 (July): 258–65. See esp. pp. 263–65.

Butterfield, Fox. 2003. "Politics and Economics Join in University Crisis." *New York Times,* July 22, sec. A.

Byrne, John A. 2003. "Goodbye to an Ethicist." *Business Week,* February 10, 38. Praise of Marvin Bower, once leader of McKinsey & Co.

Cahn, Steven M. 2003. "Unequal Professors." *New York Times,* September 6, sec. A.

Caplow, Theodore, and Reece J. McGee. 1958. *The Academic Marketplace.* New York: Basic Books. Identifies warning signs of the split between research and teaching, with teaching devalued; older but acute insights still relevant.

Cardwell, D. S. L. 1972. *Turning Points in Western Technology: A Study of Technology, Science and History.* New York: Neale Watson. Cardwell, who was head of history of science and technology at the University of Manchester, examines the relationship between science and technology through the mid-twentieth century.

Carnochan, W. B. 1993. *The Battleground of the Curriculum: Liberal Education and American Experience.* Stanford: Stanford Univ. Press. Provides historical perspective on the modern incarnation of liberal education since the late 19th century, using Stanford and Harvard as examples. Underscores the importance of personal models, and the ultimate aims of citizenship and democracy.

Catlin, Daniel, Jr. 1982. *Liberal Education at Yale: The Yale College Course of Study, 1945–1978.* Washington, DC: Univ. Press of America. Overview of Yale strategies and rationale.

Chait, Richard P. 1995. *The New Activism of Corporate Boards and the Implications for Campus Governance.* AGB Occasional Paper no. 26. Washington, DC: Association of Governing Boards of Universities and Colleges.

————. 2000. "Trustees and Professors: So Often at Odds, So Much Alike." *CHE,* August 4, B4–5.

Chaker, Anne Marie. 2003. "Tuition Soars at State Schools." *Wall Street Journal,* June 4, sec. D.

Chapman, John W. 1983. "The Western University on Trial." In *The Western University on Trial,* ed. Chapman. Berkeley and Los Angeles: Univ. of California Press.

Chronicle of Higher Education (CHE). The annual Almanac issue provides useful statistics.

Clark, Burton, R. 1983. *The Higher Education System: Academic Organization in Cross-National Perspective.* Berkeley and Los Angeles: Univ. of California Press. Comparative ways of setting up higher learning with some emphasis on liberal education. Does not argue for a single system.

Cohen, Morris R. 1944. *A Preface to Logic.* New York: Henry Holt. Incisive comments on the role of metaphor in knowledge. The title is misleading in that Cohen also discusses the arts and sciences, ethics and moral philosophy.

Coles, Robert. 1978. "The Humanities and Human Dignity." *Change* 10, no. 2 (February): 9, 63. What matters more about the humanities—specialized knowledge or something deeper?

Collins, Randall. 1979. *The Credential Society.* New York: Academic Press. On the disconnection between the degree of education actually needed to perform most jobs in the American economy and our perception of those education requirements. Collins originated the term *credentialism;* see pp. 15–16, 54, 91.

Collis, David. 1999. "When Industries Change: Scenarios for Higher Education." In *Forum Futures 1999,* ed. Maureen E. Devlin and Joel W. Meyerson, 47–70. Cambridge, MA: Forum for the Future of Higher Education. Collis continues his challenging analysis of the way in which higher education is changing economically—and rapidly—in *Forum* papers for 2000 and 2001.

Compton, Karl Taylor. 1955. *A Scientist Speaks.* Cambridge, MA: MIT Undergraduate Association. The president of MIT for nearly 20 years (1930–49) discusses education in science and the relationship of research to engineering and technical applications.

Condition of Education, The. Washington, DC: Department of Education, National Center for Education Statistics. Annual digest of statistics.

Connery, Robert H., ed. 1970. *The Corporation and the Campus.* New York: Praeger. See esp. Charles B. McCoy's "Criteria for Corporate Aid," 166–74.

Constans, H. Philip. 1980. *Fit for Freedom.* Washington, DC: Univ. Press of America. Explores the sad case of how we educate students—or rather don't—to be citizens. Centers on public schools.

Cox, Richard H. 1995. Introduction to John Locke, *Second Treatise of Government,* ed. Cox. Wheeling, IL: Harlan Davidson.

Creighton, Joanne V. 2000. Letter to the editor, *Nation* (June 5): 2.

Crosson, William. 1998/99. "'Only Connect': The Goals of a Liberal Education." *Key Reporter* 64, no. 2 (Winter): 2–4, adapted from his essay in *American Scholar* (Autumn 1998).

Daly, William T. 1994. "Teaching and Scholarship: Adapting American Education to Hard Times." *Journal of Higher Education* 65 (January–February): 45–57. See esp. p. 49.

Damrosch, David. 1995. *We Scholars: Changing the Culture of the University.* Cambridge, MA: Harvard Univ. Press. Universities need communities of the mind, not fiefs; fragmentation, selfishness, and entrenched camps are inimical to the best spirit of university life.

Dangerfield, Anthony. 1999. "The Myth of Utilitarian Education." *Loyola Magazine,* Winter, 15–19.

Davis, Michael. 1999. *Ethics and the University.* New York: Routledge. Informative on rise of professional ethics; claims links between universities and businesses should not endanger their fundamental differences but gives no specific examples.

Delbanco, Andrew. 1997. "The University Ideal vs. the Marketplace: Which Values Should Shape Our Financial Aid Policy?" *College Board Review* 181 (July): 17–30. Investigates the many complications in balancing the needs of institutions, students, and society. No prescriptive answers but strong analysis.

———. 1999. "The Decline and Fall of Literature." *New York Review of Books,* November 4, 32–38. Traces upheavals in recent teaching of literature and calls for a less materialistic, professionalistic attitude—a return to literature as a calling rather than an adjunct to other concerns.

Dembner, Alice. 2000. "Research Integrity Declines." *Boston Globe,* August 22, sec. E. Reports on Bethesda, MD, conference where evidence showed that economic motives had extensively infiltrated research ("profits do drive this business").

Devlin, Maureen E., and Joel W. Meyerson, eds. 2001. *Forum Futures 2000.* San Francisco: Jossey-Bass. These editors also compiled the 1998 and 1999 *Forum Futures;* the volumes contain valuable essays on the economics of higher education and challenges of technology, but other topics as well.

Dewey, John. 1916. *Democracy and Education.* New York: Macmillan. Cogent case for thinking about the two together; continues to inspire reflection (e.g., see Orrill, below).

Digest of Education Statistics. Washington, DC: Department of Education, National Center for Education Statistics. Published annually and supplies such information as national scores in the SAT and GRE exams and the national totals of degrees granted broken down by discipline.

"Distinctively American: The Residential Liberal Arts Colleges." 1999. Special issue of *Daedalus* (Winter). See esp. essays by Neely and by McPherson and Schapiro (cited below).

Donnelly, Fred. 2003. Review of Eric Gould, *The University in a Corporate Culture,* in *University Affairs* (7095 November), http://www.universityaffairs.ca/pdf/past_articles/2003/november/bookreview.pdf.

Drucker, Peter F. 1999. "Beyond the Information Revolution." *Atlantic Monthly,* October, 47–57. Knowledge workers, rather than capitalists, will increasingly call the shots.

"Drug Company's Efforts to Silence a Researcher, A: The Case of Nancy Olivieri." 1999. *Academe* (November–December): 25.

D'Souza, Dinesh. 1991. *Illiberal Education: The Politics of Race and Sex on Campus.* New York: Free Press. Sees common academic views as promoting conformity and a regime of correctness that stifles independent thought. A scalpel (or hatchet, depending on your view) ably sharpened.

Eden, Kathy. 2000. "Great Books in the Undergraduate Curriculum." *Literary Imagination* 2, no. 2 (Spring): 125–33. First published in *Academic Questions* 13, no. 2 (Spring 2000): 63–69. A sane, intelligent, calm, historically informed comment on the issue by the present director of Columbia University's common undergraduate curriculum.

Edmundson, Mark. 1997. "On the Uses of a Liberal Education: As Lite Entertainment for Bored College Students." *Harper's,* September, 39–49. Places the blame on society as much as or more than on educational institutions, which must reflect society. Cf. Shorris 1997b.

Ehrenberg, Ronald G. 2000a. "Private-College Trustees Must Control Costs." *CHE,* September 29, B14–15.

———. 2000b. *Tuition Rising: Why College Costs So Much.* Cambridge, MA: Harvard Univ. Press.

———. 2004. "Don't Blame Faculty for High Tuition." Annual Report on the Economic Status of the Profession 2003–04. *Academe* (March–April): 21–31.

Ehrenberg, Ronald G., and James Monks. NBER Working Paper 7227 on impact of *US News & World Report College Rankings,* http://nberws.nber.org.

Ehrenfield, David. 2000. "War and Peace and Conservation Biology." *Conservation Biology* 14 (February): 105–12.

Elfin, Mel. 2003. "Longtime Observer Gives Low Grade to Trends in U.S. Higher Education." *Key Reporter* 68, no. 2 (Winter): 9, 14. A former editor of the *US News & World Report College Guide* reflects on college costs, credentializing, standards, technology, and trustees—issues discussed in chaps. 2 and 3. Pithy and worth attention.

Eliot, Charles W. 1884. "What Is a Liberal Education?" *Century Magazine,* n.s., 6:203–12. A comprehensive view from more than a century ago, of both historical and continued interest.

———. 1913. *The Tendency to the Concrete and the Practical in Modern Education.* Boston: Houghton Mifflin.

Elliott, Deni, ed. 1995. *The Ethics of Asking: Dilemmas in Higher Education Fund Raising.* Baltimore: Johns Hopkins Univ. Press. Revealing; strong bibliography.

Elliott, Lloyd H. 2000. "How Much Does a College President Deserve to Be Paid?" *CHE*, March 10, A64. Worries over the drive to make higher education more like a business and its effects on educational CEOs.

Ellis, John. 1997. *Literature Lost*. New Haven: Yale Univ. Press. A thoughtful, not a knee-jerk, indictment of many developments in the humanities.

Engell, James. 2001. "The Idea of Organic Growth in Higher Education." In *Forum Futures 2000,* ed. Maureen E. Devlin and Joel W. Meyerson, 43–64. San Francisco: Jossey-Bass.

Engell, James, and Anthony Dangerfield. 1998. "The Market-Model University: Humanities in the Age of Money." *Harvard Magazine,* May–June, 48–55, 111.

Eulau, Heinz, and Harold Quinley. 1970. *State Officials and Higher Education.* New York: McGraw-Hill.

Fact Book on Higher Education, 1997 ed. 1998. New York: American Council on Education and Oryx Press. *Fact Book on Higher Education, 1989–90.* New York: American Council on Education and Macmillan, 1989–. A handy reference for trends in degrees granted, though the earlier edition—owing to later changes in format of the graphs—is easier to use and interpret.

Faculty Salary Survey of Institutions Belonging to National Association of State Universities and Land-Grant Colleges. Stillwater: Office of Institutional Research, Oklahoma State University. Published annually since 1974–75, this is the most authoritative source of information on trends in faculty salaries by discipline.

Fairweather, James Steven. 1996. *Faculty Work and Public Trust: Restoring the Value of Teaching and Public Service in American Life.* Needham Heights, Mass.: Allyn and Bacon. A more recent study tending to concur with Yuker 1984. See, e.g., pp. 86 and 110.

Federal Funds for Research, Development and Other Scientific Activities. Washington, DC: National Science Foundation. Series of reports covering the years 1950–81. With clear graphs and tables, these reports were very helpful in showing not only which agencies supported scientific research but also the extent and nature of that support. In 1979 the title of the series changed slightly, to *Federal Funds for Research and Development,* and shortly thereafter it was terminated, its only continuation being unreadable "detailed statistical tables."

Fellman, Bruce. 1999. "For God, For Country, and For Sale." *Yale,* March, 32–36. Products marketing colleges and vice versa.

Finn, Chester E. 1978. *Scholars, Dollars, and Bureaucrats.* Washington, DC: Brookings Institution. Notes, p. 117, that private institutions may be compelled to turn to "tuitions and fees" to make up losses in federal support.

Fisher, James L. 1997. "Advancement Professionals Who Would Be Presidents." In *The Advancement President and the Academy: Profiles in Institutional Leadership,* ed. Mary Kay Murphy, pp. 10–22. Phoenix: American Council on Education and the Oryx Press.

Fisher, James L., and Martha W. Tack, eds. 1988. *Leaders on Leadership: The College Presidency.* San Francisco: Jossey-Bass.

Foard, Douglas. 2001. "A Secretary's Reflections." *Key Reporter* 66, no. 4 (Summer): 1.

"Forum: Who Needs the Great Works?" 1989. *Harper's,* September, 43–52. Transcribed conversation and debate of prominent scholars on the question of a canon or core of humanistic readings. This exchange does not bifurcate along predictable lines.

Frank, Robert H. 2001. "Higher Education: The Ultimate Winner-Take-All Market?" In *Forum Futures 2000,* ed. Maureen E. Devlin and Joel W. Meyerson, 3–12. San Francisco: Jossey-Bass. Summarizes the importance and pressures of ranking and competition driven to their limits.

Freedman, James O. 1996. *Idealism and Liberal Education.* Ann Arbor: Univ. of Michigan Press. Intelligent and humane, occasionally utopian. Fine connections between law and literature.

———. 1999. "The Bully Lectern: Getting College Presidents Back on the Public Stage." *Harvard Magazine,* January–February, 36–39, 95. One key point: the lack of time for presidents to read, think, and reflect.

———. 2003. *Liberal Education and the Public Interest.* Iowa City: Univ. of Iowa Press. Essays by a veteran college president. "Preserving Liberal Education" is especially worthwhile.

French, Howard W. 2001. "Hypothesis: A Scientific Gap. Conclusion: Japanese Custom." *New York Times,* August 7, sec. A. Underscores economic importance of basic over narrowly conceived applied research.

Frye, Northrop. 1967. "The Instruments of Mental Production." In *The Knowledge Most Worth Having,* ed. Wayne Booth. Chicago: Univ. of Chicago Press.

"Future of the Research University." 2000. *Harvard Magazine,* September–October, 46–57, 102–5. Roundtable discussion with university presidents, deans, professors, and commentators.

Galbraith, John Kenneth. 1971. *The New Industrial State.* 2nd ed. rev. Boston: Houghton Mifflin. Key is "Education and Emancipation," pp. 372–80.

Garvin, David A. 1980. *The Economics of University Behavior.* New York: Academic Press. Explains how "prestige" is of greater practical value to an institution than "quality" and how more prestige can entail less quality.

Gass, William H. 1999. "In Defense of the Book." *Harper's,* November, 45–51. A defense and exposition of literate culture, the culture of reading.

Geiger, Roger L. 1993. "Research Universities in a New Era: From the 1980s to the 1990s." In *Higher Learning in America, 1980–2000,* ed. Arthur Levine, 67–85. Baltimore: Johns Hopkins Univ. Press.

Harvard University, Committee on the Objectives of a General Education in a Free Society. *General Education in a Free Society.* 1945. Cambridge, MA: Harvard University Press. Commonly known as *The Red Book.* Harvard's plan for liberal education developed under James Conant flourished from just after WWII to the late 1970s.

Getz, Malcolm, and John J. Siegfried. 1991. "Costs and Productivity in American Colleges and Universities." In *Economic Challenges in Higher Education,* ed. Charles T. Clotfelter et al. Chicago: Univ. of Chicago Press. On pp. 296–97, they express the reasonable presumption of funding agencies that external funding will not support more than its designated project.

Giamatti, A. Bartlett. 1981. *The University and the Public Interest.* New York: Atheneum. The chapters on liberal education and the humanities dovetail with his call for universities as a public trust.

———. 1988. *A Free and Ordered Space: The Real World of the University.* New York: W. W. Norton. His last major statement is eloquent. Battered by labor and faculty rifts at Yale, Giamatti managed in seven years to name new deans and heads to almost every faculty and college; that he could retain idealism is a tribute to the strength and effectiveness of his ideals.

Gibson, Eric. 2002a. "Big Shows, Crowds: J. Carter Brown's Troubled Legacy." *Wall Street Journal,* June 20, sec. D.

———. 2002b. "Forget Lord Elgin: New Museum Head Faces Heavier Woes." *Wall Street Journal,* July 19, sec. W.

Gitlin, Todd. "The Liberal Arts in an Age of Info-Glut," http://chronicle.com /colloquy/98/liberalarts/background.shtml. Emphasis on democratic spirit of liberal arts—how it can avoid being drowned out.

Givler, Peter. 1999. "Scholarly Books, the Coin of the Realm of Knowledge." *CHE,* November 12, A75. University presses as responsible for publishing scholarship, but pressed for money.

Goethals, George, Gordon Winston, and David Zimmerman. 1999. "Students Educating Students: The Emerging Role of Peer Effects in Higher Education." In *Forum Futures 1999,* ed. Maureen Devlin and Joel W. Meyerson, 25–45. Cambridge, MA: Forum for the Future of Higher Education.

Goldberger, Marvin L., Brendan A. Maher, and Pamela Flattau. 1995. *Research-Doctorate Programs in the United States: Continuity and Change.* Washington, DC: National Academy Press. An important study conducted by the National Research Council documenting changes in research-doctorate programs grouped according to discipline and quality ranking; see esp. pp. 45–50.

Golden, Daniel. 2001. "How Colleges Reject the Top Applicants—and Boost Their Status." *Wall Street Journal,* May 29, sec. A.

———. 2003. "At Many Colleges, the Rich Kids Get Affirmative Action." *Wall Street Journal,* February 20, sec. A.

Gombrich, Richard F. 2000. "British Higher Education Policy in the Last Twenty Years: The Murder of a Profession," http://www.ucl.ac.uk/~ucgadkw /position/gombrich/uk-higher-education.html. A passionate account of the negative effects that practical incentives and quantitative measures have visited on British universities.

Goodheart, Eugene. 1997. "Reflections on the Culture Wars." *Daedalus* (Fall): 153–75. A truly wise reflection.

Gould, Eric. 2003. *The University in a Corporate Culture.* New Haven: Yale Univ. Press. Strong points include a call for greater education in the service of democracy, but the book assumes that the corporate university and its trends are "hegemonic" (see discussion in chap. 1).

Graham, Hugh Davis, and Nancy Diamond. 1997. *The Rise of American Research Universities.* Baltimore: Johns Hopkins Univ. Press. Among other things, questions the validity of the NRC's ranking of research-doctorate programs. But see also p. 83 for remarks on the painful contraction of institutions following excessive expansion.

Grant, Daniel. 2002. "Show and Sell? Gottlieb Exhibition Crosses a Line." *Wall Street Journal,* October 31, sec. D.

Grant, George. 1975. "The University Curriculum and the Technological Threat." In *The Sciences, the Humanities, and the Technological Threat,* ed. W. Roy Niblett. London: Univ. of London Press.

Grassmuck, Karen. 1991. "Throughout the 80's, Colleges Hired More Non-teaching Staff Than Other Employees." *CHE,* August 14, A22. Administrative growth nationwide.

Gray, Hanna H. 1980. Interview, *Educational Record* 61, no. 4 (Fall): 6–11. The then president of the University of Chicago looks ahead to a decade that would bring more competition and constraints; the interview ranges widely and most remains directly relevant.

Griswold, Alfred Whitney. 1959. *Liberal Education and the Democratic Ideal and Other Essays.* New Haven: Yale Univ. Press. One of several works to cement democratic ideals with liberal education as mutually dependent.

Gustafson, James M. 1991. "Ethics: An American Growth Industry." *Key Reporter* 56, no. 3 (Spring): 1–5.

Haack, Susan. 1998. *Manifesto of a Passionate Moderate: Unfashionable Essays.* Chicago: Univ. of Chicago Press. Pertinent for the humanities and for values of learning at large. Chaps. 3, 8 (on multiculturalism), and 11 ("Preposterism and Its Consequences") are most germane. Haack decries the corruption of the academy by money, economic self-interest, and false professionalism.

Hafner, Katie. 2002. "Lessons Learned at Dot-Com U." *New York Times,* May 2, sec. E. Distance education experiences a rough start: "The groves of academe are littered with the detritus of failed e-learning startups."

Hand, Learned. 1959. *The Spirit of Learned Hand.* Ed. Irving Dilliard. New York: Alfred A. Knopf.

Hansen, W. Lee. 1985. "Salary Differences across Disciplines." *Academe* 71 (July–August): 6–7.

Hansmann, Henry. 1990. "Why Do Universities Have Endowments?" *Journal of Legal Studies* 19 (January): 3–42. Extremely interesting analysis.

———. 1999. "Higher Education as an Associative Good." In *Forum Futures 1999,* ed. Maureen E. Devlin and Joel W. Meyerson, 11–24. Cambridge, MA: Forum for the Future of Higher Education. The fact that students care who their peers are affects the economics of higher education.

Hanson, Victor Davis, and John Heath. 1998. *Who Killed Homer? The Demise of Classical Education and the Recovery of Greek Wisdom.* New York: Free Press. A well-argued case for the ancient Western classics and their broader place in the college curriculum; has upset some specialists.

Haskins, Charles Homer. 1957 [1923]. *The Rise of the Universities.* Ithaca: Cornell Univ. Press.

Hawkins, Brian L., and Patricia Battin, eds. 1998. *The Mirage of Continuity: Reconfiguring Academic Information Resources for the 21st Century.* Washington, DC: Council on Library and Information Resources and Association of American Universities. The quality of these essays on the digital revolution is uneven but hits high spots. John Seely Brown and Paul Duguid's "Universities in the Digital Age" (pp. 39–60) is good on what universities do, less so on what they should do. Some essays touch on broader issues, for the premise of the volume is that the digital revolution changes everything.

Healy, Patrick. 2000. "Glitch Releases College 'Ranks' Early." *Boston Globe,* August 31, sec. B.

Hearn, James. 1992. "The Teaching Role of Contemporary American Higher Education: Popular Imagery and Organizational Reality." In *The Economics of American Higher Education,* ed. William E. Becker and Darrell R. Lewis. Norwell, MA: Kluwer Academic Publishers. Traces the growing emphasis on specialization and specialized research back to the rise of majors and departments in the early 20th century; includes striking accounts of the distaste for teaching exhibited by many bright and ambitious academics.

Heath, Douglas. 1976. "What the Enduring Effects of Higher Education Tell Us about a Liberal Education." *Journal of Higher Education* 47, no. 2 (March–April): 173–90.

Heinzelman, Kurt. 1986. "The English Lecturers at Austin: Our New M.I.A.'s." *Academe* (January–February): 25–31.

Heisenberg, Werner. 1974. *Across the Frontiers.* Translated by Peter Heath. New York: Harper & Row.

Heller, Scott. 2000. "The Lessons of a Lost Career." *CHE,* May 26, A18–22.

Herschbach, Dudley. 1996. "Teaching Chemistry as a Liberal Art." *Liberal Education* 82 (Fall): 2–9. A renowned scientist argues how science is part of "the human adventure."

Hesburgh, Theodore M. 1980. "Presidential Leadership: The Keystone for Advancement." In *Presidential Leadership in Advancement Activities,* ed. J. L. Fisher. San Francisco: Jossey-Bass.

———. 1981. "The Future of Liberal Education." *Change* 13 (April): 40–46. Direct and sensible.

Hirsch, E. D., Jr. 1987. *Cultural Literacy: What Every American Needs to Know.* Boston: Houghton-Mifflin. In clear language makes an indispensable point too often ignored in education that has become too theory laden and averse to general knowledge, surveys, or any memorization. The book has spawned others and an institute.

Hirsch, Werner Z., and Luc E. Weber, eds. 1999. *Challenges Facing Higher Education at the Millennium.* Phoenix: American Council on Education and Oryx Press. Aside from Ikenberry's essay (see below), those by David P. Gardner and Hirsch are among the noteworthy.

Hoenack, Stephen A. 1990. "Costs within Higher Education Institutions." In *The Economics of American Universities: Management, Operations, and Fiscal Environment,* ed. Hoenack and Eileen L. Collins. Albany: State Univ. of New York Press. See pp. 143–45 on the benefits to certain administration objectives of "incomplete and ambiguous information" regarding the internal allocation of university resources; see p. 148 on the lack of empirical studies of actual rates of depreciation.

Hoffmann, Roald. 2003. "Why Buy That Theory?" *Cornell University Arts and Sciences Newsletter,* Summer, 3–4, 6. Reprinted from *American Scientist* 91, no. 1 (2003). This Nobel laureate touches on the importance of narrative and storytelling for scientific investigation.

Hofstadter, Richard. 1963. *Anti-intellectualism in American Life.* New York: Knopf. Valuable as a fine historical account of how intellectualism—typified by the humanities—could ever fall into such low esteem in the United States, and as an eloquent argument for the life of the mind.

Hofstadter, Richard, and Wilson Smith, eds. 1961. *American Higher Education: A Documentary History.* 2 vols. Chicago: Univ. of Chicago Press. A cache of primary materials covering more than three centuries.

Holub, Robert C. 1994. "Professional Responsibility: On Graduate Education and Hiring Practices." *Profession,* 79–86. Criticizes the widespread and unscrupulous overproduction of Ph.D.'s—see esp. p. 83.

Hook, Sidney, Paul Kurtz, and Miro Todorovich, eds. 1974. *The Idea of a Modern University.* Buffalo, NY: Prometheus Books. Essayists include Daniel P. Moynihan, Oscar Handlin, and Nathan Glazer.

Hopkins, David S. P., and William F. Massy. 1981. *Planning Models for Colleges and Universities.* Stanford: Stanford Univ. Press. Massy's earlier, more status-quo view of internal allocations at research universities.

"How to Influence People and Gain Degrees." 2002. *Financial Times,* March 30–31, 7.

Hoxby, Caroline M. 2001. "The Return to Attending a Highly Selective College: 1960 to the Present." In *Forum Futures 2000,* ed. Maureen E. Devlin and Joel W. Meyerson, 13–42. San Francisco: Jossey-Bass.

Huber, Bettina J. 1992. "Characteristics of Foreign Language Requirements at US Colleges and Universities: Findings from the MLA's 1987–89 Survey of Foreign Language Programs." *ADFL Bulletin* 24 (Fall): 8–16. See esp. p. 13, where Huber reports that "one-year requirements appear to have gained ground during the 1980s."

Hutchins, Robert Maynard. 1936. *The Higher Learning.* New Haven: Yale Univ. Press. The University of Chicago's famous president—appointed at age 30—outlines views forcefully. Chap. 3 is entitled "General Education."

———. 1952. *The Great Conversation: The Substance of a Liberal Education.* Vol. 1 of *Great Books of the Western World.* Chicago: Encyclopaedia Britannica. Some find here the best case for a curriculum based on key common ideas and texts.

Ikenberry, Stanley O. 1999. "The University and the Information Age." In *Challenges Facing Higher Education at the Millennium,* ed. Werner Z. Hirsch and Luc E. Weber. Phoenix: American Council on Education and Oryx Press. Synoptic but considerably more thoughtful than many essays on the subject.

Institute for Higher Education Policy. 1998. *Reaping the Benefits: Defining the Public and Private Value of Going to College.* March. Washington, DC: The Institute.

Jacoby, Russell. 1994. *Dogmatic Wisdom: How the Culture Wars Divert Education and Distract America.* New York: Doubleday.

Jaffe, Bernard. 1976. *Crucibles: The Story of Chemistry: From Ancient Alchemy to Nuclear Fission.* 4th ed. New York: Dover.

James, Estelle. 1986. "Cross-Subsidization in Higher Education: Does It Pervert Private Choice and Public Policy?" *Private Education and Public Policy,* ed. Daniel C. Levy. New York: Oxford Univ. Press. Since the late 1970s, James's research has raised the possibility of "cross-subsidization."

Johnstone, D. Bruce. 1995. "Learning Productivity: A New Imperative for American Higher Education." In *Higher Education in Crisis: New York in National Perspective,* ed. William C. Barba. Speaks more of intellectual than economic productivity, a distinction at times unclear and which itself cries out for analysis without gainsaying the economic value of much intellectual work.

Jones, Howard Mumford. 1959. *One Great Society.* New York: Harcourt, Brace.

Kampf, Louis. 1968. "The Humanities and Inhumanities." *Nation,* September 30, 309–13. Incisive analysis of a trend that would become dominant in the following three decades: education serving business.

Kane, Thomas J. 2001. "Assessing the U.S. Financial Aid System: What We Know, What We Need to Know." In *Ford Policy Forum,* ed. Maureen Devlin, pp. 25–34. Cambridge, MA: Forum for the Future of Higher Education. A paper delivered to the forum in 2000.

Karabell, Zachary. 1998. *What's College For? The Struggle to Define American Higher Education.* New York: Basic Books. Sharp commentary mindful of the variety of higher education in the U.S. Warns we cannot expect it to be a panacea.

Katz, Seth R. 1995. "Graduate Programs and Job Training." *Profession*, 63–67. The pressure to publish within a "teaching institution," p. 64.

Katz, Stanley. 2001. "Don't Confuse a Tool with a Goal: Making Information Technology Serve Higher Education, Rather Than the Other Way Around." In *The Internet and the University*, ed. Maureen Devlin, Richard Larson, and Joel Meyerson, 29–43. Cambridge, MA: Forum for the Future of Higher Education and Educause. The question of means and ends wisely applied to technology.

Kauffman, Joseph. 1993. "Governing Boards." In *Higher Learning in America, 1980–2000*, ed. Arthur Levine. Baltimore: Johns Hopkins Univ. Press, pp. 222–39. One of the best short pieces on governing boards. See also his 1980 *At the Pleasure of the Board: The Service of the College and University President* (Washington, DC: American Council on Education).

Kaufmann, Walter. 1977. *The Future of the Humanities.* New York: Reader's Digest Press.

Kelley, Michael A. 2000. "Political Science and Post-Tenure Review." *PS: Political Science & Politics* (June), www.findarticles.com/cf_0/m2139/2_33 /63787150/. Astute study of complexities of post-tenure review, not at all confined to political science.

Kennedy, Donald. 1997. *Academic Duty.* Cambridge, MA: Harvard Univ. Press. Among good observations rests a too easily satisfied sense that things are not so bad and that conflicts of interest can be handled without much fuss.

———. 2002. "The New School Spirit." *New York Times,* January 5, sec. A. The former president of Stanford muses on the changing landscape of academic loyalty: "I confess I rather liked the old world in which loyalty was easier to keep track of."

Keohane, Nannerl O. 2001. "Becoming Nimble, Overcoming Inertia." *Harvard Magazine,* January–February, 55–56.

Kernan, Alvin, ed. 1997. *What's Happened to the Humanities?* Princeton: Princeton Univ. Press. A conspectus of views, well-articulated, looking over the last quarter of the 20th century.

———. 1999. *In Plato's Cave.* A memoir of his academic life as professor and administrator. Diffuse, occasionally strong insights; seems deeply conflicted on developments since the 1970s.

Kerr, Clark. 1963. *The Uses of the University.* Cambridge, MA: Harvard Univ. Press. The title rightly suggests Kerr's somewhat utilitarian, pragmatic outlook, too sanguine about the connections between universities, large corporations, and businesses, and too satisfied to see the generation of a multiversity. His later *Great Transformation in Higher Education, 1960–1980* (Albany: SUNY Press, 1991) is a more diffuse continuation of themes established earlier.

Kerr, Clark, and Marian L. Gade. 1987. "The Contemporary College President." *American Scholar* (Winter): 29–44. Stresses circumstance as well as character and claims that the results of leadership are hard to ascribe to one over the other.

Kimball, Bruce. 1995. *Orators and Philosophers: A History of the Idea of Liberal Education.* New York: College Entrance Examination Board.

Kimball, Roger. 1990. *Tenured Radicals: How Politics Has Corrupted Our Higher Education.* New York: Harper & Row. Akin to Sykes's books (see below) but more sophisticated; not a book to be dismissed out of hand.

Kirn, Walter. 2002. "Acceptance." *New York Times Magazine,* August 25, 15–16. Discusses admissions, merit, the need to be selective, and the "Princeton hacking scandal." Kirn concludes that the idea or myth of meritocracy is deeply cherished.

Kirp, David L. 2000. "The New U." *Nation,* April 17, 25–29. Reviews Stanley Aronowitz's *The Knowledge Factory* and James J. Duderstadt's *A University for the 21st Century;* identifies the mix of commercial markets and learning as key to higher education; unafraid to make judgments.

———. 2001. "Hurricane Hugo: Following the Stormy Departure of Its President, the University of Chicago Reconsiders His Legacy." *Lingua Franca* 11, no. 3 (April). Balanced report on tensions between money and mission at a university proud of its unique emphasis on the latter, but troubled by a chronic shortfall of the former.

———. 2004. "And the Rich Get Smarter." *New York Times,* April 30, sec. A. A cogent summary of arguments against giving market forces their head.

Kirp, David L., et al. 2003. *Shakespeare, Einstein, and the Bottom Line: The Marketing of Higher Education.* Cambridge, MA: Harvard Univ. Press. This book offers useful, readable explorations of how budget choices are being made at targeted institutions from various strata—chiefly elite schools, but with forays into distance learning. Generally critical of recent trends, the criticisms are dotted about rather than developed as a set of cohesive arguments.

Kirschling, Wayne R. 1979. "Conceptual Problems and Issues in Academic Labor Productivity." In *Academic Rewards in Higher Education,* ed. Darrell R. Lewis and William E. Becker Jr. Cambridge, MA: Ballinger. Useful in providing yet another review of ways one might think about "productivity" in higher education.

Knight Foundation, Commission on Intercollegiate Athletics. 2001. *A Call to Action: Reconnecting College Sports and Higher Education.* Miami: John S. and James L. Knight Fund. An incisive analysis of college sports in relation to the goals of higher education, this superb report includes historical background and specific reforms.

Konrad, Alison M., and Jeffrey Pfeffer. 1990. "Do You Get What You Deserve? Factors Affecting the Relationship between Productivity and Pay." *Administrative Science Quarterly* 35 (June): 258–85. More on the thorny concept of "productivity."

Kors, Alan Charles, and Harvey A. Silverglate. 1998. *The Shadow University.* New York: Free Press. Includes thoughtful analysis of speech codes and enforced political correctness.

Krimsky, Sheldon. 2003. *Science in the Private Interest: Has the Lure of Profits Corrupted Biomedical Research?* Lanham, MD: Rowman & Littlefield. The author sees, and documents, increasing conflicts of interest that taint the integrity of scientific research (see discussion in chap. 1).

Krueger, Alan B., and Mikael Lindahl. 2000. *Education for Growth: Why and for Whom?* NBER Working Paper 7591. Cambridge, MA: National Bureau of Economic Research. Challenges the research indicating that increases in educational attainment are unrelated to economic growth.

Kuh, George D., et al. 2001. *National Survey of Student Engagement: Technical and Norms Report.* Bloomington: Indiana University Center for Postsecondary Research and Planning. A commendably painstaking and rigorous digest of student self-reports on the quality of their college experience. Prefatory comments on methodology are useful and self-aware about limitations. Not for casual reading but a valuable resource.

Labaree, David F. 1997. *How to Succeed in School without Really Learning: The Credentials Race in American Education.* New Haven: Yale Univ. Press. Adeptly contrasts three sometimes compatible, sometimes competing educational objectives: democratic equality, social efficiency, and social mobility.

LaFleur, Richard A. 1993. "Foreign Languages, the Classics, and College Admissions." *ADFL Bulletin* 24 (Spring): 29–35. The late 1960s through the 1970s were the darkest days for foreign-language programs; measures taken in response have borne some fruit.

Langer, Susanne K. 1974. *Philosophy in a New Key: A Study in the Symbolism of Reason, Rite, and Art.* 3rd ed. Cambridge, MA: Harvard Univ. Press. This classic work dovetails with discussions in chaps. 6, 8, and 9 and complements the work of Vico and Bruner; it argues powerfully for the interrelated nature of human intellectual and cultural activities and retains vital implications for education at large.

Lapham, Lewis. 1988. *Money and Class in America: Notes and Observations on Our Civil Religion.* New York: Weidenfeld & Nicolson.

Lasch, Christopher. 1979. *The Culture of Narcissism.* New York: W. W. Norton. Implications for education at every level.

Lennington, Robert. 1996. *Managing Higher Education as a Business.* Phoenix: American Council on Education and Oryx Press.

Leonhardt, David. 2004. "As Wealthy Fill Top Colleges, New Efforts to Level the Field," http://www.nytimes.com/2004/04/22/education/22COLL.html.

Levine, Arthur. 1980. *When Dreams and Heroes Died: A Portrait of Today's College Student.* San Francisco: Jossey-Bass and the Carnegie Foundation for the Advancement of Teaching. Pinpoints trends in student attitudes that grew pronounced in the ensuing decades: loss of idealism, worry over money, higher education as job training, diminished curiosity.

————, ed. 1993. *Higher Learning in America, 1980–2000.* Baltimore: Johns Hopkins Univ. Press.

————. 1997. "How the Academic Profession Is Changing." *Daedalus* (Fall): 1–20. Relying on inclusive surveys, Levine finds reassuringly little change in professors' dedication to teaching; once one concentrates on institutions with an established research culture, however, the picture changes markedly.

Levine, Arthur E. 2001. "Transforming Technologies." *Harvard Magazine,* January–February, 59–60.

Lewin, Tamar. 2003. "4 Highest-Paid University Presidents Top $800,000 a Year." *New York Times,* November 10, sec. A.

Lewis, Lionel S., and Philip G. Altbach. 1996. "Faculty versus Administration: A Universal Problem." *Higher Education Policy* 9:255–58.

Lewontin, Richard. 2000. *The Triple Helix.* Cambridge, MA: Harvard Univ. Press. Begins with a meditation on the use of metaphor in science.

Lipset, Seymour Martin. 1994. "In Defense of the Research University." In *The Research University in a Time of Discontent,* ed. Jonathan R. Cole, et al. Baltimore: Johns Hopkins Univ. Press. The status quo has many advocates; this essay is especially enthusiastic for things as they are.

Liu, Alan. 1999. "Knowledge in the Age of Knowledge Work." *Profession,* 113–24. One of the best analyses of the changing relation of education to business with regard to the knowledge both seek; see also Liu's website: http://humanitas.ucsb.edu/liu/palinurus/.

Lively, Kit, and Scott Street. 2000. "The Rich Get Richer: The Wealthiest Universities Report Spectacular Returns on Investments." *CHE,* October 13, A49–52. Endowments, their growth and spending.

Losco, Joseph, and Brian L. Fife. 2000. "Higher Education Spending: Assessing Policy Priorities." In *Higher Education in Transition: The Challenges of the New Millennium,* ed. Losco and Fife. Westport, CT: Bergin & Garvey. Their analysis of expenditures is highly useful.

Lueck, Sarah. 2000. "University of Pennsylvania Will End Gene-Therapy Research on Humans." *Wall Street Journal,* May 25, sec. A.

MacIntyre, Alasdair. 1999. "The Recovery of Moral Agency?" *Harvard Divinity Bulletin* 28, no. 4: 6–10. Assesses contemporary moral issues; theorizes that theory is insufficient: the moral life is personal and active or nothing.

Maher, Brendan A. 1996. "The NRC's Report on Research-Doctorate Programs: Its Uses and Misuses." *Change* (November–December): 54–59.

Mamet, David. 1997. *True and False: Heresy and Common Sense for the Actor.* New York: Random House. Another pertinent kind of education.

Mancing, Howard. 1994. "A Theory of Faculty Workload." *ADFL Bulletin* 25

(Spring): 32–37. See esp. p. 33 on institutional hypocrisy and pp. 36–37 on unfair weighting of teaching time.

Mander, Jerry. 1978. *Four Arguments for the* Elimination *of Television.* New York: Quill. Cranky and abrupt at times, but a strong argument.

Mangan, Katherine S. 2000. "Harvard Weighs a Change in Conflict-of-Interest Rules: The University May Relax Financial Restrictions to Prevent Researchers from Leaving." *CHE,* May 19, A47–48.

Marc, David. 1995. *Bonfire of the Humanities: Television, Subliteracy, and Long-Term Memory Loss.* Syracuse: Syracuse Univ. Press.

Marcum, Deanna, and Clifford Lynch. 2002. "Preservation of Scholarship: The Digital Dilemma." Paper presented at the Forum for the Future of Higher Education, Aspen.

Mariantes, Liz. 2000. "What Ivory Tower?" *Christian Science Monitor,* January 25, 20.

Martin, Everett Dean. 1926. *The Meaning of Liberal Education.* New York: W. W. Norton. Holds more than historical interest. This and Van Doren's book (see below) reveal marked continuities as well as change.

Martin, Randy, ed. 1998. *Chalk Lines: The Politics of Work in the Managed University.* Durham, NC: Duke Univ. Press.

Marx, Anthony W. 2003. "Academia for Sale (Standards Included)." *New York Times,* May 17, sec. B.

Marx, Leo. 1975. "Technology and the Study of Man." In *The Sciences, the Humanities, and the Technological Threat,* ed. W. Roy Niblett, 3–20. London: Univ. of London Press.

Massy, William F. 1990. "Commentary." In *Higher Education in a Changing Economy,* ed. Katharine H. Hanson and Joel W. Meyerson, 78–84. New York: Macmillan. Candidly expresses the growing persuasion of the vice president for business and finance at Stanford University that "cross-subsidization" of research and graduate studies by undergraduate studies indeed exists.

Massy, William F., and Robert Zemsky. 1994. "Faculty Discretionary Time: Departments and the 'Academic Ratchet.'" *Journal of Higher Education* 65 (January–February): 1–22.

Mathews, Anna Wilde. 2002. "Entertainment Companies Aim to Thrill Museum Throngs." *Wall Street Journal,* November 25, sec. B.

Maull, Nancy. 1998. Unpublished paper. Harvard University.

McCullough, David. 2002. "History?" *Reader's Digest,* December, 87–89. A short reflection—and warning—about the direction in which the study of history is heading in higher education, written by a Pulitzer Prize–winning historian and biographer.

McDowell, George R. 2001. *Land-Grant Universities and Extension into the 21st Century: Renegotiating or Abandoning a Social Contract.* Ames: Iowa

State Univ. Press. Deeply thoughtful on the fate of land-grant institutions. This study covers technical education, service, extension, and community outreach. Treats different faculties with equity and urges a more engaged stance, a renewal of the original vision.

McGinn, Daniel. 2000a. "Poison Ivy: Campaigns on Campus." *Newsweek,* February 28, 50–52.

———. 2000b. "Failing Grades: A Small College Hits the Skids." *Newsweek,* September 25, 62.

McGinn, Daniel, and John McCormick. 2000. "The Boom Generation." *Newsweek,* February 7, 26–29.

McKeon, Richard. 1964. "The Liberating Arts and the Humanizing Arts in Education." In *Humanistic Education and Western Civilization: Essays for Robert M. Hutchins,* ed. Arthur A. Cohen. New York: Holt, Rinehart and Winston.

McPherson, Michael S., and Morton Owen Schapiro. 1999. "The Future Economic Challenges for the Liberal Arts Colleges." In "Distinctively American: The Residential Liberal Arts Colleges," special issue of *Daedalus* (Winter): 47–75.

———. 2001. "Beyond One-Upsmanship." *Harvard Magazine,* January–February, 58–59. Some institutions, such as Harvard, can help break the deadlock of positional ranking competition.

McPherson, Michael S., Morton Owen Schapiro, and Gordon C. Winston. 1993. *Paying the Piper: Productivity, Incentives, and Financing in U.S. Higher Education.* Ann Arbor: Univ. of Michigan Press. Chap. 3, "The Concept of Productivity," is germane to topics in this book. Chap. 13, "Why Are Capital Costs Ignored by Nonprofit Organizations and What Are the Prospects for Change?" is a fascinating look at how colleges and universities often fail to account for real—and large—capital costs.

Mead, George Herbert. 1967 [1934]. *Mind, Self, and Society; from the Standpoint of a Social Behaviorist.* Chicago: Univ. of Chicago Press. Examines the growth and education of the self in light of the phenomenon of language (see chap. 8).

Meltz, Barbara F. 2003. "With TV So Loud, No One's Listening." *Boston Globe,* November 6, sec. H.

Menand, Louis. 1990. "Lost Faculties." *New Republic,* July 9–16, 36–40.

———, ed. 1996. *The Future of Academic Freedom.* Chicago: Univ. of Chicago Press. Cogent essays by various hands.

Merritt, Jennifer. 2002. "For MBAs, Soul-Searching 101." *Business Week,* September 16, 64, 66.

Merton, Robert K. 1970. *Science, Technology and Society in Seventeenth-Century England.* New York: Howard Fertig. First published in 1938, this volume seeks the origins of the impact of experimental science on society and education.

————. 1973. *The Sociology of Science: Theoretical and Empirical Investigations.* Chicago: Univ. of Chicago Press.

Middaugh, Michael F., and David E. Hollowell. 1992. "Examining Academic and Administrative Productivity Measures." In *Containing Costs and Improving Productivity in Higher Education,* ed. Carol S. Hollins. San Francisco: Jossey-Bass. For administrative expansion, see pp. 61–62.

Miles, Jack. 1999. "The Liberal Arts and Intellectuals in Exile." *Cross Currents* 49 (Fall): 304–19. The senior adviser to the president at the J. Paul Getty Trust makes a plausible case that those practicing the liberal arts will find themselves a small minority on campuses; the new home of the liberal arts may be institutions and venues other than colleges and universities.

Miller, Zell. 2000. "10 Crucial Things the Next President Should Do for Colleges." *CHE,* July 14, B4–6. Former governor of Georgia, now professor at the University of Georgia, has recommendations a cut above what most politicians offer.

Minogue, Kenneth R. 1973. *The Concept of a University.* London: Weidenfield and Nicolson. A wonderful book by a political scientist, unfortunately given little play in America; especially pertinent is the chap. "The Academic and the Practical Worlds."

Montgomery, David C. 2003. "Marketing Science, Marketing Ourselves." *Academe,* www.aaup.org/publications/Academe/03so/03somont.htm.

Moore, Robert M., and Jeanne Rattenbury. 2004. "10 Practical Questions about Branding." *Trusteeship* (March–April): 13–17. Advice culled from "campus marketing professionals." Institutions of higher learning are discussed in terms that make them all but indistinguishable from commercial enterprises.

Mortenson, Thomas. 1999. "Educational Opportunity by Family Income 1970 to 1997." *Postsecondary Educational Opportunity,* no. 86 (August).

Moulakis, Athanasios. 1994. *Beyond Utility: Liberal Education for a Technological Age.* Columbia: Univ. of Missouri Press. Cogent and intelligent but handicapped by a format of numerous, disjointed short chapters.

Mowery, David C., and Richard R. Nelson, et al. 2001. "The Growth of Patenting and Licensing by U.S. Universities: An Assessment of the Effect of the Bayh-Dole Act of 1980." *Research Policy* 30:99–119. This fine study with excellent historical background stresses the new role played by biotechnology in more closely linking research to immediate use. They conclude that the 1980 act did not discourage basic research, still healthy, but that it possibly inhibits sharing the results of that research.

Muller, Steven. 1981. "Higher Education and Free Enterprise: Making Common Cause." *Educational Record* (Winter): 21–22. Calls for a mutually beneficial alliance between higher education and business.

Munn, R. F. 1989. "The Bottomless Pit, or the Academic Library as Viewed from the Administration Building." *College & Research Libraries* 50:635–37. Why administrators wince at library costs, and the future of libraries.

Murphy, Mary Kay, ed. 1997. *The Advancement President and the Academy: Profiles in Institutional Leadership.* Phoenix: American Council on Education and Oryx Press.

National Commission on the Role and Future of State Colleges and Universities. 1986. *To Secure the Blessings of Liberty.* Washington, DC: American Association of State Colleges and Universities.

National Research Council, Board on Human-Resource Data and Analyses. 1978. *A Century of Doctorates: Data Analyses of Growth and Change.* Washington, DC: National Academy of Sciences. Good graphs and tables for rates of change in the granting of doctorates.

National Salary Survey by Discipline and Rank. Washington, DC: College and University Personnel Association. This study, published annually since 1982–83 in two volumes—one for public institutions, one for private—includes data from a great many smaller colleges. The *Faculty Salary Survey of Institutions* (cited above), however, is more consistent.

National Science Foundation. 1964. *Comparisons of Earned Degrees Awarded 1901–1962.* Washington, DC.

Neely, Paul. 1999. "The Threats to Liberal Arts Colleges." In "Distinctively American: The Residential Liberal Arts Colleges," special issue of *Daedalus* (Winter): 27–45.

Nelson, Cary, and Stephen Watt. 1999. *Academic Keywords: A Devil's Dictionary for Higher Education.* New York: Routledge. Alphabetical entries include affirmative action, tenure, and the like; points out great inequalities in higher education (e.g., large, growing underclass of untenured teachers); criticizes the economics of higher education; research and anecdote.

Nelson, Deborah, and Rick Weiss. 2000. "Penn Ends Gene Trials on Humans." *Washington Post,* May 25, sec. A.

Nevins, Allan. 1962. *The State Universities and Democracy.* Urbana: Univ. of Illinois Press. A wonderfully balanced history, with analysis and intellectual depth, of the first century of these institutions.

"New Chancellor Calls for Businesslike Oxford." 2003. *Boston Globe,* June 26, sec. A.

Newman, John Henry. *The Idea of a University.* 1996 [1859, 1873]. Ed. Frank M. Turner. New Haven: Yale Univ. Press. A text that must be read; this edition contains critical essays.

Niblett, W. Roy, ed. 1975. *The Sciences, the Humanities, and the Technological Threat.* London: Univ. of London Press. Not as reactionary as the title suggests. Leo Marx's essay is sharp, as are those by George Grant, George Tolley, and Richard S. Peters (Marx, Grant, Peters listed here).

Nicklin, Julie L., and Goldie Blumenstyk. 1993. "Number of Non-Teaching Staff Members Continues to Grow in Higher Education." *CHE,* January 6, A43–46. Administrative growth nationwide (4.5 percent in two years during the early 1990s recession).

Nisbet, Robert. 1971. *The Degradation of the Academic Dogma: The University in America, 1945–1970.* New York: Basic Books. Universities serve society indirectly but are becoming enmeshed in doing so directly, a mistake. Although he can seem absolute, even reactionary, Nisbet is learned, not naive, and has excellent historical perspective.

Nixon, Andrew. 2003. "An Unfair Deal for Part-Time UMass Faculty." *Boston Globe,* November 12, sec. A.

Noam, Eli. 1998. "Electronics and the Decline of Books: The Transformation of the Classroom." In *Forum Futures 1998,* ed. Maureen E. Devlin and Joel W. Meyerson, 83–88. New Haven, CT: Forum Publishing. A virtual screed against books in the name of the virtual—certainly, in some fields, better, but Noam is a prophet of apocalyptic change.

Noll, Roger G., and William P. Rogerson. 1998. "The Economics of University Indirect Cost Reimbursement in Federal Research Grants." In *Challenges to Research Universities,* ed. Noll. Washington, DC: Brookings Institution. Frank and clear, their benchmark scheme seems a real improvement over current practices.

"Numbers." 1999. *Time,* August 16, 21.

Nussbaum, Martha C. 1997. *Cultivating Humanity: A Classical Defense of Reform in Liberal Education.* Cambridge, MA: Harvard Univ. Press. Many good points but some untested assumptions, particularly in characterizing others who may not agree with those good points; the fine chapter "The Narrative Imagination" dovetails with chap. 8 in the present volume.

O'Brien, Dennis. 1998. *All the Essential Half-Truths about Higher Education.* Chicago: Univ. of Chicago Press. Somewhat impatient and desultory, but chap. 10, "Synthetic Morality," pp. 170–201, is a highlight.

O'Donnell, James. 1998. *Avatars of the Word: From Papyrus to Cyberspace.* Cambridge, MA: Harvard Univ. Press. Classics and the history of the book through the electronic age; chaps. 7 and 8 focus on ramifications of technological change for liberal and higher education.

O'Harrow, Robert, Jr. 2000. "Academic Research under the Microscope: Faculty Members' Business Interests Stir Controversy." *Washington Post,* August 5, sec. A.

O'Neill, June. 1971. *Resource Use in Higher Education: Trends in Ouputs and Inputs, 1930–1967.* Berkeley: Carnegie Commission on Higher Education. See esp. pp. 4–6.

Opdyke, Jeff D. 2000. "An Athletic Arms Race." *Wall Street Journal,* August 23, sec. B.

Orrill, Robert, ed. 1997. *Education and Democracy: Re-imagining Liberal Learning in America.* New York: College Entrance Examination Board. A valuable book with strong essays, e.g., Charles W. Anderson, "Pragmatism, Idealism, and the Aims of Liberal Education"; Douglas C. Bennett (president of Earlham), "Innovation in the Liberal Arts and Sciences"; and Alexander W. Astin (listed above).

Palmer, Stuart. 1998. *The Universities Today: Scholarship, Self-Interest, and Politics.* Washington, DC: Univ. Press of America. Not synthetic in overall argument—minichapters on specific subjects make that impossible—but passionate, informed, and clear-sighted on several topics, including the need for leadership and fair-mindedness rather than continued internal wrangling and defensiveness.

Park, Shelley M. 1996. "Research, Teaching, and Service: Why Shouldn't Women's Work Count?" *Journal of Higher Education* 67, no. 1 (January–February): 46–84. Much of what she says about women faculty in general could be said about humanities faculty; of all fields, the percentage of women is highest in the humanities.

Parkinson, C. Northcote. 1957. *Parkinson's Law.* Cambridge, MA: Riverside Press.

Pattenaude, Richard L. 2000. "Administering the Modern University." In *Higher Education in Transition,* ed. Joseph Losco and Brian L. Fife, 159–75. Westport, CT: Bergin & Garvey. Commonsensical, the ideas are not bad but rather bland, often platitudes. Does not discuss knotty academic or intellectual issues; adopts a vague business model.

Paulos, John Allen. 1988. *Innumeracy.* New York: Hill and Wang. Not only do we not use numbers well, but using numbers isn't always the best method to measure complex human realities.

Payton, Robert L. 1989. "The Ethics and Values of Fund Raising." In *The President and Fund Raising,* ed. James L. Fisher and Gary H. Quehl. New York: Macmillan and the American Council on Education. Warns against dollars as the only measure of presidential success, yet recognizes importance of fund-raising.

Peirce, C. S. 1940. *The Philosophy of Peirce: Selected Writings.* Ed. Justus Buchler. London: Routledge & Kegan Paul.

Pelikan, Jaroslav. 1992. *The Idea of the University: A Reexamination.* New Haven: Yale Univ. Press. A superb commentary, studded with insights and relevance, on Newman's original text.

Peters, Richard S. 1975. "Subjectivity and Standards." In *The Sciences, the Humanities, and the Technological Threat,* ed. W. Roy Niblett. London: Univ. of London Press.

Petersen, Melody. 2003a. "Scientists Urge Journal Policy on Disclosures." *New York Times,* August 22, sec. A.

———. 2003b. "Uncoupling Campus and Company." *New York Times,* September 23, sec. F.

Pfinster, Allan O. 1984. "The Role of the Liberal Arts College: A Historical Overview of the Debates." *Journal of Higher Education* 55, no. 2 (March–April): 145–70. Focuses on three periods of significant change in American liberal arts and sciences colleges.

Podgórecki, Adam. 1997. *Higher Faculties: A Cross-National Study of University Culture.* Westport, CT: Praeger. One of a few international comparative studies; based on extensive interviews and research.

Popper, Karl Raimund. 1963. *The Open Society and Its Enemies,* vol. 2: *The High Tide of Prophecy.* 4th ed. rev. New York: Harper & Row.

Postman, Neil. 1985. *Amusing Ourselves to Death.* New York: Viking Penguin. Critique of the pervasive influence of entertainment and TV: everything, including higher education, becomes entertainment to be consumed, or else passed by as too difficult.

————. 1993. *Technopoly.* New York: Vintage. A denunciation of the willingness of society to indenture itself to technology, coupled with a warning that culture is succumbing to "information glut."

————. 1995. *The End of Education: Redefining the Value of School.* New York: Knopf. Intelligent and important.

Powell, Alvin. 2000. "Rising Research Tide Lifts Math, Physical Sciences." *Harvard University Gazette,* December 14, 4. Reports on importance of basic research and its eventual, unforeseen impacts.

President's Committee on the Arts and the Humanities. 1997. *Creative America: A Report to the President.* Washington, DC: The Committee. John Brademas's committee sees a national role for the humanities.

Pritchett, Henry S. 1905. "Shall the University Become a Business Corporation." *Atlantic Monthly,* September, 289–99. His question and answers remain provocative.

Proctor, Robert. 1988. *Education's Great Amnesia: Reconsidering the Humanities from Petrarch to Freud.* Bloomington: Indiana University Press. An attempt to regain principles and goals; concentrates on humanities.

Pruitt, George A. 1988. "Some Good Advice." In *Leaders on Leadership: The College Presidency,* ed. James L. Fisher and Martha W. Tack, 31–35. San Francisco: Jossey-Bass. And it is. Pruitt served as president of Thomas A. Edison State College, Trenton.

Ransom, Harry Huntt. 1982. *The Conscience of the University and Other Essays.* Ed. Hazel H. Ransom. Austin: Univ. of Texas Press. A mixed collection but some outstanding words on basic university governance and policy.

Rauch, Jonathan. 1993. *Kindly Inquisitors: The New Attacks on Free Thought.* Chicago: Univ. of Chicago Press. Sees a rising tide of censorship, including within higher education.

Readings, Bill. 1996. *The University in Ruins.* Cambridge, MA: Harvard Univ. Press. Thought-provoking analysis of changes in the function of universities, a bit vitiated by speculations about decline of the nation-state.

Reeves, Hubert. 1984. *Atoms of Silence.* Cambridge, MA: MIT Press.

Reich, Robert B. 2000. "How Selective Colleges Heighten Inequalities." *CHE,* September, B7–10. Argues that selective higher education is worsening the gap between well-to-do and just-getting-by.

Reuben, Julie A. 1996. *The Making of the Modern University: Intellectual Transformation and the Marginalization of Morality.* Chicago: Univ. of Chicago Press. A broadly intelligent historical survey of, and commentary on, the tensions between fact, objectivity, moral authority, and ethical education in American higher education.

Rivlin, Alice M. 1961. *The Role of the Federal Government in Financing Higher Education.* Washington, DC: Brookings Institution.

Roche, George. 1994. *The Fall of the Ivory Tower: Government Funding, Corruption, and the Bankrupting of American Higher Education.* Washington, DC: Regnery. Lacking in understanding of and unsympathetic to higher learning, but not wholly wrong in some of its criticism.

Rojstaczer, Stuart. 1999. *Gone for Good: Tales of the University Life after the Golden Age.* New York: Oxford Univ. Press. Things have not changed for the better, but instead of proposing reforms or raising strong protests, this book tries to make the best of what has become worse.

Root-Bernstein, Robert Scott. 1984. "Creative Process as a Unifying Theme of Human Cultures." *Daedalus* (Summer): 197–219.

Rosenberg, Nathan. 2000. *Schumpeter and the Endogeneity of Technology: Some American Perspectives.* London: Routledge. Excellent chapters on the relationship between science and technology and American universities as "endogenous institutions."

Rosovsky, Henry. 1990. *The University: An Owner's Manual.* New York: W. W. Norton. Telling anecdotes and pragmatic advice on administration. Glances at educational policy and ideas.

———. 2002. "No Ivory Tower: University and Society in the Twenty-first Century." In Werner Z. Hirsch and Luc E. Weber, *As the Walls of Academia Are Tumbling Down.* London: Economica.

Roszak, Theodore. 1994. *The Cult of Information.* Berkeley and Los Angeles: Univ. of California Press.

Rothschild, Michael, and Lawrence J. White. 1993. "The University in the Marketplace: Some Insights and Some Puzzles in Studies of Supply and Demand." In *Higher Education,* ed. Charles T. Clotfelter and Michael Rothschild. Chicago: Univ. of Chicago Press. Argues (pp. 13–16) against Estelle James by asserting that undergraduates and parents wouldn't pay so much for an education at research universities if they weren't getting something in return; no doubt they are getting "something," but too often it is not rigorous classroom instruction.

Rowland, Christopher. 2004. "Firms Abandoning Antibiotics Research." *Boston Globe,* March 13, sec. A.

Rudolph, Frederick. 1962. *The American College and University: A History.* New York: Knopf.

———. 1977. *Curriculum: A History of the American Undergraduate Course of Study since 1636.* San Francisco: Jossey-Bass.

Russell, Susan Higley. 1991. *Profiles of Faculty in Higher Education Institutions, 1988.* Washington, DC: Department of Education, National Center for Education Statistics. See table 3.17 on p. 114 for a general idea of the significance of consulting income in various disciplines.

Rutenberg, Jim. 2002. "Big MTV on Campus?" *New York Times,* February 18, sec. C. Inroads of institutionally approved televised entertainment in colleges, much of it with nil intellectual content.

Said, Edward W. 1999. "Restoring Intellectual Coherence." *MLA Newletter* (Spring): 3–4. Said tries to turn humanists back to larger purposes, not infighting; warns of possible negative effects of a "deepening alliance" between universities and corporations.

Sapir, Edward. 1921. *Language.* New York: Harcourt, Brace.

Sarason, Seymour B. 1998. "Some Features of a Flawed Educational System." *Daedalus* (Fall): 1–12. Rightly emphasizes the need for systemic reform and the failure of views pointing the finger at one issue only.

Schiffrin, André. 1999. "Payback Time: University Presses as Profit Centers." *CHE,* June 18, B4–5.

Schubert, William Henry. 1980. *Curriculum Books: The First Eighty Years.* Washington, DC: University Press of America. Useful, with fine bibliography.

Schumpeter, Joseph A. 1950. *Capitalism, Socialism, and Democracy.* 3rd ed. New York: Harper & Brothers.

———. 1991. *The Economics and Sociology of Capitalism.* Ed. Richard Swedberg. Princeton: Princeton Univ. Press.

Schuster, Jack H. 1995. "Speculating about the Labor Market for Academic Humanists: 'Once More unto the Breach.'" *Profession,* 56–61. A tellingly guarded intimation of renewed interest in teaching.

"Science Economy, The." 2000. *Harvard University Gazette,* December 14, 1, 4.

Scott, Peter. 1984. *The Crisis of the University.* London: Croom Helm. A sharp, trenchant English perspective. Scott edited the *Times Higher Education Supplement.*

Sellers, M. N. S., ed. 1994. *An Ethical Education: Community and Morality in the Multicultural University.* Oxford: Berg.

"Selling Out? Corporations on Campus." 2001. Special issue of *Academe* (September–October). See esp. essays by Nancy P. Goldschmidt and James H. Finkelstein on college presidents populating corporate boards, and Jennifer L. Croissant on the "conflation of student and consumer."

Shapiro, Harold. 1997. "Cognition, Character, and Culture in Undergraduate Education: Rhetoric and Reality." In *The American University: National Treasure or Endangered Species,* ed. Ronald G. Ehrenberg, pp. 58–99. Ithaca: Cornell Univ. Press.

Shils, Edward. 1997a. *The Calling of Education: The Academic Ethic and Other Essays on Higher Education,* ed. Steven Grosby. Chicago: Univ. of Chicago

Press. Lays out basic tenets of responsibilities and duties of academic life and appointments; defines and defends academic freedoms.

———. 1997b. *The Order of Learning: Essays on the Contemporary University.* New Brunswick, NJ: Transaction. Blunt and informative, full of insight, occasionally dismissive and authoritarian. Regards the humanities as betrayed by childish opportunists who will never help govern the universities, whose basic values they question simplistically.

Shorris, Earl. 1997a. *New American Blues.* New York: W. W. Norton. Includes observations on the perversity of the culture wars in the humanities.

———. 1997b. "On the Uses of a Liberal Education: As a Weapon in the Hands of the Restless Poor." *Harper's,* September, 50–59. The liberating effects of education for some of those long without it.

Shulman, James L., and William G. Bowen. 2001. *The Game of Life: College Sports and Educational Values.* Princeton: Princeton Univ. Press.

Signs of Trouble and Erosion: A Report on Graduate Education in America. 1983. Washington, DC: National Commission on Student Financial Assistance.

Simon, John G., Charles W. Powers, and Jon P. Gunnemann, eds. 1972. *The Ethical Investor: Universities and Corporate Responsibility.* New Haven: Yale Univ. Press. Discusses not only university investments but the more complex links between education, business, profits, and academic freedom.

Singh, Jagjit. 1959. *Great Ideas of Modern Mathematics: Their Nature and Use.* New York: Dover. Helpful on the history of the relationship between, and the reciprocity of, "pure" and "utilitarian" science and mathematics.

Slaughter, Sheila, and Larry L. Leslie. 1997. *Academic Capitalism: Politics, Policies, and the Entrepreneurial University.* Baltimore: Johns Hopkins Univ. Press. Significant research and careful findings; more descriptive than driven by a vision of what should or might be.

Sleeper, Jim. 2001. "Harvard's New Leader, Global Capitalism, and the Liberal Arts." *CHE,* April 13, B20.

Smith, Charles W. 2000. *Market Values in American Higher Education: The Pitfalls and Promises.* Lanham, MD: Rowman & Littlefield. Astute analyses; see esp. "Why Education Seems So Expensive," "Expanding Academic Administration," and "Real Issues Confronting Higher Education."

Smith, Hedrick. 1995. *Rethinking America.* New York: Random House.

Stauffer, Thomas M. 1980. "Higher Education's Responsibilities for Economic Renewal." *Educational Record* 61 (Fall): 4–5. As the nation sees itself slipping economically, higher education is asked to contribute to the rescue because the economic health of both are seen to be linked.

Stein, Ronald H., and Stephen Joel Trachtenberg. 1993. *The Art of Hiring in America's Colleges and Universities.* Buffalo, NY: Prometheus Books.

Steinberg, Jacques. 2003. "A New College Ranking System, Wanted or Not." *New York Times,* October 8, sec. A.

Steneck, Nicholas H. 1994. "Ethics and the Aims of Universities in Historical

Perspective." In *An Ethical Education: Community and Morality in the Multicultural University,* ed. M. N. S. Sellers. Oxford: Berg.

Stille, Alexander. 1998. "The Betrayal of History." *New York Review of Books,* June 11, 15–20. Reviewing textbooks in American history, Stille uncovers the distortion, dumbing down, and jazzing up that characterize many. He finds Joy Hakim's *A History of US* a refreshing exception.

———. 2001. "Grounded by an Income Gap." *New York Times,* December 15, sec. A. Relates the persistent and at times widening income gaps in the U.S. to education and college education in particular.

Straub, Hans. 1964 [1949]. *A History of Civil Engineering.* Translated by Erwin Rockwell. Cambridge, MA: MIT Press. Instructive on how disjointed and then seredipitous the relation of pure science to engineering technology can be.

Strauss, Valerie. 2000. "For Students, No Dodging the Drafts." *Washington Post,* May 23, sec. A. Developments in student writing.

Sullivan, Constance. 1999. "The Corporatized Research University and Tenure in Modern Language Departments: Notes from Minnesota." *Profession,* 86–95.

Sykes, Charles. 1988. *Profscam: Professors and the Demise of Higher Education.* Washington, DC: Regnery Gateway.

———. 1990. *The Hollow Men: Politics and Corruption in Higher Education.* Washington, DC: Regnery Gateway. This and his earlier book document— who doubted it?—real abuses and ideological cadres; will sober the naive idealist, but Sykes has his own ideological edge, too. Anecdote threatens to overwhelm evidence.

Symonds, William C. 2003. "College Admissions: The Real Barrier Is Class." *Business Week,* April 14, 66, 68.

Taylor, John. 1989. *Circus of Ambition: The Culture of Wealth and Power in the Eighties.* New York: Warner Books.

Teitel, Jay. 2001. "Something Rotten in the State of the Arts." *University of Toronto Magazine,* Spring, 12–17. The arts can and do have a healthy relationship to the market; their usefulness is underrated.

Thresher, B. Alden. 1966. *College Admissions and the Public Interest.* New York: College Entrance Examination Board.

Tompkins, Ellsworth, and Walter H. Gaumnitz. 1954. "The Carnegie Unit: Its Origin, Status, and Trends." U.S. Department of Health, Education, and Welfare Bulletin 7, 1–58. A helpful description of the Carnegie Unit, with arguments for and against its utility in secondary education. Since it has fallen out of favor, we have lost our closest approximation to an objective measure of quantity of foreign-language instruction—and in language acquisition quantity of classroom time is a component of quality of learning.

Toulmin, Stephen. 1972. *Human Understanding.* Princeton: Princeton Univ. Press.

Traub, James. 1997. "Drive-Thru U." *New Yorker,* October 20–27, 115–23. Discusses the phenomenon of Phoenix "University" and market pressures for utilitarian education.

Trevor-Roper, Hugh. 1976. *Men and Events.* New York: Octagon.

Truman, Harry S. n.d. "On Reading." Post-presidential Files, Desk File, Box 3, The Harry S. Truman Presidential Library, Independence, MO.

Tye, Larry. 1999. "Medical Journal's Top Editor Is Fired." *Boston Globe,* July 26, sec. A.

Van Doren, Mark. 1943. *Liberal Education.* New York: Henry Holt.

Vargas Llosa, Mario. 2001. "Why Literature: The Premature Obituary of the Book." *New Republic,* May 14, 31–36.

Veblen, Thorstein. 1918. *The Higher Learning in America: A Memorandum on the Conduct of Universities by Business Men.* New York: B. W. Huebsch. Warns against the economic co-opting of universities that turns them into utilitarian machines. Veblen wrote this just as business and learning were beginning to fuse.

Verene, Donald Phillip. 2002. *The Art of Humane Education.* Ithaca: Cornell Univ. Press. A Vico scholar offers a rare, impassioned, but subtle exposition of teaching in the humanities. This short work is a gem.

Veysey, Laurence R. 1965. *The Emergence of the American University.* Chicago: Univ. of Chicago Press. This exceptionally well-researched study traces the rise of great public institutions and the metamorphosis of private ones from the Civil War to the earlier 20th century. Its second chapter contains significant, balanced insights on the nature of "utility" and utilitarian education pursued by universities. It pertains to chaps. 2, 3, 8, 9, and 10 in the present volume.

Vico, Giambattista. 1968 [1744]. *The New Science of Giambattista Vico.* Trans. Thomas Goddard Bergin and Max Harold Fisch. Ithaca: Cornell Univ. Press. References in the text are, by tradition, to paragraph number, not page.

———. 1990 [1709]. *On the Study Methods of Our Time.* Trans. Elio Gianturco. Preface by Donald Phillip Verene, with his translation of "The Academies and the Relation between Philosophy and Eloquence." Ithaca: Cornell Univ. Press.

Weaver, Frederick Stirton. 1991. *Liberal Education: Critical Essays on Professors, Pedagogy, and Structure.* New York: Teachers College.

Wegener, Charles. 1978. *Liberal Education and the Modern University.* Chicago: Univ. of Chicago Press. Chap. 1 is history, chaps. 3 and 4 on liberal education with keen insights.

Weinbach, Jonathan. 2000. "Luxury Learning." *Wall Street Journal,* November 10, sec. W.

Weinberg, Steven. 2000. "Five and a Half Utopias." *Atlantic Monthly,* January, 107–14. Skeptical of a technological utopia, this physics Nobel laureate is concerned about the threat to basic research posed by profit motives and immediate economic utility.

———. 2001. "The Future of Science, and the Universe." *New York Review of Books*, November 15, 58–63. A reflection on the nature of science, where it can lead us, and what it cannot tell us as well.

Weingartner, Rudolph H. 1999. *The Moral Dimensions of Academic Administration*. Lanham, MD: Rowman & Littlefield. The subtlety and care of his distinctions are derived both from philosophic training and from practical tests.

Whildin, Sara Lou, Susan Ware, and Gloriana St. Clair. 2001. "The Disquieting Dilemmas of Digital Libraries." In *Technology Enhanced Learning: Opportunities for Change,* ed. Paul S. Goodman, 123–52. Mahwah, NJ: Lawrence Erlbaum. Excellent overview of problems and opportunities facing the technologically enhanced library.

Whitehead, Alfred North. 1929. *The Aims of Education and Other Essays*. New York: Macmillan. Pertinent, surprisingly fresh.

———. 1956. *Dialogues of Alfred North Whitehead*. Ed. Lucien Price. New York: Mentor. Scattered insights, historical and philosophical, on learning.

Wiener, Norbert. 1954. *The Human Use of Human Beings: Cybernetics and Society*. Garden City: Doubleday. A half century later, still a bracing and sweeping view of human activity, learning, and communication by a towering figure.

Wilcove, David S., and Thomas Eisner. 2000. "The Impending Extinction of Natural History." *CHE*, September 15, B24.

Wilkinson, Rupert. 1964. *Gentlemanly Power: British Leadership and the Public School Tradition, a Comparative Study in the Making of Rulers*. Oxford: Oxford Univ. Press. Explores the tension between reason and tradition that characterizes higher education; explores both perils and contributions of traditionalism.

Wilshire, Bruce. 1990. *The Moral Collapse of the University: Professionalism, Purity, and Alienation*. Albany: State Univ. of New York Press. Argues that the modern university ignores the whole human being in favor of solely empirical knowledge. See "The Reactionary Response of Positivism: Cementing Purification, Professionalism, Segmentation in the University," pp. 201–21.

Wilson, Woodrow. 1909. "What Is a College For." *Scribner's Magazine,* July–December, 570–77. Recognizes forces of accelerating change and attempts to establish basic principles in an altered modern world.

Winn, James Anderson. 1998. *The Pale of Words: Reflections on the Humanities and Performance*. New Haven: Yale Univ. Press.

Winston, Gordon C. 1998. "Do Private Colleges Make Big Profits?" *Forum Futures 1998,* ed. Maureen E. Devlin and Joel W. Meyerson, 25–34. New Haven, CT: Forum Publishing.

———. 2000. "The Positional Arms Race in Higher Education." Discussion Paper no. 54 of the Williams College Project on the Economics of Higher

Education. Excellent analysis of current competition among colleges as an arms race of rankings with real negative effects. Also summarized in *Forum Futures 2001,* ed. Maureen Devlin, pp. 19–22 (Cambridge, MA: Forum Publishing, 2001).

Wolf, Alison. 2002. "Knowledge Economy Fails the Test." *Financial Times* (May 25–26): II. Wolf also published in 2002 *Myths about Education and Economic Growth* (London: Penguin).

Woolf, Virgina. 1929. *A Room of One's Own.* New York: Harcourt, Brace.

Yardley, Jonathan. 2003. "Higher Education, Upping the Ante." *Washington Post,* April 24, sec. C.

Yuker, Harold E. 1984. *Faculty Workload: Research, Theory, and Interpretation.* ASHE-ERIC Higher Education Research Report no. 10. Washington, DC: Association for the Study of Higher Education. Concentrates on research-oriented institutions. See pp. 34–56 for findings on faculty interest in teaching, variation in preparation time among disciplines, typical overvaluation of class size and class level as measures of time expended, and the role of consulting.

Zammuto, Raymond F. 1984. "Are the Liberal Arts an Endangered Species?" *Journal of Higher Education* 55, no. 2 (March–April): 184–211.

Zernike, Kate. 1999a. "Crimson Eclipse." *Boston Globe,* August 20, sec. A.

———. 1999b. "Alumni Carry on a 'Painful' Legacy." *Boston Globe,* September 20, sec. A.

———. 2000. "Fortunes of Colleges Are Shown to Rise, Fall with Rankings." *Boston Globe,* February 7, sec. A.

———. 2001. "2 'Spokesguys' Pause for a Word about Their College Sponsor." *New York Times,* July 19, sec. A. Advertisements and commercial messages now in the fabric of colleges.

Zhao, Yilu. 2002. "As Endowments Slip at Colleges, Big Tuition Increases Fill the Void." *New York Times,* February 23, sec. A. Stock market slump forces many institutions to hike tuition above rate of inflation.

Ziman, John. 2000. "Post Academic Science: Constructing Knowledge with Networks and Norms." In *Beyond the Science Wars,* ed. Ullica Segerstråle, 135–54. Albany: SUNY Press. Despite the title, this is not a soft piece on science as constructed knowledge but a thoughtful one on the standards of science and the relationship of science to society. Ziman was trained as a physicist and as an economist of science.

INDEX